Postcard History Series

Yuma and La Paz Counties

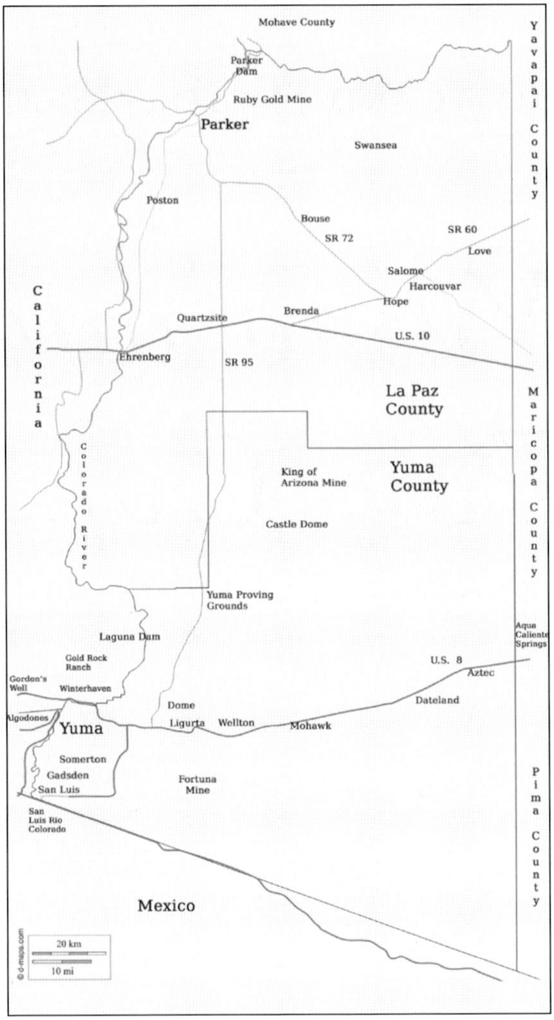

Yuma and La Paz County Map. This map shows the towns and communities, past and present, that are mentioned in this book. (Author's collection.)

On the Front Cover: East Entrance, c. 1940s (Real-Photo Postcard). The Yuma sign once proudly hung over Highway 80 (Fourth Avenue) at Eighth Street. The town of Yuma ended at Eighth Street, as did the paved highway. From there on, the highway remained dirt across the rest of the state until the 1930s, when most of the highway was paved. (Published by L.L. Cook Co., author's collection.)

On the Back Cover: Parker, Street Scene, c. 1950s (Real-Photo Postcard). Parker's population has remained relatively small since its beginnings in the early 1900s. In 1910, as the town began to move northward to its present location, the population was only 420 people. Twenty years later, in 1930, the population reached 1,315. By 1950, two years after incorporating, the town actually lost residents, with a population of 1,201. The town doubled in size by 1980, reaching a population of 2,897. Parker's highest population was in 2000, when the population reached 3,140. Since 2000, the population has slowly declined, and by 2016, the population was estimated to be 3,026. (Published by W.M. Cline Co., photograph by Gene Aiken, author's collection.)

POSTCARD HISTORY SERIES

Yuma and La Paz Counties

Rick Sprain

ARCADIA
PUBLISHING

ISBN 978-1-4671-0256-8

Published by Arcadia Publishing
Charleston, South Carolina

Printed in the United States of America

Library of Congress Control Number: 2018947602

For all general information contact Arcadia Publishing at:
Telephone 843-853-2070
Fax 843-853-0044
E-mail sales@arcadiapublishing.com
For customer service and orders:
Toll-Free 1-888-313-2665

Visit us on the Internet at www.arcadiapublishing.com

This book is dedicated to the best parents a guy could have asked for,
Dee and Dale Sprain.

CONTENTS

Acknowledgments		6
Introduction		7
1.	Yuma: The Town	9
2.	Staying in Town: Hotels and Snowbirds	33
3.	Getting to Yuma: Riding the Rails and Roadways	47
4.	Yuma County Communities: Towns Past and Present	61
5.	Military and Prison: Serving Your Country and Serving Time	71
6.	Wedding Chapels: Get'n Hitched	81
7.	Native Americans: First People to Yuma	87
8.	Miscellaneous: From Agriculture to the River	93
9.	La Paz County: The Old Yuma County	105
10.	Just across the Border: Near Yuma County	123

Acknowledgments

My fondness for Yuma and its history goes back many years to when we would visit my grandmother in the early 1970s. Years later, my parents relocated to Yuma, and after my retirement, my fascination with the region grew. I had begun collecting postcards as a kid, and it was only natural that I ended up acquiring many from Yuma and La Paz Counties later on. These cards were the beginnings of creating this book.

I had help over the years researching historical facts, as well as from some great people who allowed me to use some of their personal collection for this book. I met John Taylor a few years back when I was researching another book. John has one of the most spectacular collections of mining cards in the nation, and he was kind enough once again to allow me to use some of his collection in this book. Others who assisted me with their collections were Mike Hawk, Eric Larson, and the California State Library. I would also like to thank Nancy Snook, Yuma's city historian and park manager of the Yuma Crossing National Heritage Area. Nancy was instrumental in helping identify locations of some of the older historical postcards. Helping keep Yuma's rich history alive are owners of the Coronado Motor Hotel, John and Yvonne Peach. As longtime residents, both John and Yvonne helped identify hard-to-find locations for me. Louie and Dee Gradias of Gadsden are two of the nicest and warmest people you will ever meet. They welcomed me into their home with stories of old Gadsden and Somerton and allowed me to use any of the postcards they owned. Lastly, I would like to thank Laurie Boone from the Arizona History Society. Laurie not only assisted in identifying some old postcards, she opened up the Arizona History Society's archives for me to use as research.

All images in this book are from my personal collection unless otherwise noted.

INTRODUCTION

The climate in winter is incomparably finer than that of Italy. It would scarcely be possible to suggest an improvement. I never experienced such exquisite Christmas weather as we enjoyed during our sojourn. Perhaps fastidious people might object to the temperature in summer, when the rays of the sun attain their maximum force, and the hot winds sweep in from the desert. . . . I have even heard complaint made that the thermometer failed to show the true heat because the mercury dried up. Everything dries; wagons dry; men dry; chickens dry; there is no juice left in anything, living or dead, by the close of summer. Officers and soldiers are supposed to walk about creaking; mules, it is said, can only bray at midnight; and I have heard it hinted that the carcasses of cattle rattle inside their hides, and that snakes find a difficulty in bending their bodies and horned frogs die of apoplexy. Chickens hatched at the season, as old Fort Yumers say, come out of the shell ready cooked.

—J. Ross Browne, "A Tour through Arizona,"
Harper's New Monthly Magazine, October 1864

Although I have never lived in Yuma, I have fond memories going back many decades. When my brother and I were children, my parents would take us to Yuma to visit my grandmother, who moved there in the early 1970s. I have always had a fascination with the Old West, and it seems Yuma fit right in. We would visit the old prison or head to the Colorado River for the day, where my brother and I would explore the desert looking for old relics of the past. Fast-forward many years to now: I go visit my parents, who at first were among the thousands of snowbirds who would stay in Yuma during the winter months. Eventually, they moved to Yuma full time, and I still visit the river and desert whenever I can.

Yuma's history goes back many centuries. Long before the first European explorers arrived around 1540, ancestors of present-day Quechan and Cocopah tribes called this area home. In 1781, the Quechans, who had been antagonized and mistreated by the Spanish soldiers for many years, rebelled, killing a number of soldiers, along with Fr. Francisco Garces and his fellow priests. Calm ensued until American explorers, followed by the forty-niners, swarmed Yuma Crossing on their way to the goldfields. The Americans and the Quechans were in good standing with one another until 1850, when John Glanton appeared in Yuma and muscled in on the ferry business. Once again, the Quechans rose against their oppressors, killing Glanton along with his gang of cutthroats, destroying the ferry, and possibly getting away with as much as $60,000.

The military first arrived in 1849, with 1st Lt. Cave J. Couts, of the 1st Dragoons, setting up a fort about a mile below the Gila River. The post moved to its permanent site on an elevated section on the west bank of the Colorado River in 1851. A year after relocating, the name of the fort was changed from Camp Yuma to Fort Yuma. Fort Yuma was abandoned on May 16, 1884, and transferred to the Department of the Interior on July 22, 1884.

Soon ferryboats were paddling up the Colorado River from the Gulf of California, and the Butterfield stage was making regular stops. In February 1863, Arizona became an official territory of the United States, making the territorial capital in La Paz, about 120 miles upriver from Yuma. Now a ghost town, La Paz was the largest city in the Yuma area; however, as the mines played out, so did La Paz. The site for Arizona City was laid out in 1866, with full incorporation in 1871. That same year, the county seat relocated from La Paz to Arizona City, and in 1873, Arizona City became Yuma. By 1877, Yuma was made accessible to the rest of the world when the Southern Pacific (S.P.) Railroad crossed the Colorado River from California.

Probably one of the most infamous Western prisons in American history opened its gates in 1876. Yuma Territorial Prison operated from 1876 through 1909, when the last of its prisoners were moved to Florence. During the prison's 33 years of operation, 3,069 prisoners, including 29 women, were locked within its walls. The prison's buildings were used from 1910 to 1914 as Yuma High School. The Southern Pacific Railroad was realigned to its current route in 1923, and in doing so, the railroad demolished portions of the prison's west walls, along with the women's cells. The City of Yuma operated the prison's museum from 1941 until 1960, when the State of Arizona took over, making the Yuma Territorial Prison the third state park.

The early settlers of Yuma proved themselves to be extremely resilient. At least four times, in 1862, 1884, 1891, and 1916, they had to rebuild their town after disastrous floods decimated the area. Each time, the town was constructed better than the last. From small adobe structures rose new and modern wood and brick two-story hotels, stores, and homes. Even some of the old buildings from the old Yuma Territorial Prison were used to rebuild after the flood of 1916.

By the turn of the 20th century, Yuma changed. It was no longer a small Wild West town but a modern city with a population of over 1,500 people. As the population grew, so did tourism and the need for people to reach out to family and friends to give firsthand accounts of their travels. Postcards were an inexpensive way for businesses to advertise their stores and hotels to the traveler. Penny postcards became extremely popular during the first half of the 20th century, with millions being sold over the years. For 2¢, a penny for the card and a penny for the postage, a father could write his family back in New York that he is doing fine while on a stopover in Yuma. A young teacher could send her mother in Kansas City a postcard of the high school she now works at while placing an X over her classroom. Or a weary traveler might send his brother a postcard of downtown Yuma in 1910, telling him how unbelievably hot it is.

In the infancy of postcards, many of the local merchants produced their own postcards for distribution. From local newspapers such as the *Yuma Examiner* to pharmacists J. Homer Smith and Joseph Jauman to Darlings Notion Store, each published their own style of postcards picturing highlights of early Yuma. Later, big-name publishers of postcards began moving into the Southwest. Companies such as Frashers Fotos, Curt Teich, and Albertype were extremely popular from the 1920s through the 1950s, selling millions of postcards each. Although color postcards were produced well back into the 1910s, it was the 1950s that saw the use of color Kodachrome postcards being published by Petley Studios and Yuma Color Cards, along with others that brought postcards into the 20th century.

Postcards are still fairly popular, although their demand has diminished over the past couple of decades. With the advent of cell phones, people are easily able to take a photograph from their device as a memento of their trip, rather than purchasing a postcard. If they want to share a photograph with family or friends, all they have to do is text, Facebook, Snapchat, or use any number other apps to send and share their pictures.

This book will look back at the history of Yuma County through postcards, some of which carry stories from the people who mailed them well over 100 years ago. Even though the county was split in two, creating La Paz County in 1983, I have included postcards that were produced prior to 1983 that now cover both Yuma and La Paz Counties.

One

Yuma
The Town

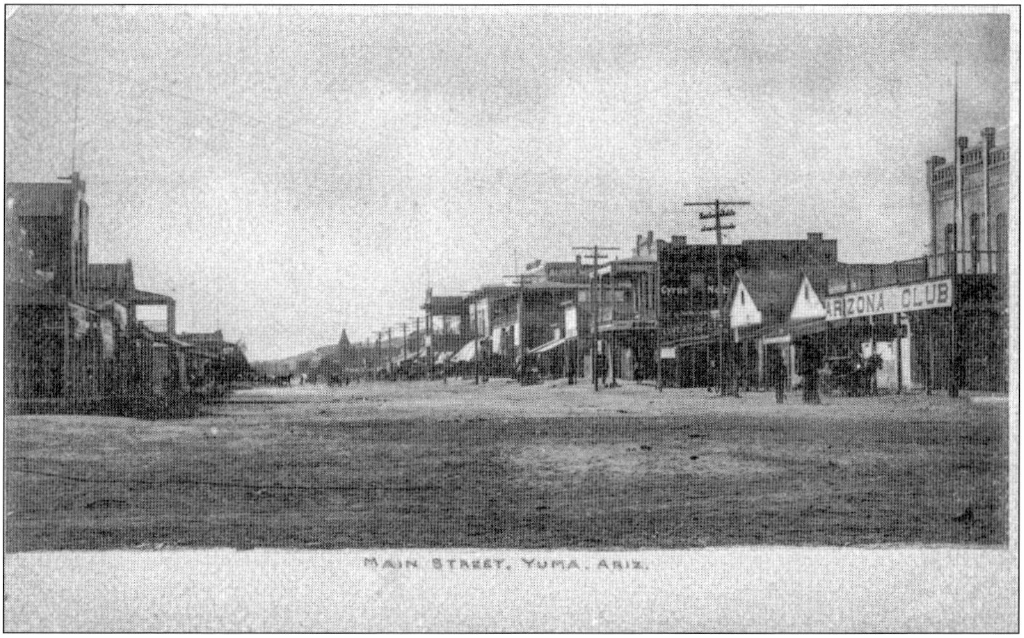

Main Street, c. 1904 (Undivided Back Postcard). Starting as a small community across the river from Fort Yuma in the 1850s, Arizona City had grown to 1,144 people by 1870. In 1873, the town's name was changed to Yuma. Over the next 30 years, to the turn of the century in 1900, Yuma had gained less than 400 people, reaching a population of 1,519. By 1910, Yuma almost doubled in size to 2,914 people. In 1930, the population reached 4,892, and in 1950, it was 9,145. The largest increase in population was between 1950 and 1960, when the population gained over 162 percent, to 23,974. By 1980, the town's size about doubled again to 42,481 people. In the 2000 census, Yuma's population reached 77,515 people, and by 2016, Yuma was estimated to have a population of 94,906 people. (Published by the Albertype Co.)

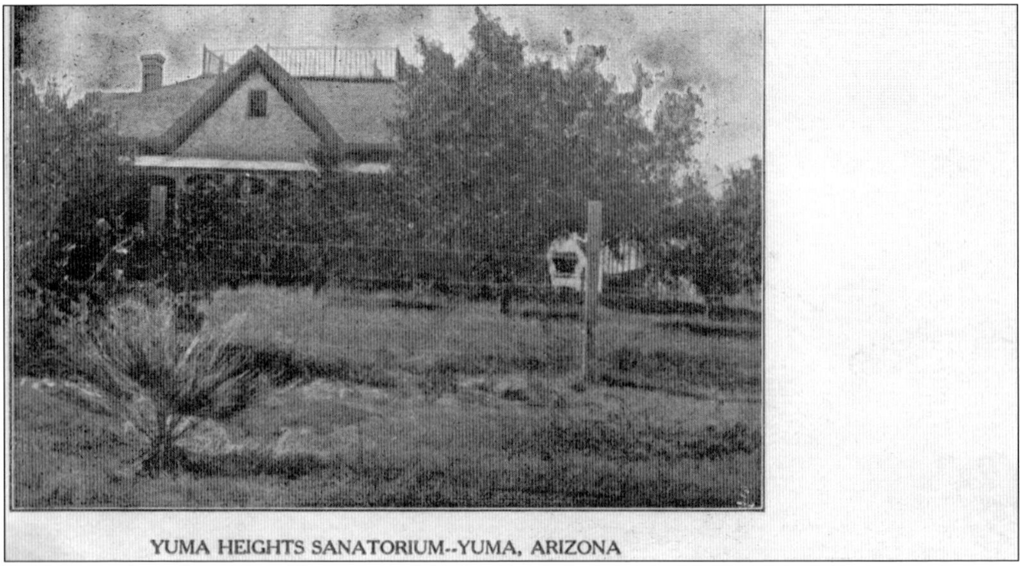

YUMA HEIGHTS SANATORIUM, C. 1905 (UNDIVIDED BACK POSTCARD). The *Medical Record* of April 20, 1907, read, "Recently the Yuma Heights Sanatorium has been opened and better accommodations are assured. The sanatorium is only open during the winter months." The *Arizona Sentinel* of March 17, 1894, reported, "The Sanitarium of the Southwest YUMA is acknowledged as a wonderful Health Resort. It is the home of the orange, lemon, banana and other tropical fruits. It is the hope of ill afflicted with any of the Pulmonary Complaints, for the air is pure, dry and invigorating. The building stands on the banks of the Colorado River. The Hotel was built and furnished with a view to accommodate the Heap Prospector, the Tourist, Families and all those desiring the accommodation of a first class hotel in every particular, on a healthy site."

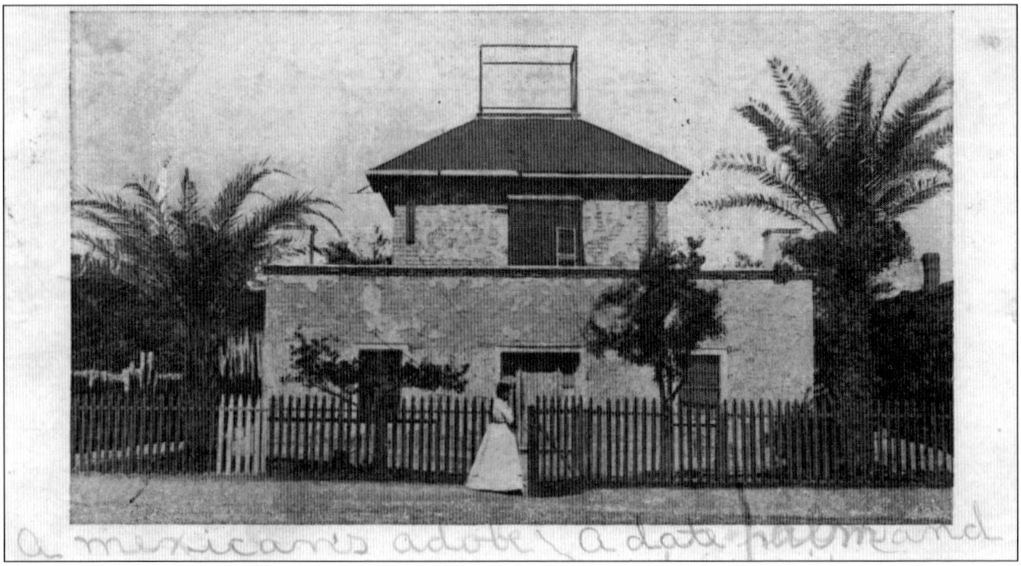

ADOBE RESIDENCE, POSTMARKED JANUARY 21, 1906 (REAL-PHOTO POSTCARD). Handwritten on the front of the card is the following: "A Mexicans adobe residence in Yuma. A date palm and its fruits." With wood and building material in short supply in early Yuma, adobe was the mainstay for constructing homes and businesses. With its thick walls, adobe kept the home cool in the summer and warm in the winter.

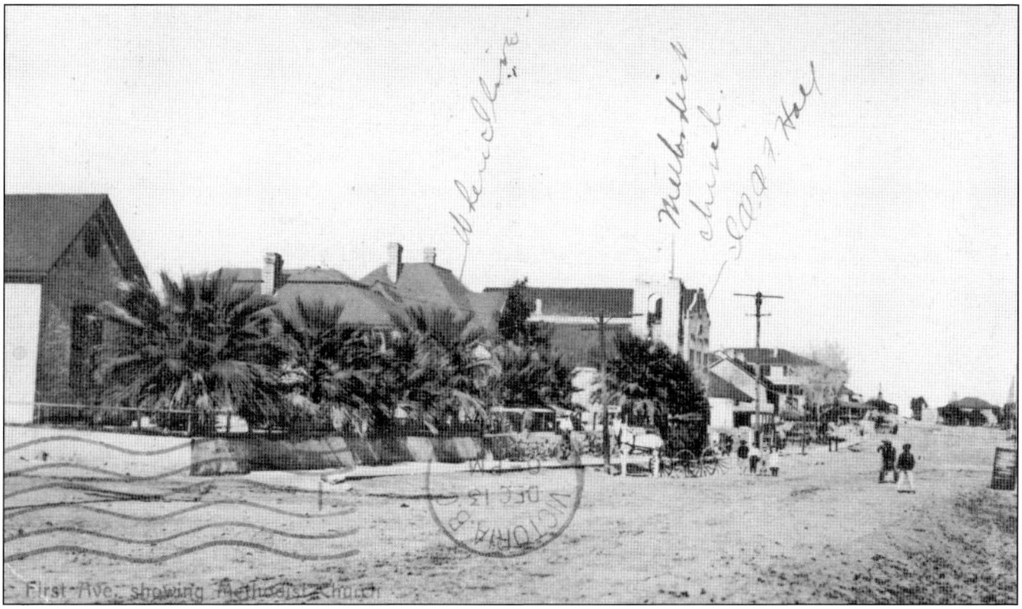

FIRST AVENUE, POSTMARKED DECEMBER 9, 1908 (HAND-COLORED POSTCARD). The photograph would have been taken from West Third Street, now known as Harold C. Giss Parkway, facing north on First Avenue. The building at 268 First Avenue is still standing and is where the person wrote, "Where I live." The Methodist church is now known as the Christian Science Society. The Ancient Order of United Workmen (AOUW) hall opened in July 1888 and became the Independent Order of Odd Fellows hall by the early 1900s. (Published by the *Yuma Examiner.*)

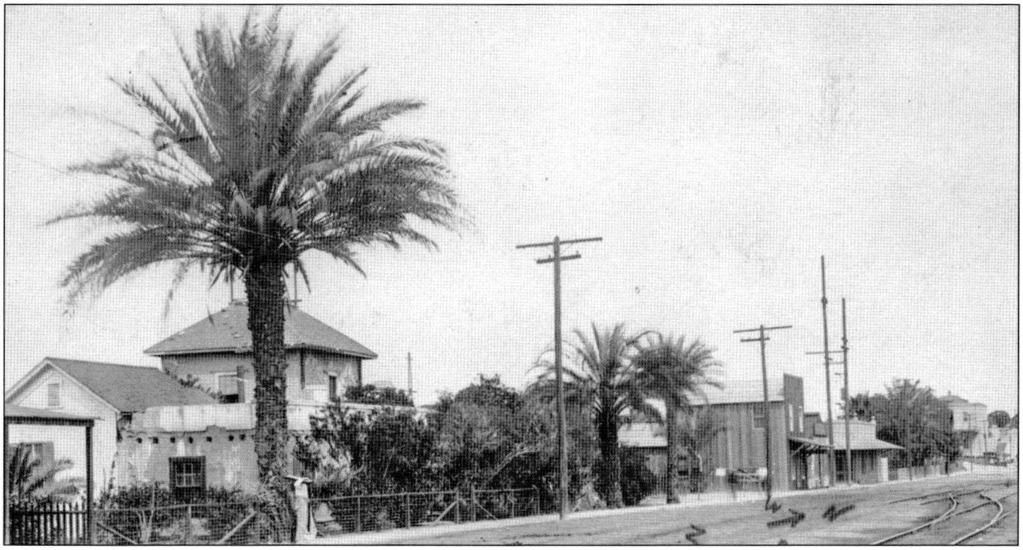

MADISON AVENUE, POSTMARKED MAY 16, 1909 (REAL-PHOTO POSTCARD). This picture was taken on Madison Avenue from about Second Street facing north towards First Street. Not a single building seen here is standing today. The area near the trees on the far portion of Madison Avenue (formally Brinley Avenue) is part of the Brinley Historic District, which includes the Mary Neahr Pancrazi adobe built in 1899, the Neahr-Laeger-Martinez House, and the Popular Drug Store, also known as the Golden Wedding Bell Chapel, built in 1891.

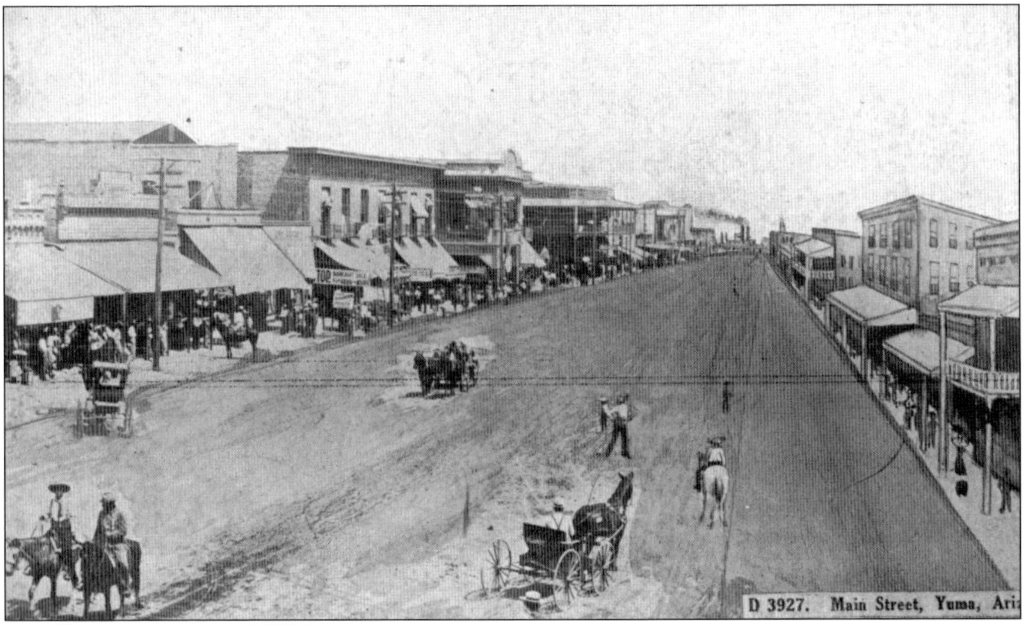

ABOVE, MAIN STREET, C. 1908 (DIVIDED BACK POSTCARD); BELOW, MAIN STREET, POSTMARKED MARCH 23, 1908 (HAND-COLORED POSTCARD). Although Yuma was not really considered part of the Wild West, it did have its share of characters. Take the Earps, for example: Warren Earp, the youngest of the Earp brothers, lived in Yuma in the early 1890s. In November 1893, Warren was arrested for assaulting a bartender with the last name of Behrens on a bridge over the Colorado River. The charges were eventually dropped when it was discovered the assault occurred 24 feet into California. Warren's older brother Wyatt and his wife, Josie, lived in Yuma around 1897 before joining the gold rush in Alaska. (Below, published by the *Yuma Examiner*.)

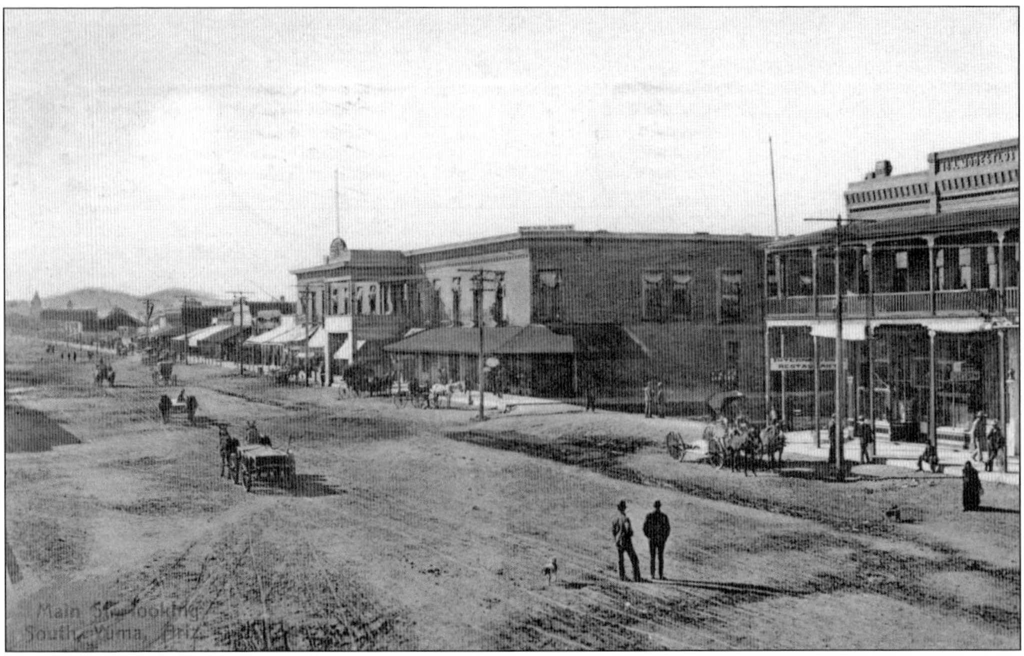

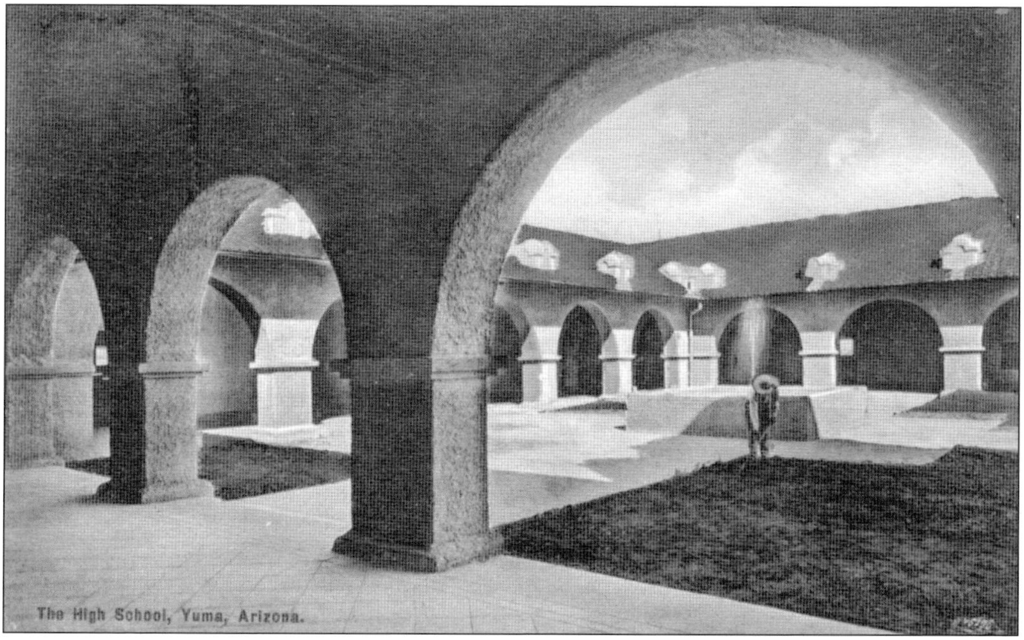

ABOVE, YUMA, HIGH SCHOOL, HAND DATED MARCH 27, 1909 (HAND-COLORED POSTCARD); BELOW, YUMA, HIGH SCHOOL, POSTMARKED MAY 12, 1914 (CURT TEICH POSTCARD). The original school, built in 1909, was located near Main and Third Streets. The school was relocated to the old prison for three years after it burned down in 1910. Since 1914, the high school has been located at 400 South Sixth Avenue. Due to its short time at the prison, the school's sports teams took on the name of the "Criminals." (Above, published by M. Rieder, Publ.; below, published by J. Homer Smith, Yuma.)

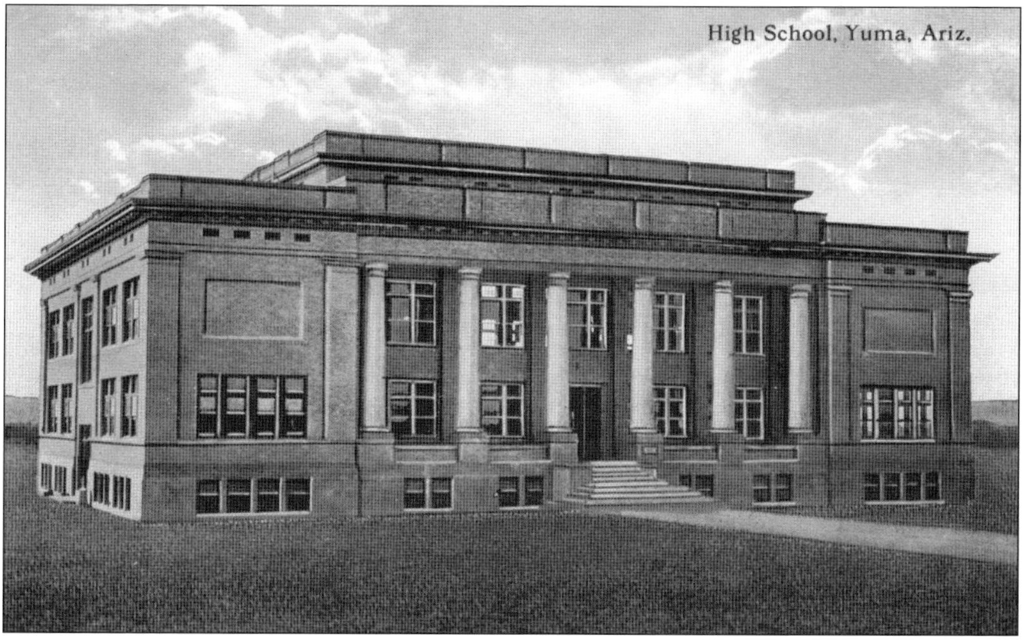

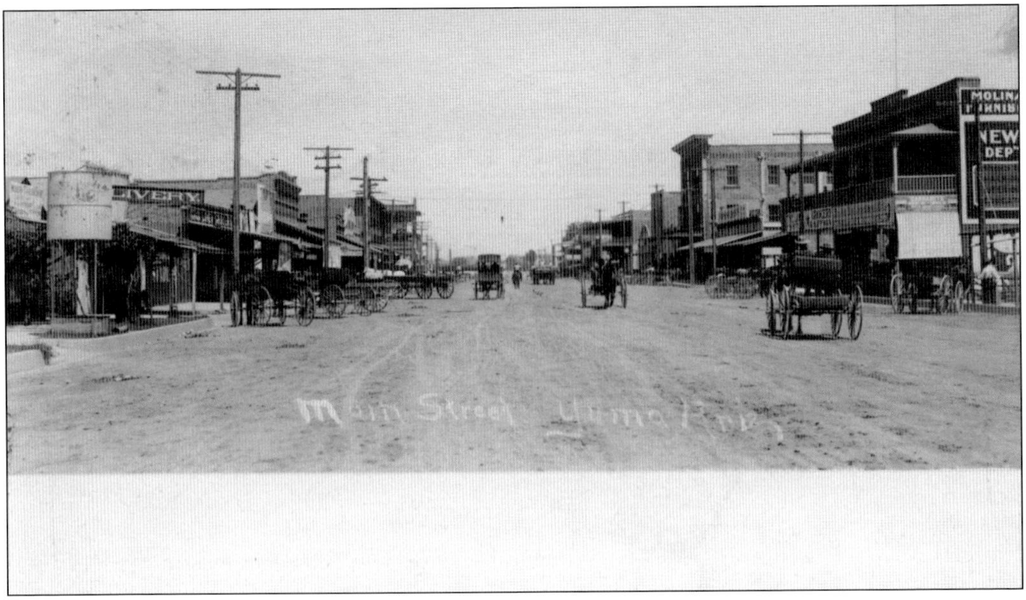

MAIN STREET, C. 1910 (REAL-PHOTO POSTCARD). In December 1905, the Yuma City Council passed a resolution that by the beginning of March 1906, the city would begin installing concrete sidewalks along the downtown streets. The dusty streets throughout downtown Yuma remained dirt until 1925, when Main Street was finally paved.

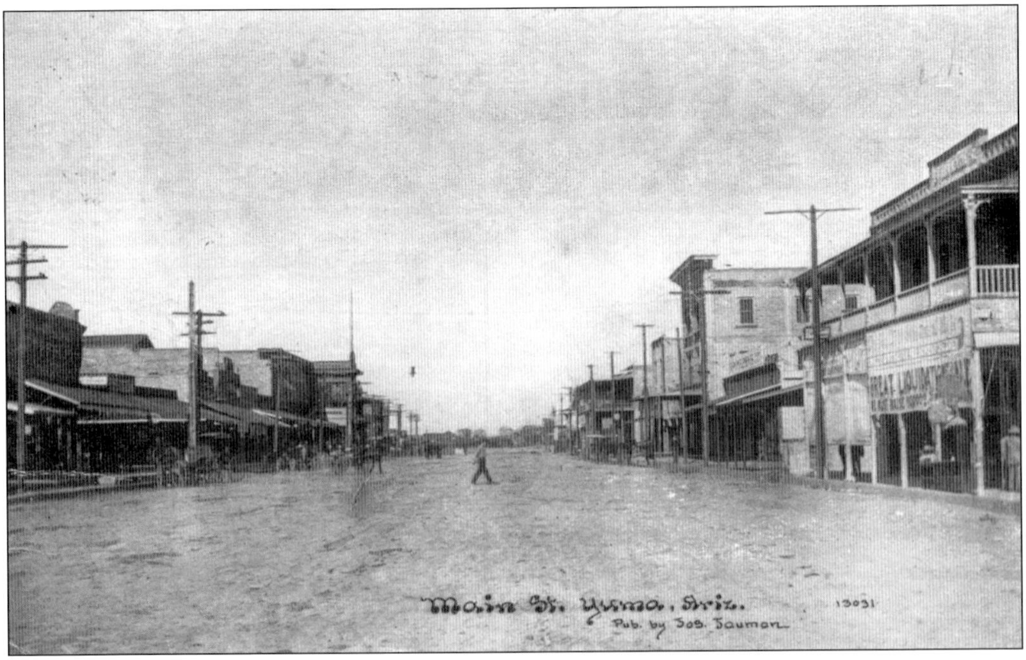

MAIN STREET, POSTMARKED OCTOBER 28, 1912 (REAL-PHOTO POSTCARD). On the back of the card, Douglas is writing to his aunt in Dover, New Jersey, saying, "Dear Aunt. This doesn't look much like Dover does it? Yesterday we had a sand storm all day long, the sand blew everywhere, you can't keep it out of the houses." (Published by Joseph Jauman.)

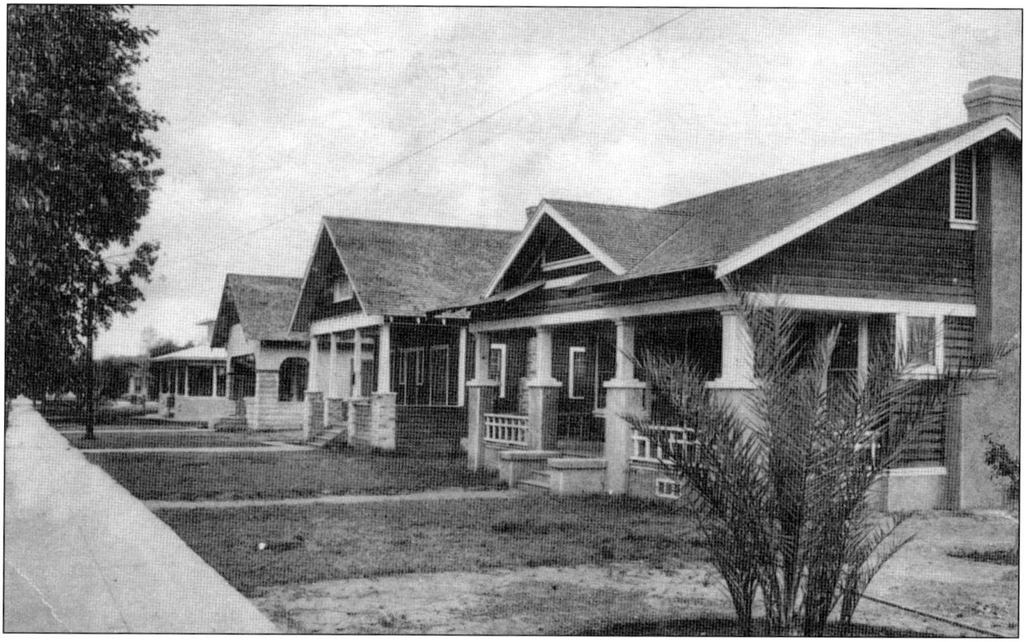

Residential Street, c. 1910 (Albertype Postcard). Pictured above is a typical street of early bungalow- and Craftsman-style homes constructed in the early 1900s near downtown. (Published by J. Homer Smith.)

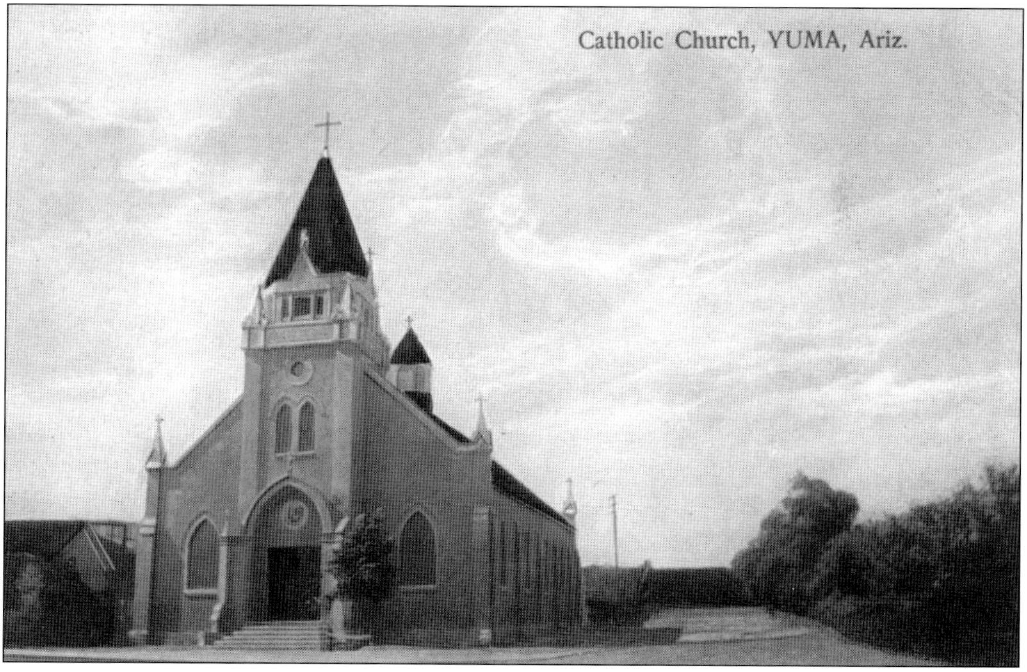

Catholic Church, c. 1910 (Hand-Colored Postcard). The first Immaculate Conception Church was built in 1866 of adobe bricks donated by local parishioners. After the parish outgrew the adobe, a new brick church was constructed in 1899 on Main Street. The church served until 1960, when a devastating fire ravaged the building. (Published by United Post Card Co.)

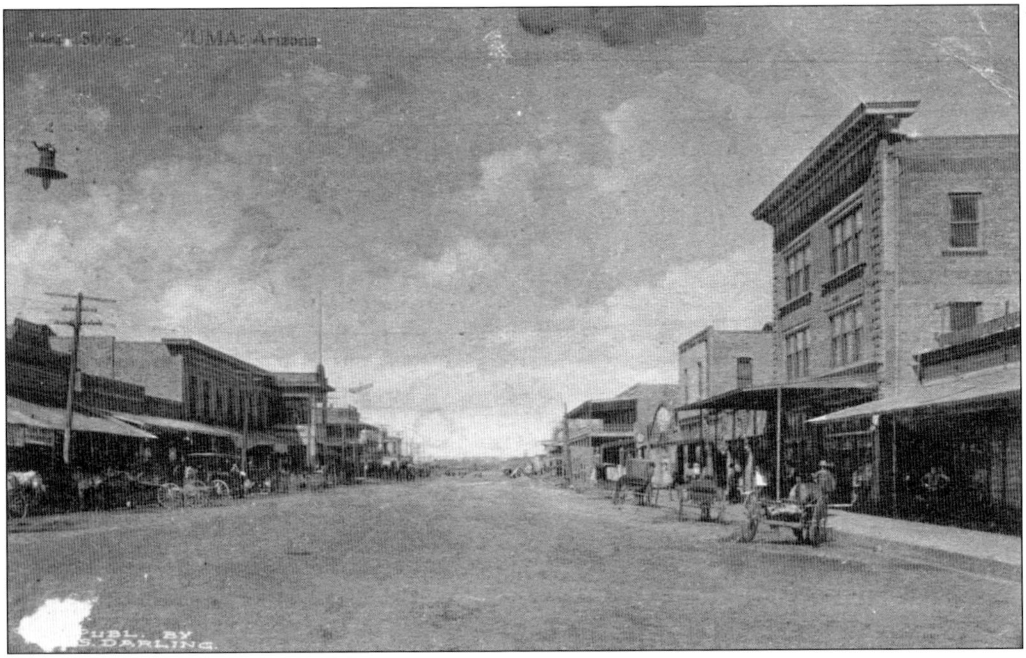

Above, Main Street, Postmarked October 29, 1913 (Real-Photo Postcard); Below, Main Street Looking North, Hand Dated November 4, 1916 (Real-Photo Postcard). Handwritten on the back of the lower card is the following: "Dear this is the Biggest Part of Yuma the Business Center of the whole city or whatever they call it I call it a jerk water because the dirty silvery Colorado River divides Ariz from Cal. everything is fine and dandy with me and hope it is the same with you hope to be with you soon Daddy." (Above, published by M.S. Darling.)

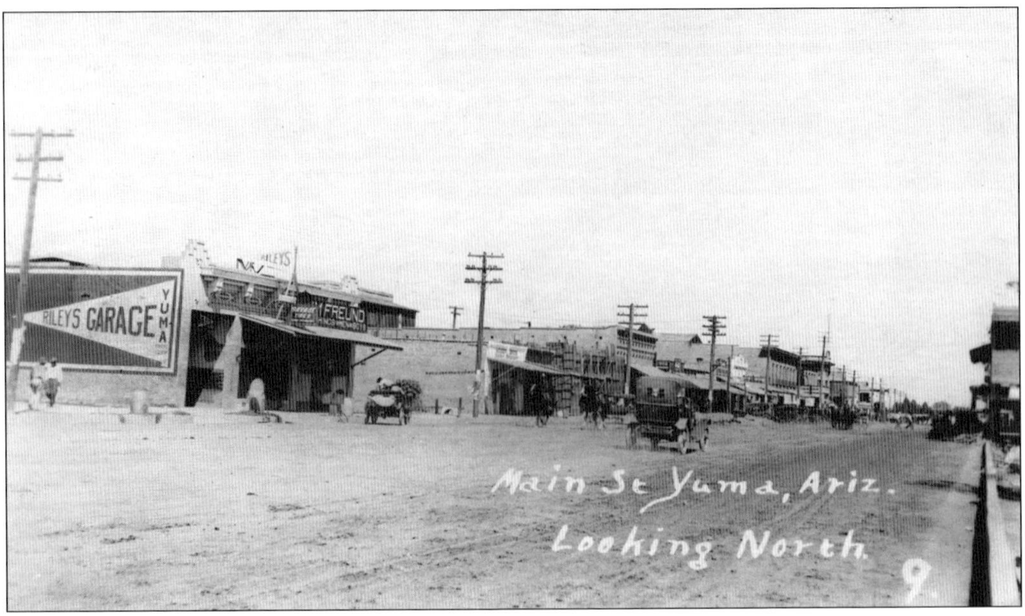

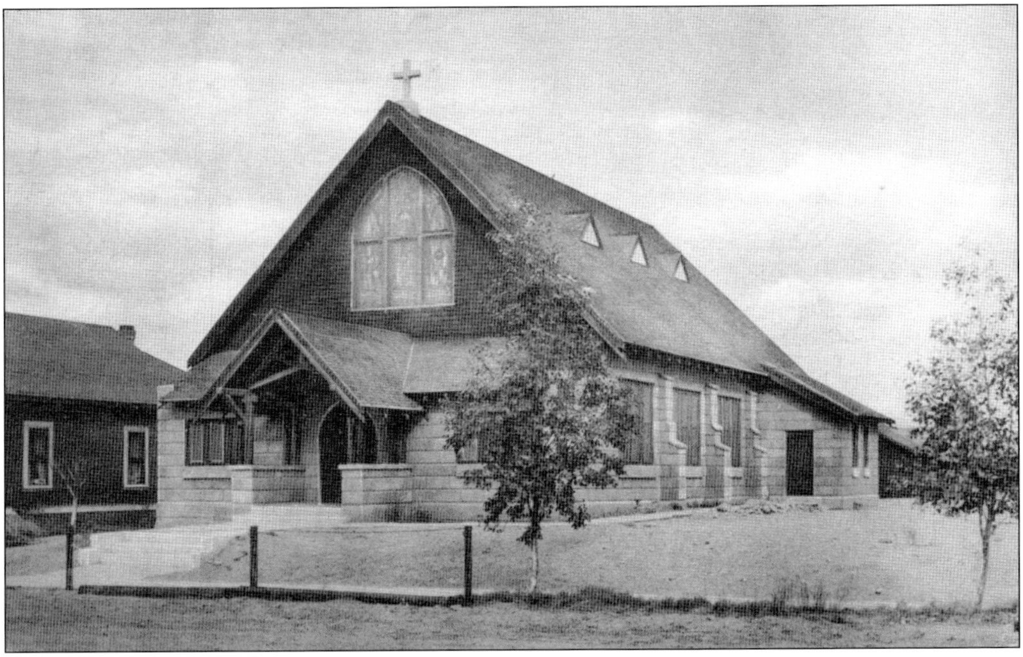

EPISCOPAL CHURCH, C. 1910S (ALBERTYPE POSTCARD). St. Paul's Episcopal Church was constructed in 1909 at 637 Second Avenue in Yuma. It was added to the National Register of Historic Places in 1982 and is currently serving as a cultural center. (Published by J. Homer Smith.)

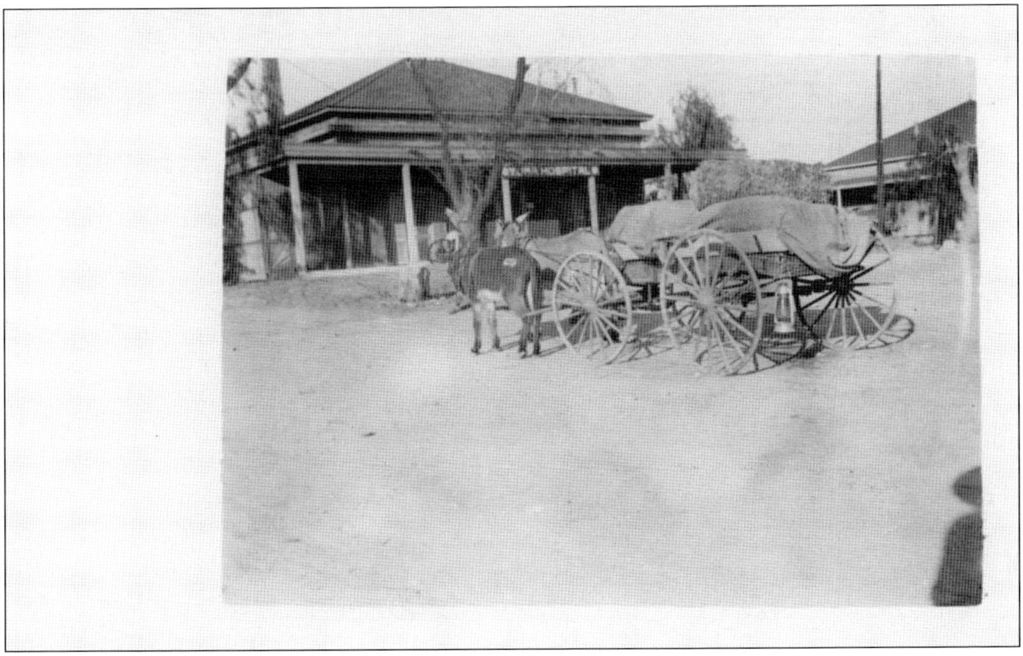

YUMA HOSPITAL, HAND DATED 1913 (REAL-PHOTO POSTCARD). In the early 1900s, Yuma's hospital was located at Fort Yuma, and by 1913, it was a teaching hospital for the Southwest. By 1915, the hospital had outgrown the old fort, and a new location was being sought. Within a few years, the hospital relocated to the county farm four miles south of town on Warrenite Boulevard.

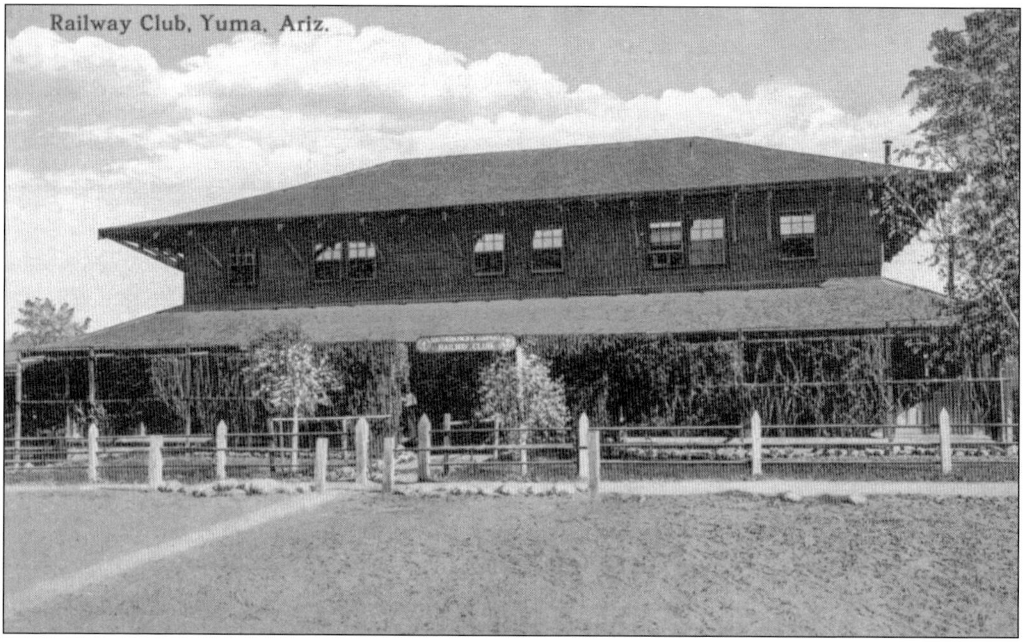

RAILWAY CLUB, C. 1915 (HAND-COLORED CURT TEICH POSTCARD). An article in the October 2, 1907, issue of the *Arizona Sentinel* read, "The new railway club house was opened and dedicated last night by a reception and dance. Those who attended had an enjoyable time." (Published by J. Homer Smith.)

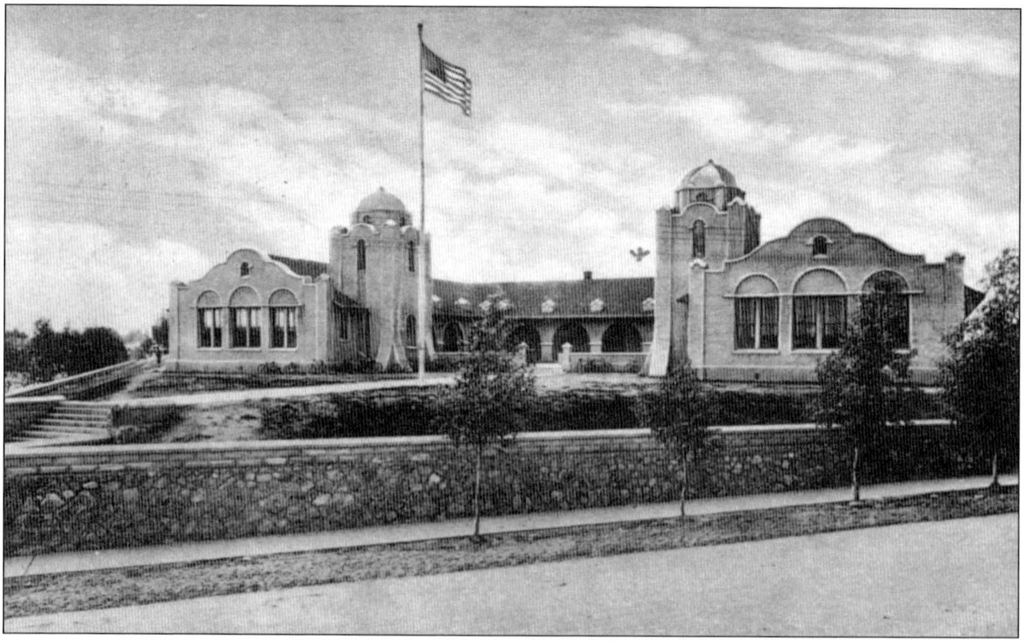

GRAMMAR SCHOOL, HAND DATED JANUARY 28, 1919 (ALBERTYPE POSTCARD). On the back of the card, a student by the name of Blanch wrote, "Dear Nana, This is my school. Where I put a cross is my room. I'm making the cutest little doll house. How are you getting along? Write me all the news. I'm having lots of fun in Yuma. Goodby with love." (Published by J. Homer Smith.)

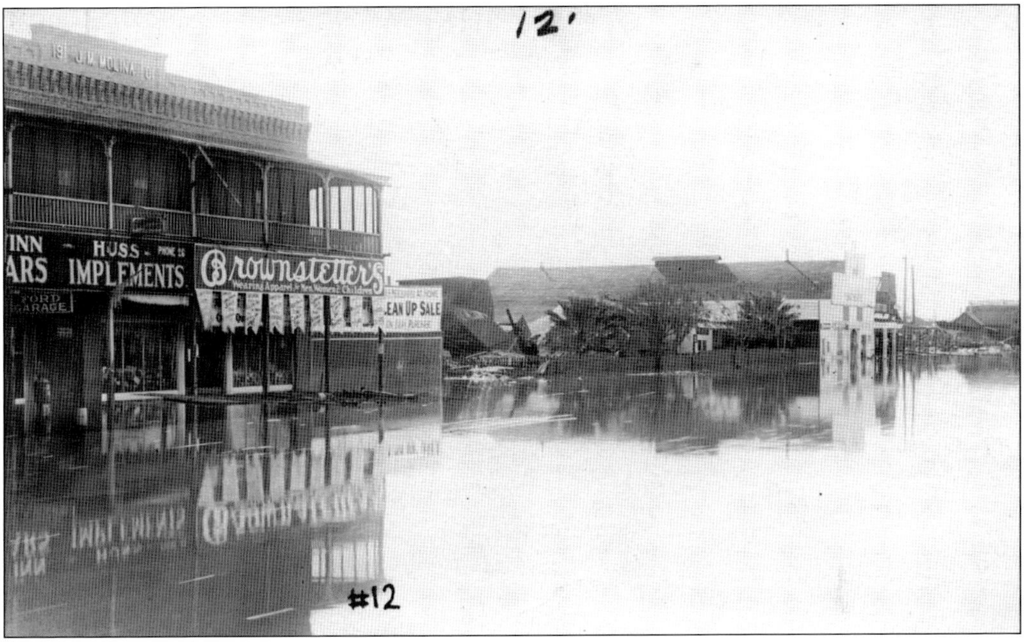

MAIN STREET, FLOOD OF 1916 (REAL-PHOTO POSTCARDS). When heavy rains in the mountains above Yuma raised the lower Gila and Colorado Rivers to dangerous levels, the rivers eventually overflowed their banks, flooding the entire downtown area. Quite a few of the downtown buildings were still constructed of adobe, and the rising waters softened the adobe walls and caused many of the oldest structures to collapse.

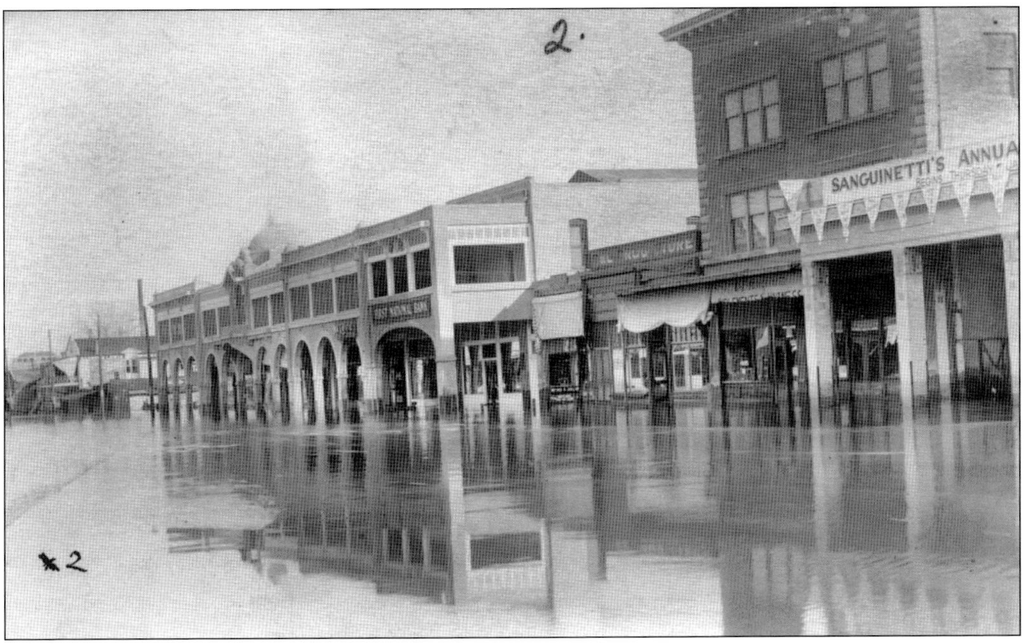

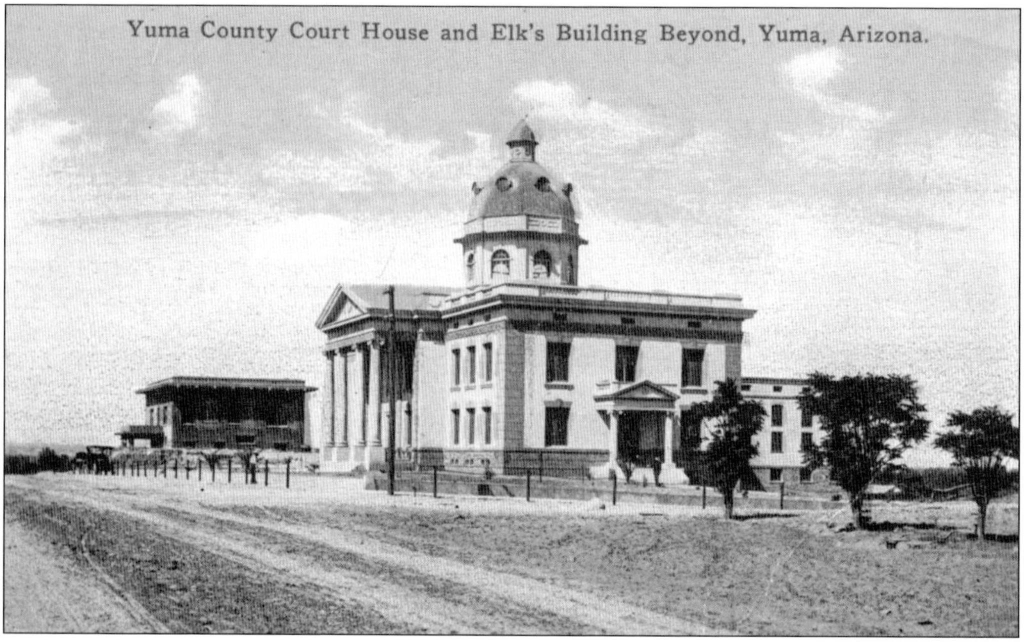

Above, Courthouse and Elks Lodge, Postmarked June 6, 1917 (Divided Back Postcard); Below, Yuma County Courthouse, c. 1940 (Real-Photo Postcard). Constructed in 1909, the courthouse suffered a devastating fire on August 18, 1927. Reopening in 1928, the redesigned courthouse added a third floor instead of replacing the dome, and the front columns were removed. Although most of the court's activities were moved to a newer adjacent courthouse, which opened in 2005, the old courthouse, designed by Ralph Swearingen and G.A. Hanseen, is still in use today. (Above, published by Yuma County Commercial Club; below, published by the L.L. Cook Co.)

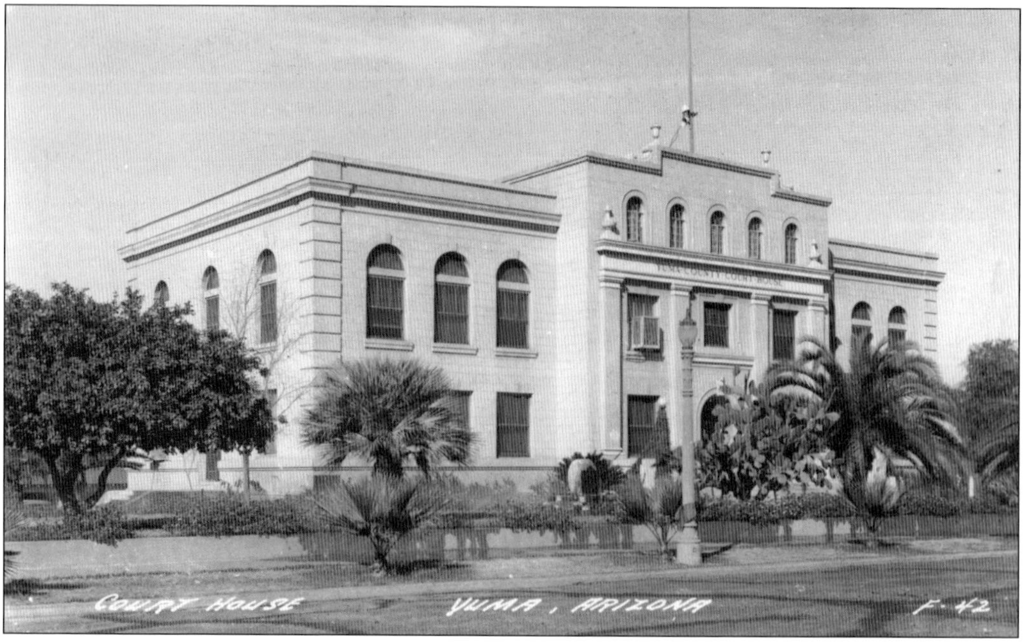

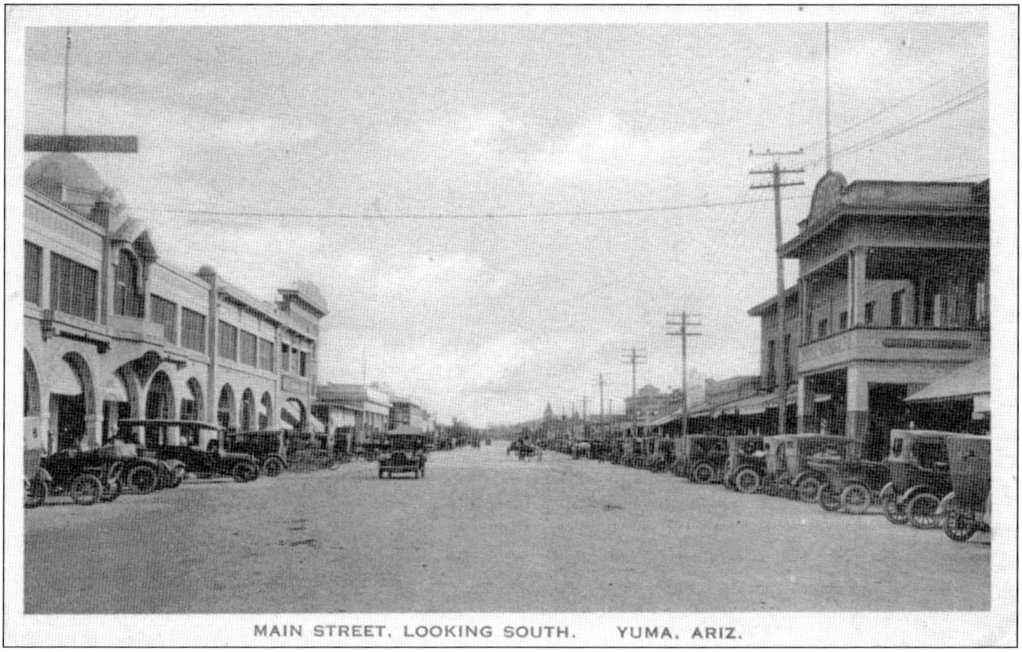

ABOVE, MAIN STREET LOOKING SOUTH, C. 1920S (ALBERTYPE POSTCARD); BELOW, MAIN STREET, C. 1920S (ALBERTYPE POSTCARD). One of the most haunted buildings in Yuma is the Lee Hotel, located at 390 South Main Street. The two-story, 30-room hotel was constructed in 1917 and is said to be haunted by three female spirits. One is the original owner, who has been seen in the halls at night knocking and rattling on doors. The second is a teenage girl carrying towels down the hall. The last one, which may predate the hotel, is an Indian woman seen hovering over guests' beds. (Both, published by J. Homer Smith.)

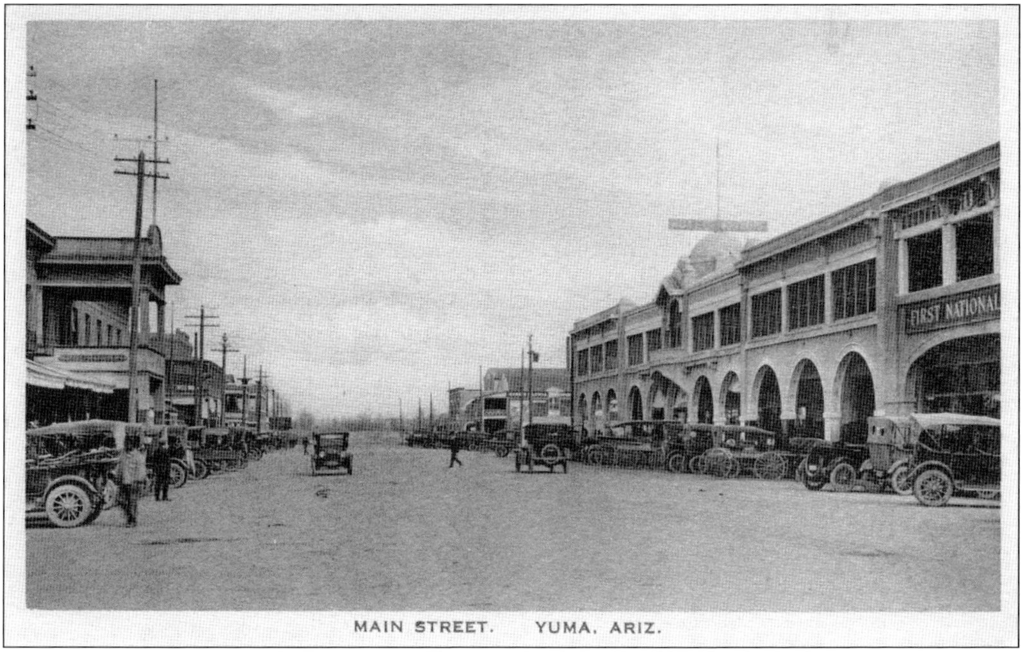

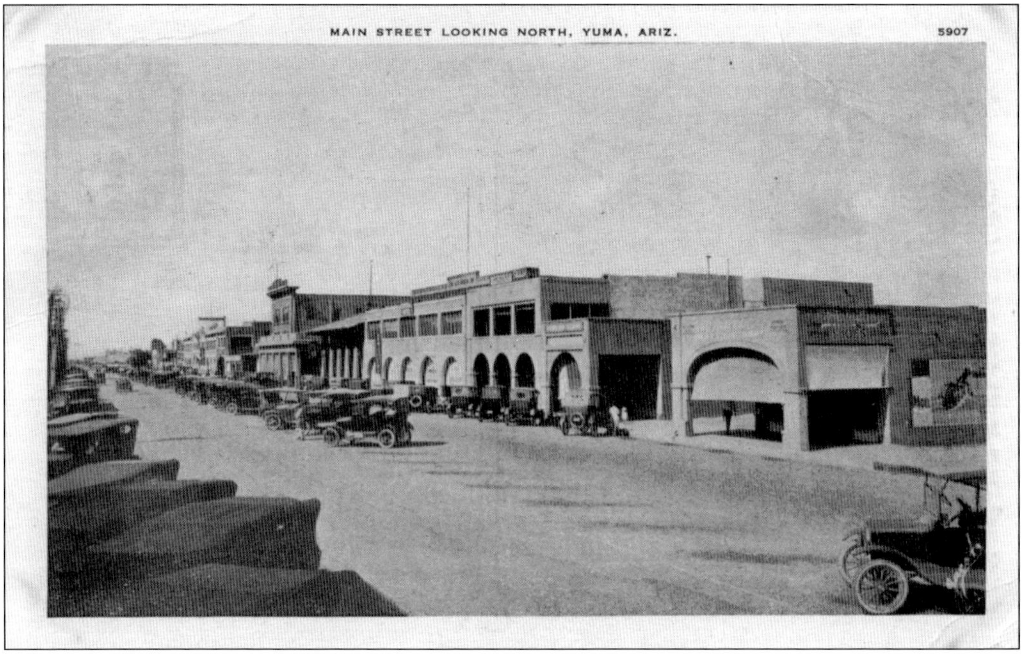

ABOVE, MAIN STREET LOOKING NORTH, HAND DATED APRIL 1, 1926 (REAL-PHOTO POSTCARD); BELOW, MAIN STREET LOOKING NORTH, POSTMARKED OCTOBER 16, 1928 (CURT TEICH POSTCARD). Most of the Main Street buildings date to the 1920s, after the devastating flood of 1916 destroyed downtown. The adobe buildings that crumbled and dissolved into mud were replaced with a modern downtown with wooden and brick structures. (Above, published by Dean's News Depot; below, published by Curt Teich & Co., which also went by CurTeich and Curt Teich, Inc.)

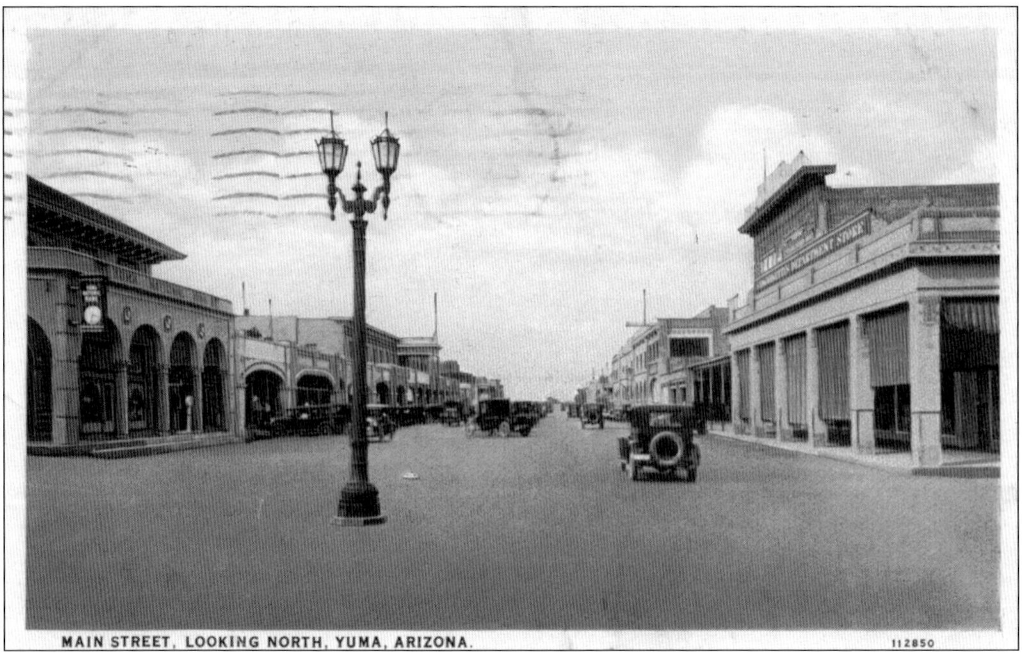

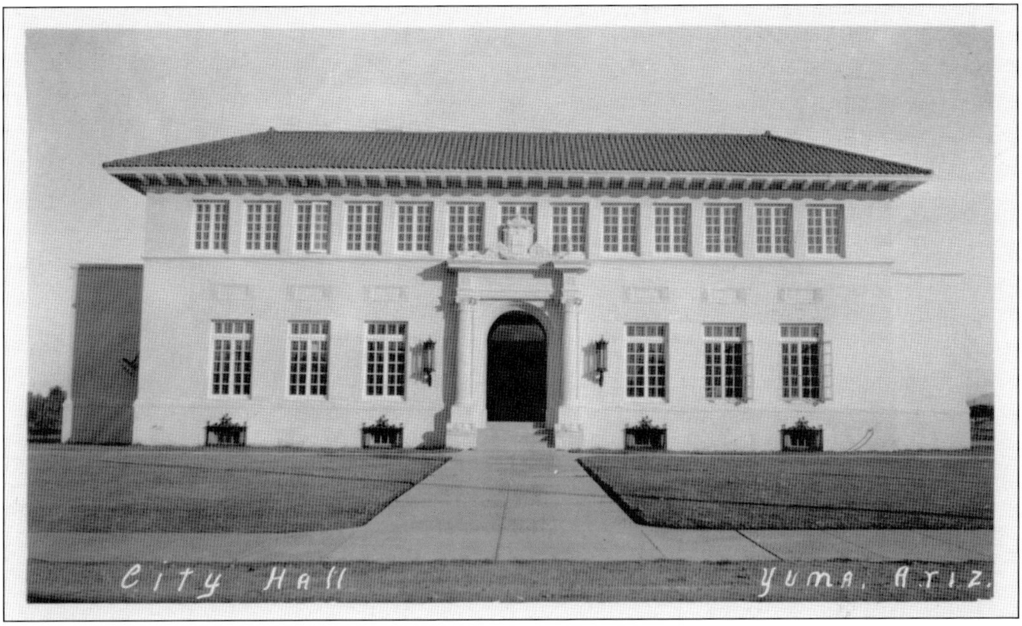

City Hall, c. 1920 (Real-Photo Postcard). On the reverse of the card, someone wrote, "The public buildings are very creditable. The fire house is directly in the rear." The former city hall was located at 180 First Street and was constructed in 1921 in the classic Spanish Colonial Revival style. The building is now home to the Yuma Crossing Heritage Area center.

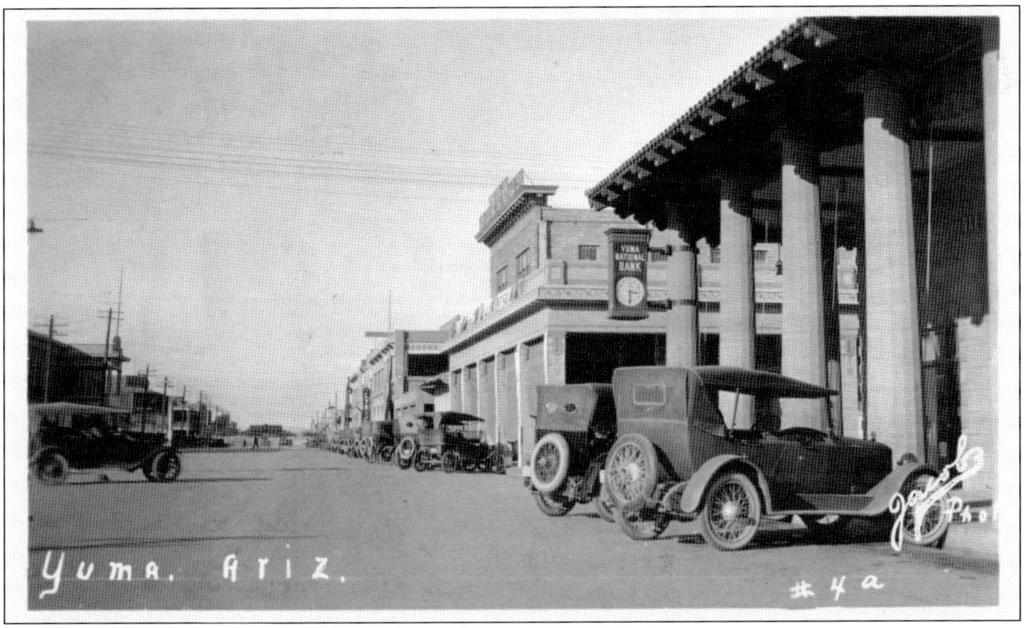

Main Street, Yuma National Bank, c. 1920s (Real-Photo Postcard). The Yuma National Bank opened on January 3, 1910, only to close its doors under a suspicious cloud three months later on April 18, 1910. The bank reorganized and reopened a few days later under new management. In 1929, Yuma National Bank absorbed the First National Bank of Yuma. The structure on Main Street was rehabilitated as the county administration building in 1990. (Published by Jacobs Photo.)

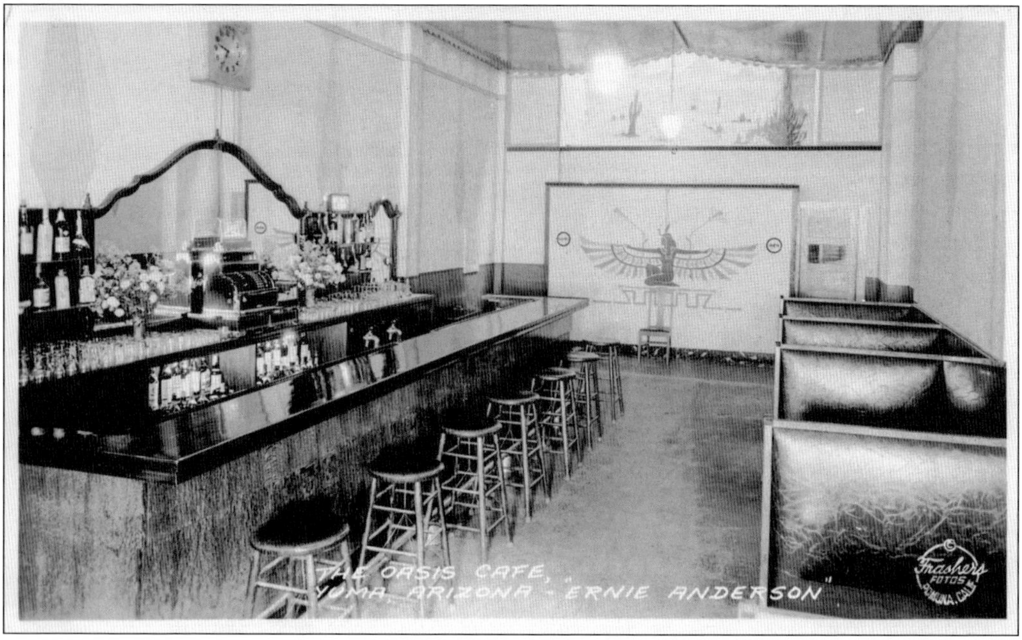

THE OASIS CAFÉ, C. 1930S (REAL-PHOTO POSTCARD). In 1934, the Oasis Café's menu included a 35¢ merchant lunch, and for 60¢, one could feast on a filet mignon in a mushroom sauce. The Oasis Café was located at 18 Second Street. (Published by Frashers Fotos, which also went by Frashers and Frashers, Inc.)

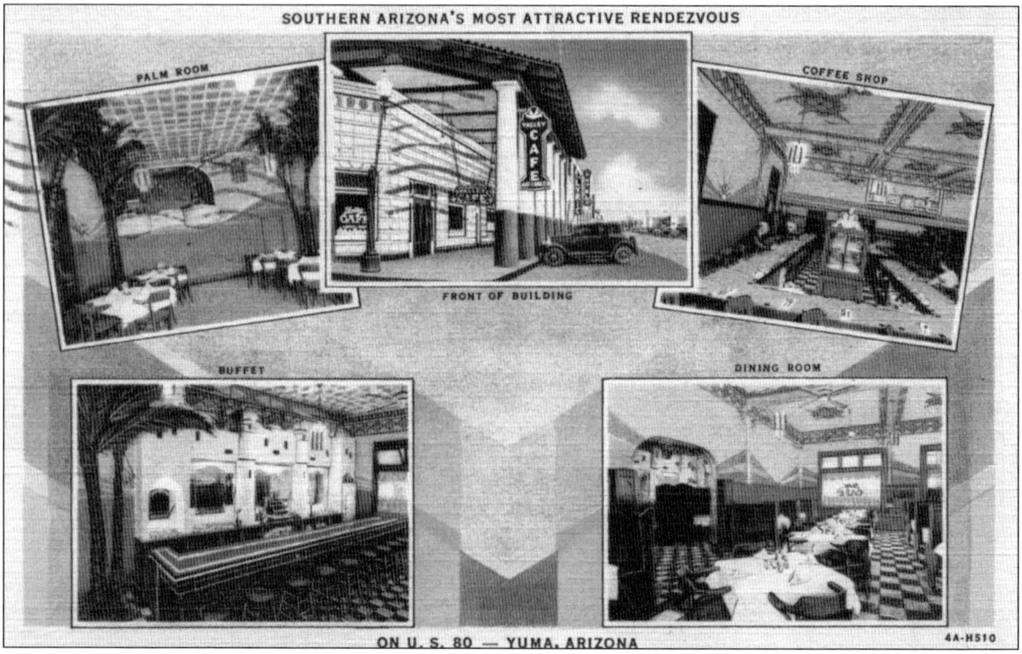

THE VALLEY CAFÉ, POSTMARKED APRIL 22, 1935 (ADVERTISING LINEN POSTCARD). The Valley Café opened on Main Street in the 1920s and was considered one of the best restaurants downtown. It closed in the late 1950s, with the Yuma First National Bank occupying the space a few years later. (Published by Curt Teich & Co.)

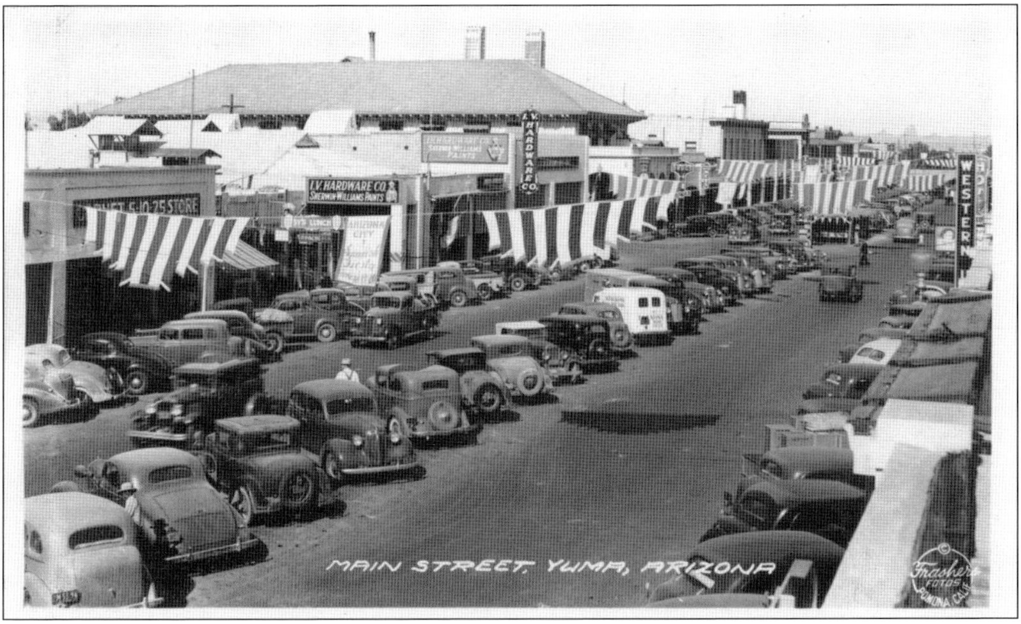

MAIN STREET, DOWNTOWN, C. 1930S (REAL-PHOTO POSTCARD). The I.V. (short for Imperial Valley) Hardware Co. store, on the left side of the street, had eight stores throughout the Imperial Valley of California and the Yuma area by the 1920s. The Yuma store downtown opened in 1926. The last store in Yuma could not compete with the new big-box stores and closed in 2000. (Published by Frashers Fotos.)

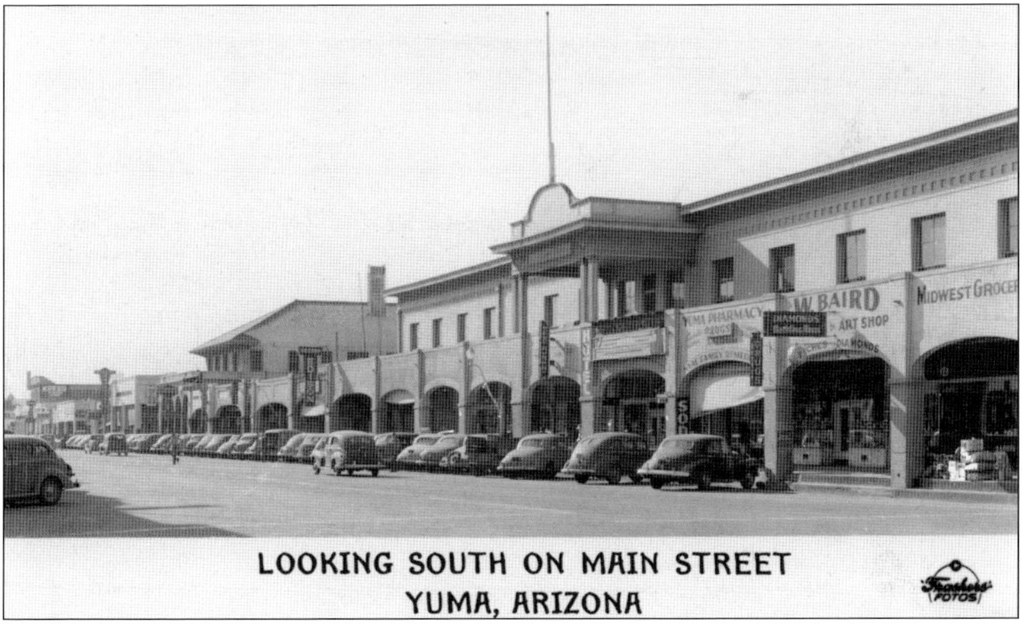

MAIN STREET LOOKING SOUTH, C. 1940S (REAL-PHOTO POSTCARD). The building on the right with the flagpole is the Hotel Santa Rita. Originally the Gandolfo Hotel, one of the finer hotels in Yuma, it became the Roosevelt Hotel in the 1930s. By the 1940s, the hotel was sold again, becoming the Hotel Santa Rita, where a room went for as low as $1.50 a night. (Published by Frashers Fotos.)

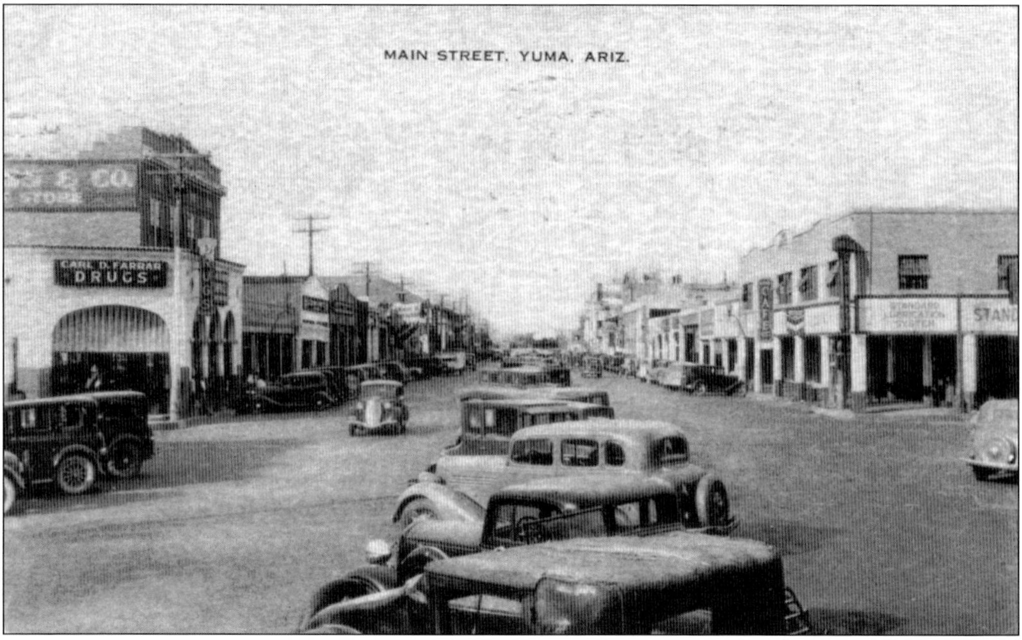

ABOVE, MAIN STREET, POSTMARKED DECEMBER 3, 1938 (REAL-PHOTO POSTCARD); BELOW, MAIN STREET, C. 1940S (REAL-PHOTO POSTCARD). The McCallum Cutrate Drug Store was located on the northwest corner of Main and Third Streets. Prior to being McCallum Drug, it was the Carl D. Farrar Drug Store. The building resembles nothing of its past and is now the local Mexican consulate. The Kress building looks quite similar today. It is now home to a number of smaller stores and the popular Kress Ultra Lounge. (Above, published by Artvue Post Card Co.; below, L.L. Cook Co.)

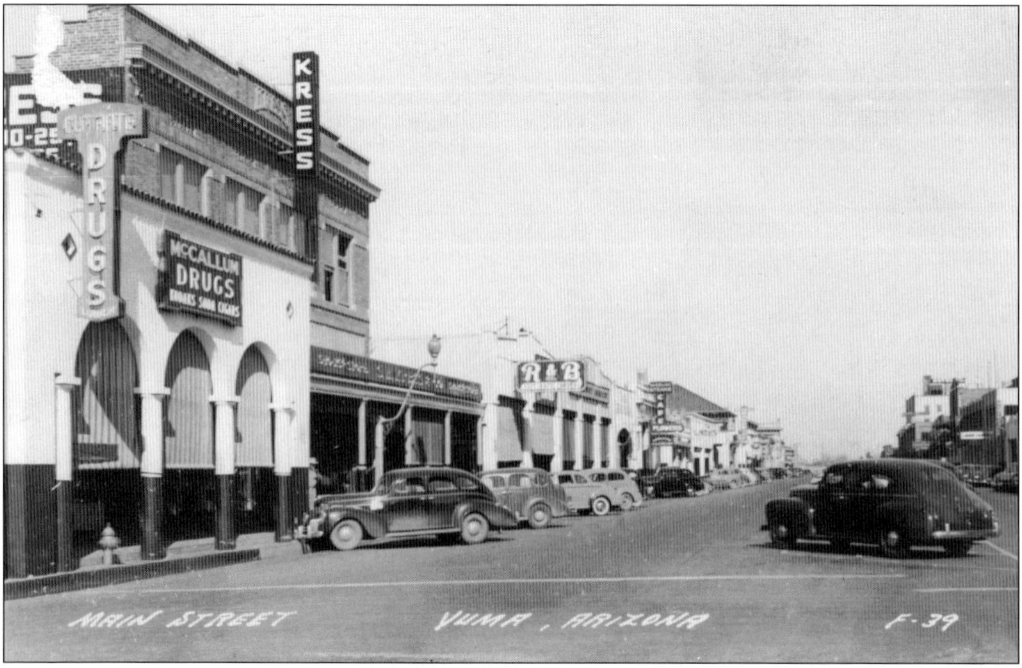

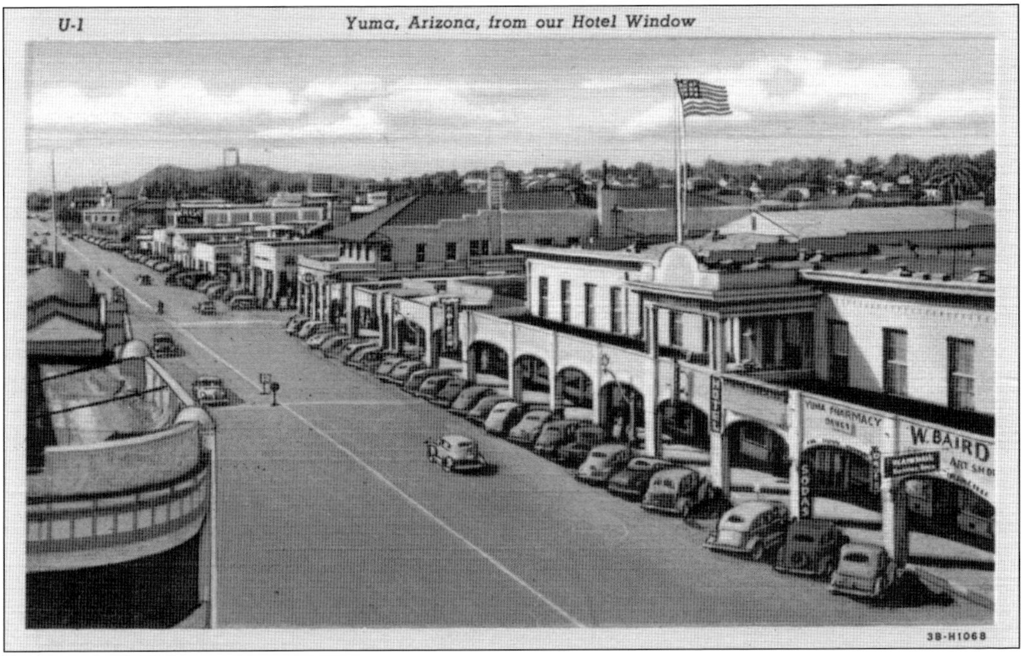

Above, Yuma from Hotel Window, c. 1943 (Curt Teich Linen Postcard); Below, Looking North on Main Street, c. 1943 (Curt Teich Linen Postcard). The above postcard would have been the view from the San Carlos Hotel looking south onto Main Street. The structure on the bottom left is the top of the Hotel Arizona. The postcard below depicts the opposite view of Main Street looking north from a location near Second Street. (Both, published by Lollesgard Specialty Co.)

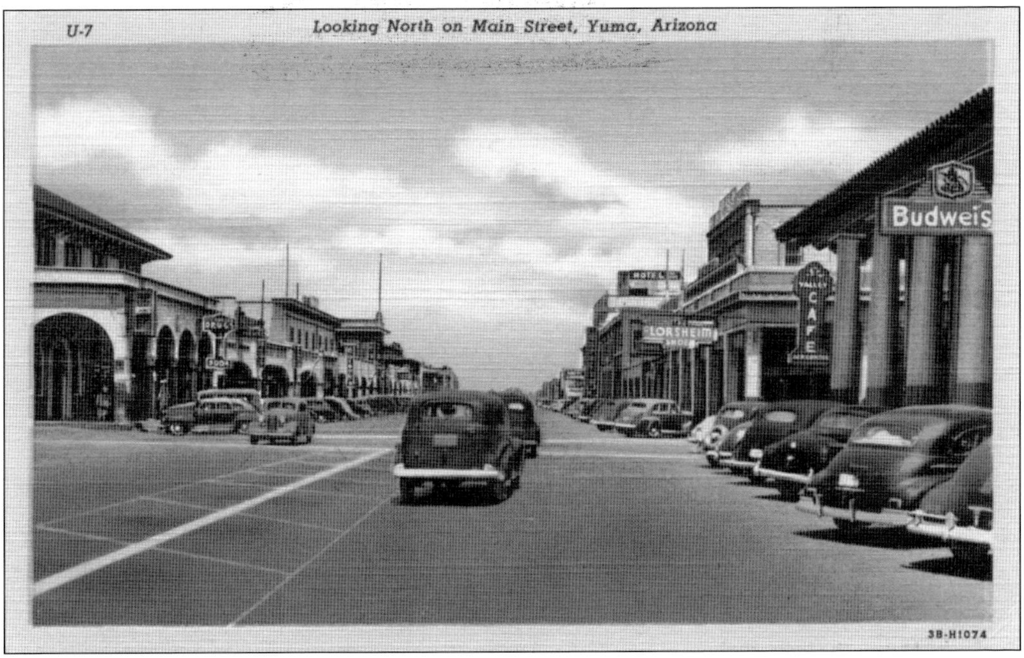

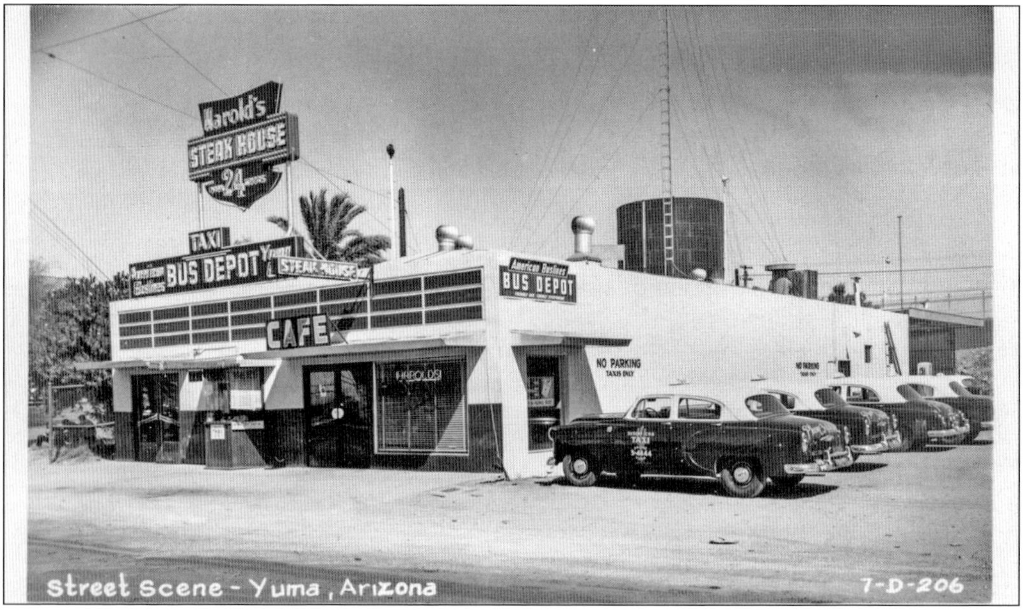

Bus Depot and Harold's Steak House, c. 1950 (Real-Photo Postcard). Located at the corner of Gila and Third Streets, the building that once was the transportation hub of Yuma still stands today across from the old Hotel Del Sol. For many years, the depot was used by the Desert Cab Company and the Greyhound Bus Lines. The building is now used by the Union Railroad.

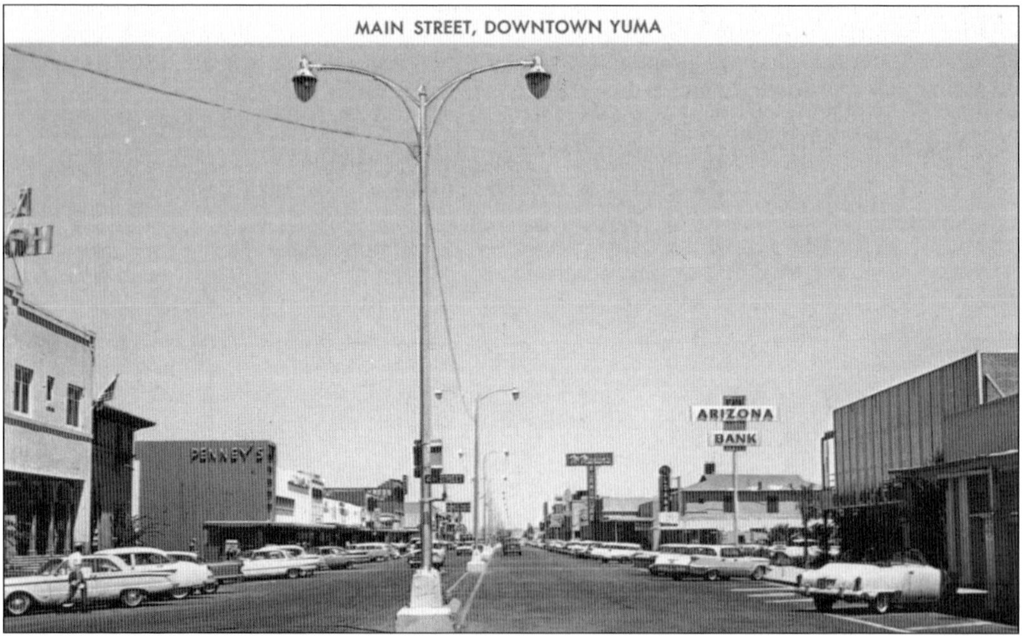

Main Street, Downtown, Postmarked December 1, 1965 (Real-Photo Postcard). A few years after this photograph was taken, Main Street was closed to vehicle traffic to make way for a pedestrian mall. In 1975, J.C. Penney (left), located at 354 Main Street since the 1950s, started looking for a larger location, eventually relocating to Southgate Mall. (Published by Yuma Color Cards.)

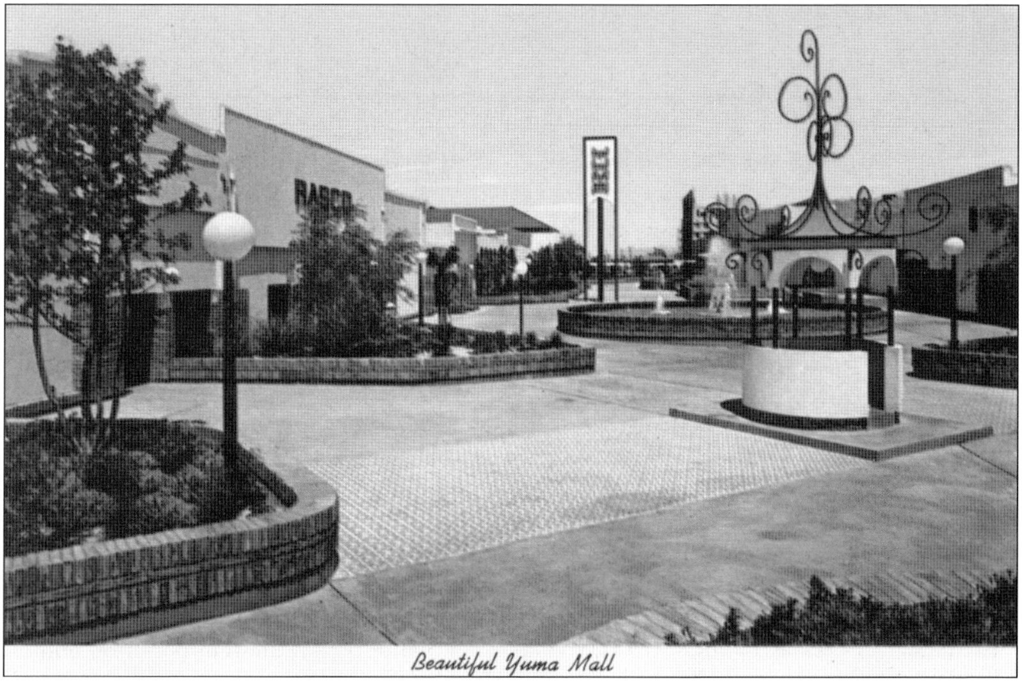

Above, Yuma Mall, c. 1970s (CurTeich Color Postcard); Below, Yuma Mall, c. 1970s (Kodachrome Postcard). In an attempt to get people into the old part of downtown, where many stores and business had closed, the city in 1969 closed off Main Street and built an outdoor pedestrian mall with walkways, a tress, and fountains. In 2005, the mall was removed, and Main Street returned to vehicle traffic. (Above, published by Yuma Distributing Service, photograph by Emil Eger; below, published by Petley Studios.)

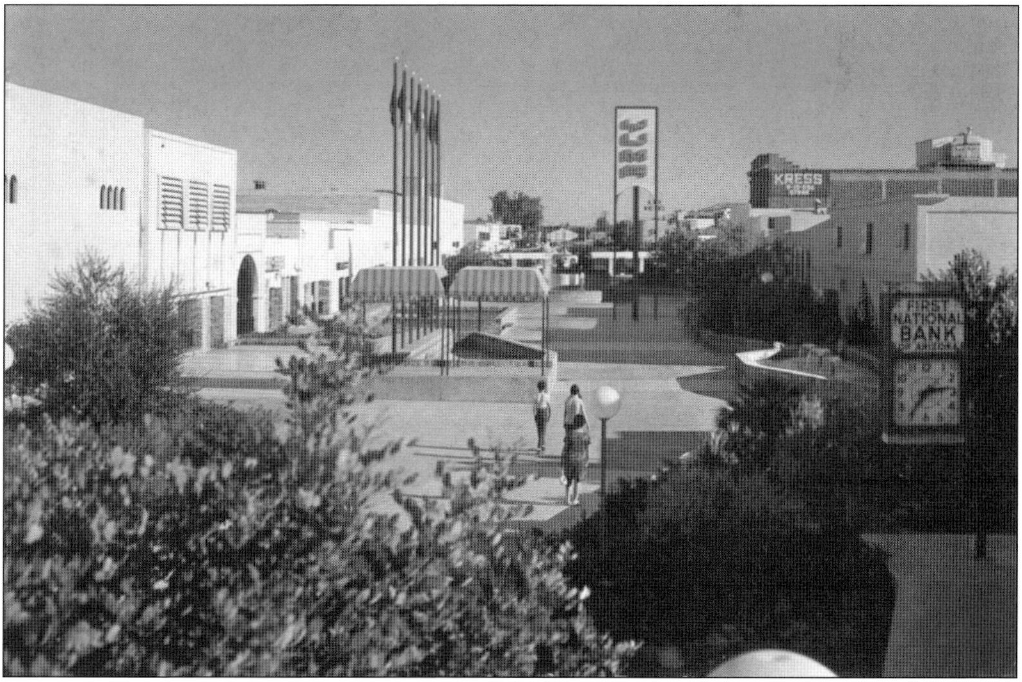

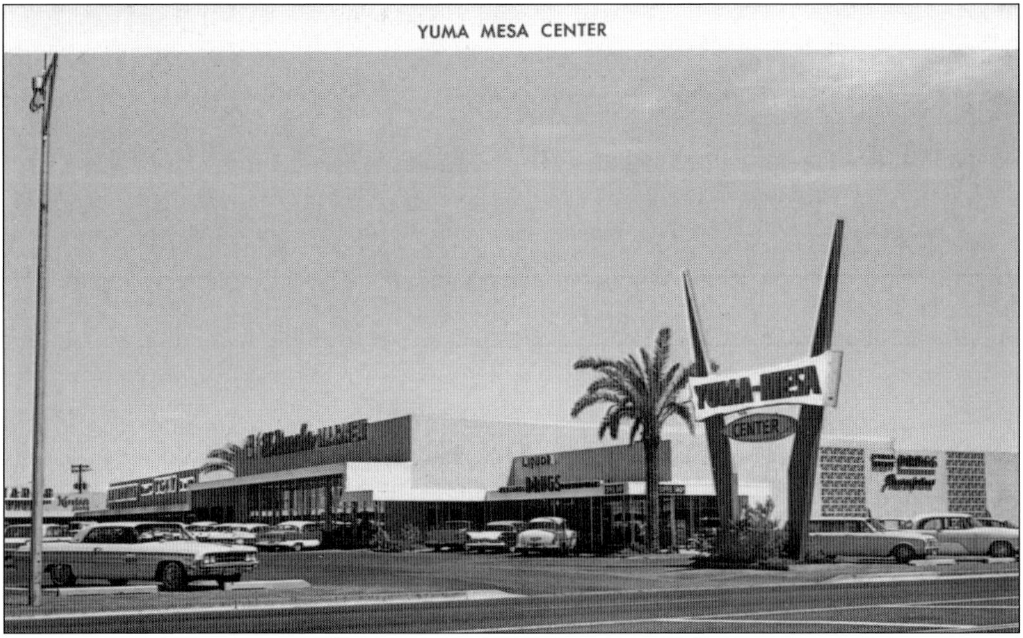

YUMA MESA CENTER, POSTMARKED FEBRUARY 5, 1965 (CURTEICH COLOR POSTCARD FOLDER). The Yuma Mesa Shopping Center held its grand opening on Wednesday, April 12, 1961. Located on the corner of Sixteenth Street and Fourth Avenue, it was one of the first shopping centers in Yuma. It has gone through many remodels over the years and many store changes, but the Mesa Center is still in operation today. (Published by Yuma Color Cards.)

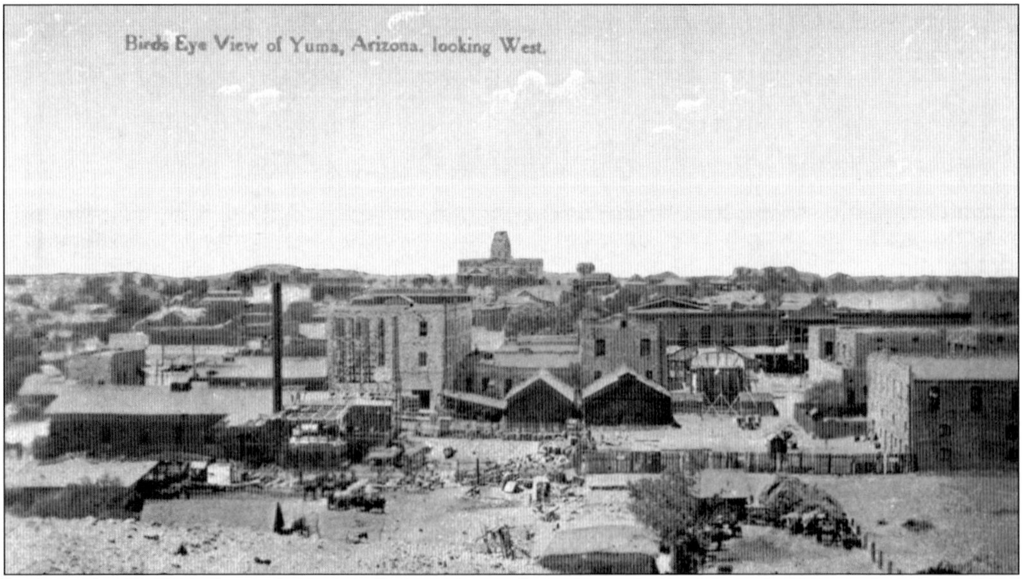

VIEW OF YUMA LOOKING WEST, C. 1910 (DIVIDED BACK POSTCARD). The tall building in the background, constructed in 1909, is the Yuma County Courthouse on South Second Street. The Gandolfo Hotel, built in 1899 on Main Street, is the structure facing forward. The three-story building, center left, is the old Sanguinetti store. Yuma County recently remodeled the structure, making it almost unrecognizable from the historic building it once was. (Published by Newman Post Card Co.)

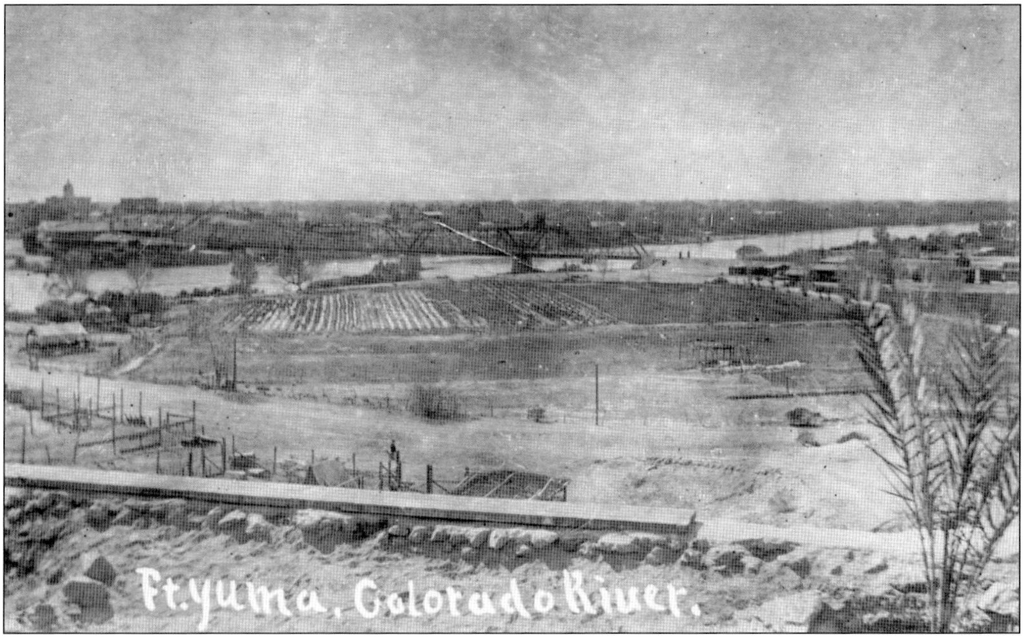

FORT YUMA, C. 1910 (REAL-PHOTO POSTCARD). This photograph was taken from the California side of the river, from Fort Yuma. The Southern Pacific Railroad bridge seen here was built in 1899 and crossed the Colorado onto Madison Avenue. The two-story building near the end of the bridge is the Southern Pacific Hotel.

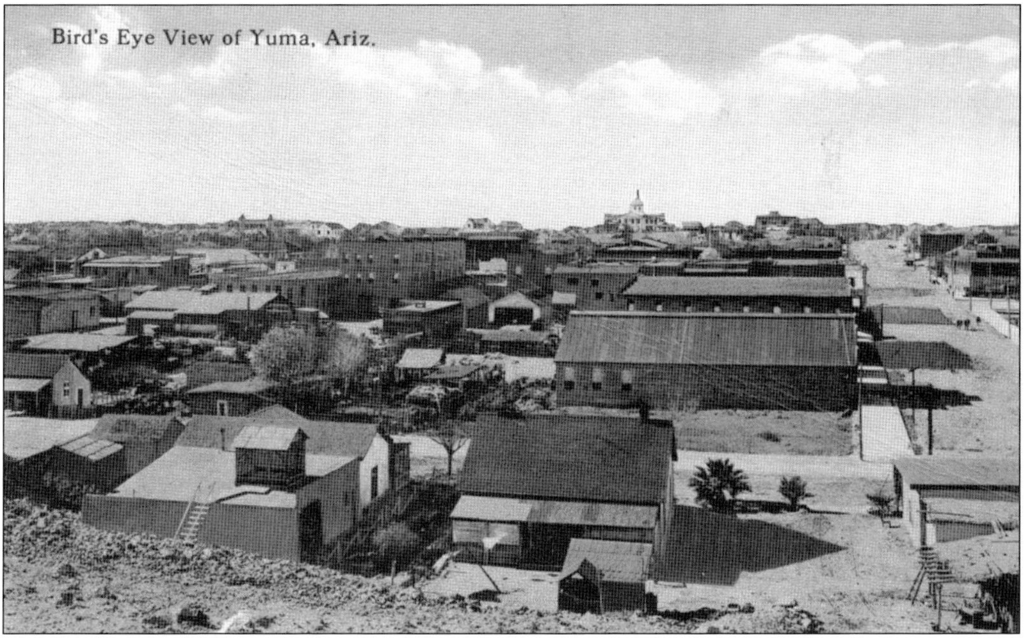

VIEW OF YUMA, C. 1915 (CURT TEICH HAND-COLORED POSTCARD). The road in the foreground is East Gila Street, with East First Street at right. The first building on First Street is now the site of the Mad Chef Restaurant. The homes in the foreground on East Gila Street are long gone, as are the buildings across from them, which is now a large parking lot. (Published by J. Homer Smith.)

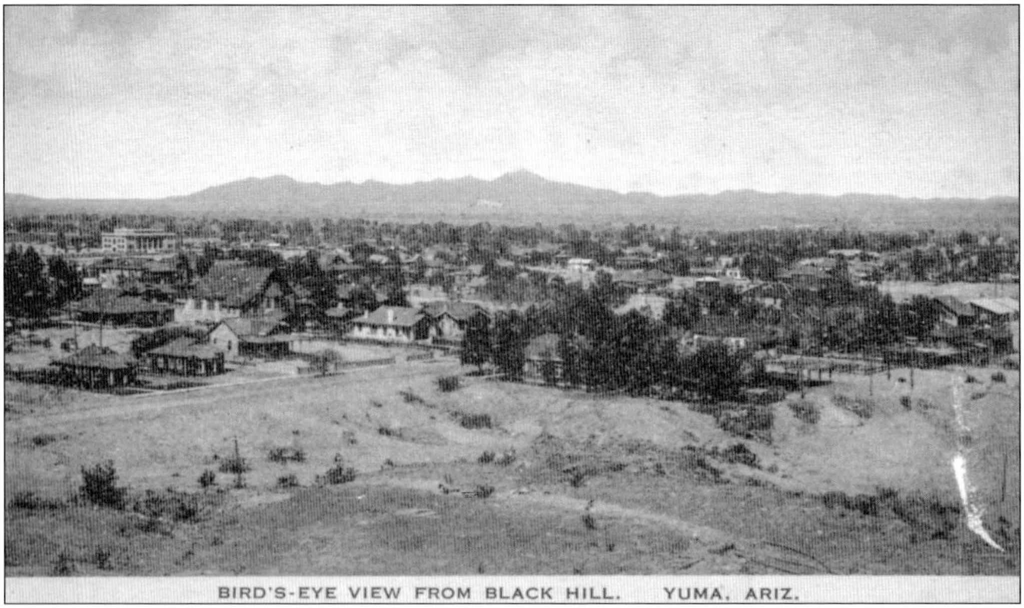

From Black Hill, c. 1910s (Albertype Postcard). The two houses on South First Street, at center and at left, are no longer there. The next three homes are still present, as is the old historic St. John's Episcopal Church behind them. Located at 637 South Second Street, St. John's was built in 1909 and added to the National Register of Historic Places in 1982. (Published by the Albertype Co.)

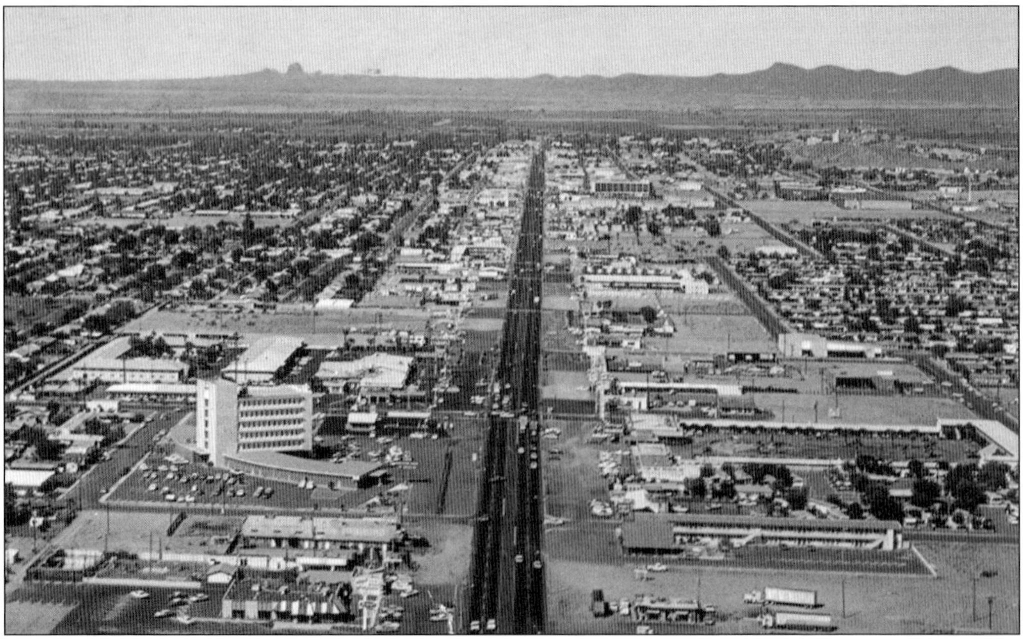

Aerial View, Postmarked May 22, 1970 (Real-Photo Postcard). This view shows South Fourth Avenue, one of the main thoroughfares through Yuma. It was also the old Highway 80 (now Interstate 8) prior to its rerouting around town. The large circular building at left is the Crescent Center, located on South Fourth Avenue and West Twenty-Fourth Street. (Published by Petley Studios.)

Two

Staying in Town
Hotels and Snowbirds

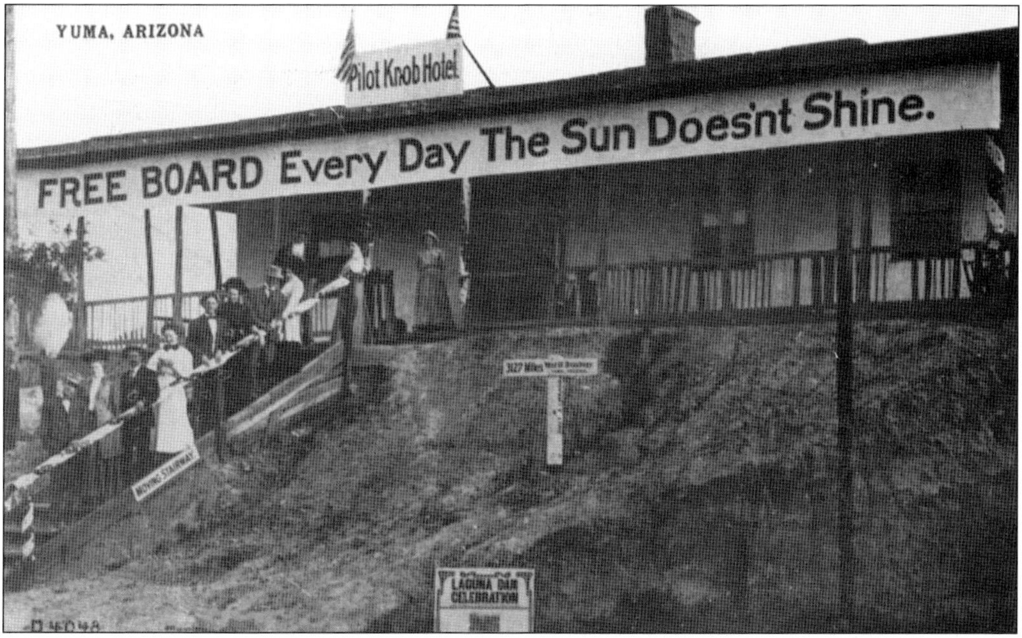

Pilot Knob Hotel, Postmarked February 23, 1917 (Real-Photo Postcard). With an average of 350 days of sunshine, it was a pretty safe bet that the Pilot Knob Hotel, located on Jones Street near Madison Avenue, did not give away too many free nights. In an article from the February 10, 1910, *Arizona Sentinel*, "Joe Henry and J.J. Waddell have raised a fund among the local businessmen to restore the sign, 'Free Board Every Day the Sun Doesn't Shine,' adorning the Pilot Knob Hotel. This sign has proved an immediate attraction to tourists, advertising one of this regions chief assets." (Published by M.S. Darling.)

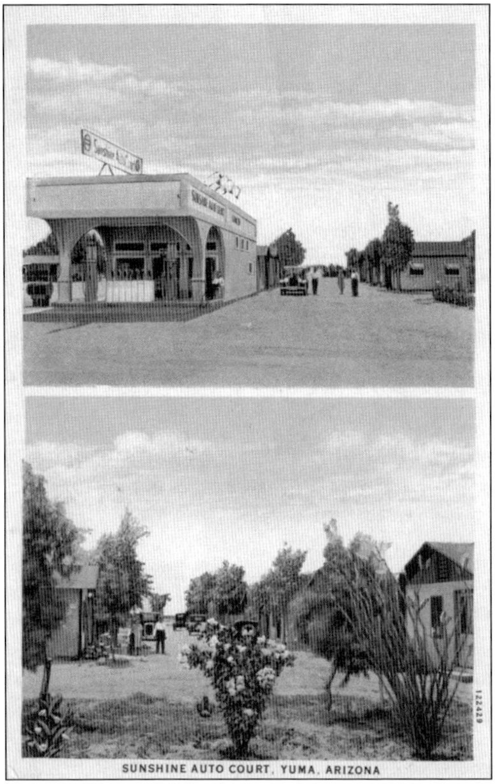

SUNSHINE AUTO COURT, C. 1920S (ADVERTISING POSTCARD). The Sunshine Auto Court was located at 1098 Fourth Avenue at the corner of West Eleventh Street. (Published by Harry Herz.)

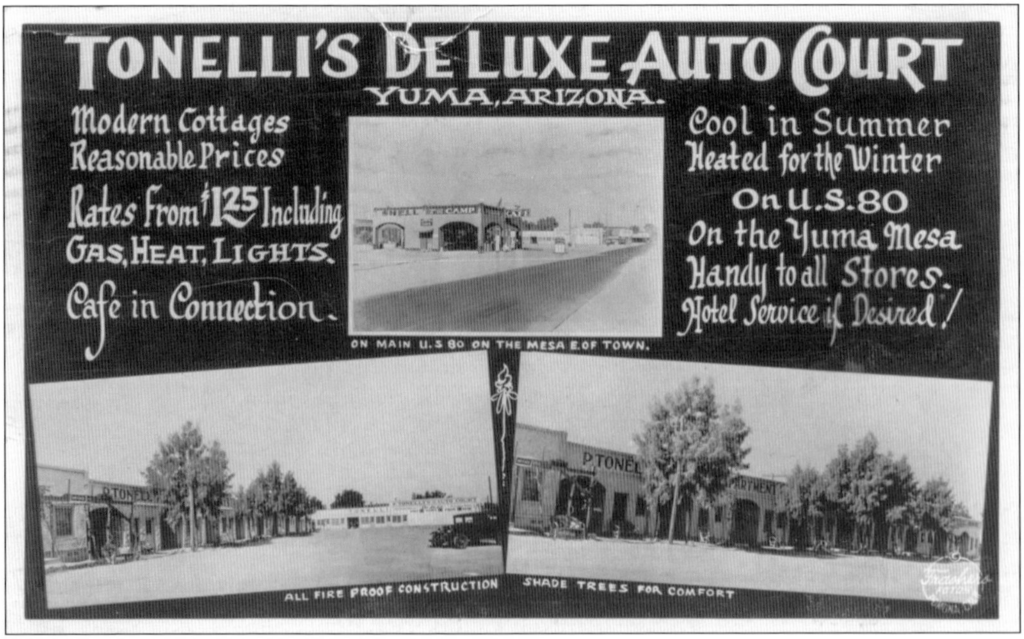

TONELLI'S DELUXE AUTO COURT, POSTMARKED JANUARY 3, 1933 (ADVERTISING POSTCARD). The postcard describes the location as being on US 80 east of town on the Yuma Mesa. Handwritten on the back of the card is "Dear Phyllis, This is a picture of our new home for the night. Love Jack." (Published by Frasher's Inc.)

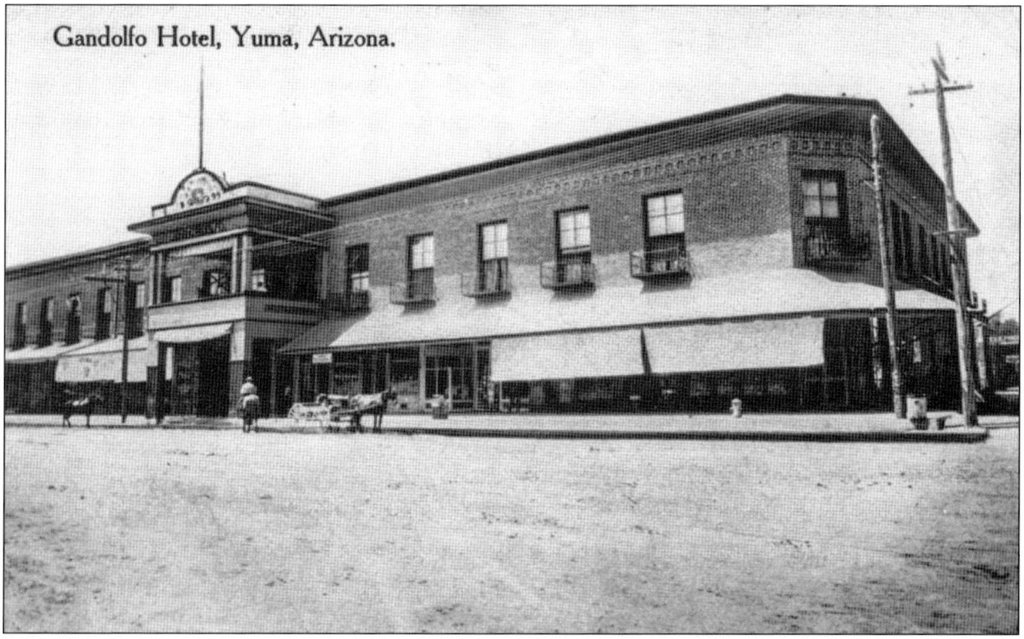

ABOVE, GANDOLFO HOTEL, C. 1908 (REAL-PHOTO POSTCARD); BELOW, GANDOLFO HOTEL, POSTMARKED SEPTEMBER 28, 1916 (HAND-COLORED POSTCARD). John Gandolfo came to Yuma in 1876 and established himself in the local business establishment. He built the Gandolfo Hotel and Gandolfo Café on the corner of Main and First Streets in 1883. The hotel had more than 50 rooms and was the largest and most elegant hotel in Yuma. In the 1930s, the Gandolfo Hotel was sold and became the Roosevelt Hotel. The hotel was eventually demolished to make room for retail stores downtown. (Below, published by J. Homer Smith.)

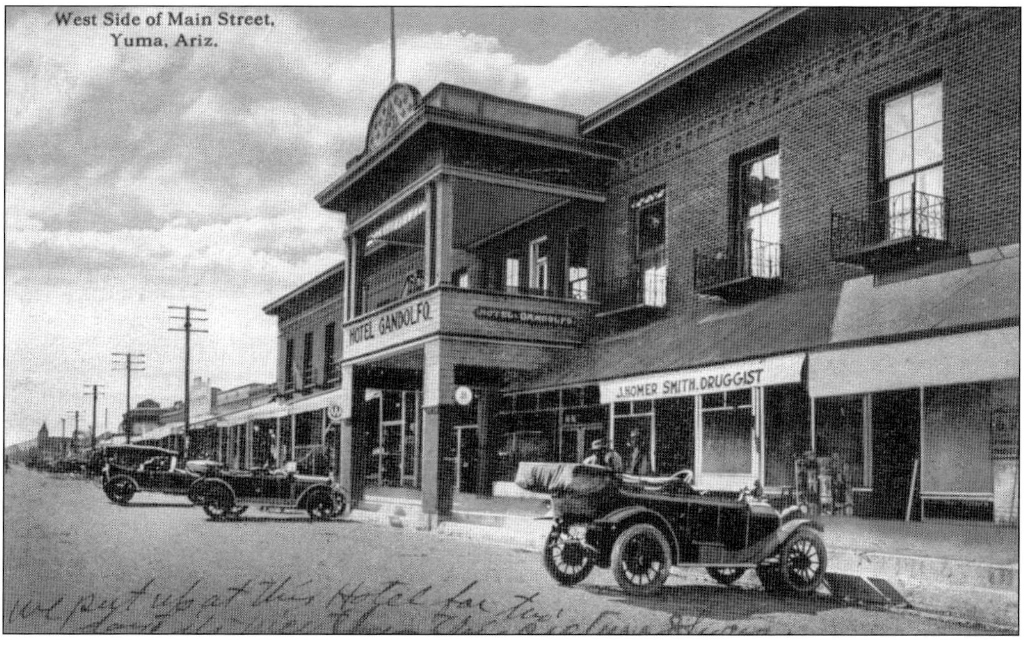

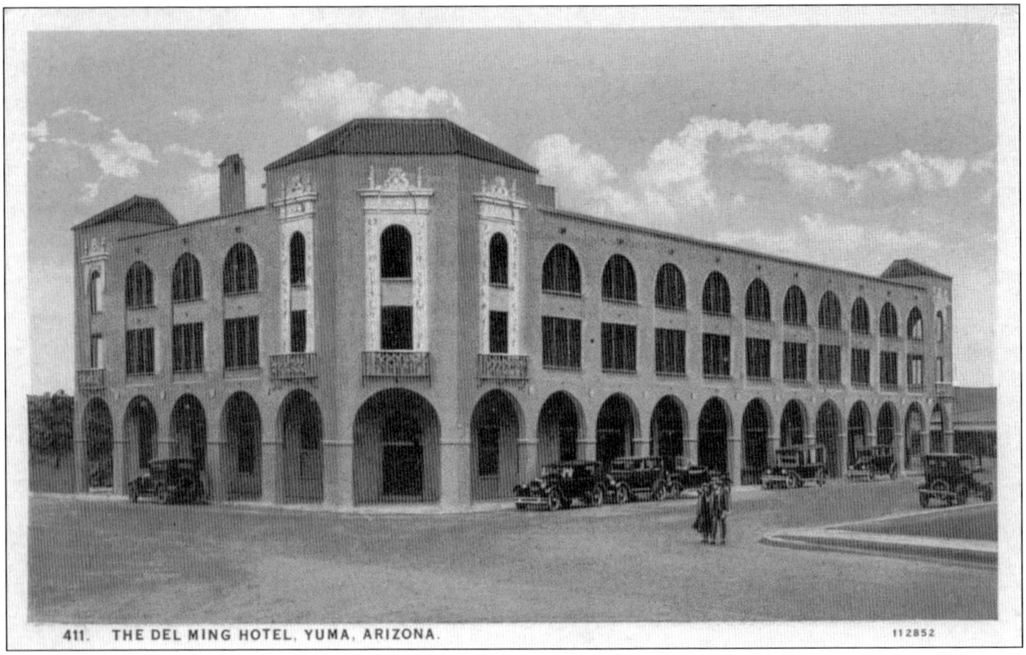

Above, Hotel Del Ming, c. 1926 (Curt Teich Postcard); Below, Hotel Del Ming, Postmarked July 12, 1939 (Real-Photo Postcard). Frank Ming came to Yuma with his wife, Anna, in 1902. For many years prior to opening the Hotel Del Ming in 1927, Ming ran the Southern Pacific Hotel and served on the Yuma City Council and later as mayor. He died in Yuma in 1930. (Below, published by Harry Herz.)

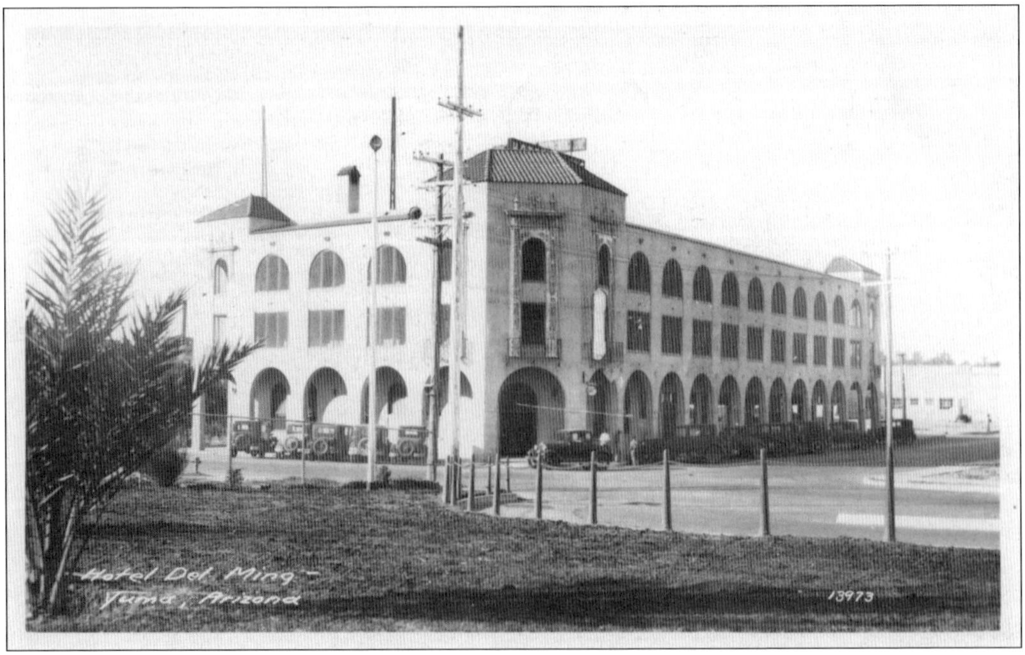

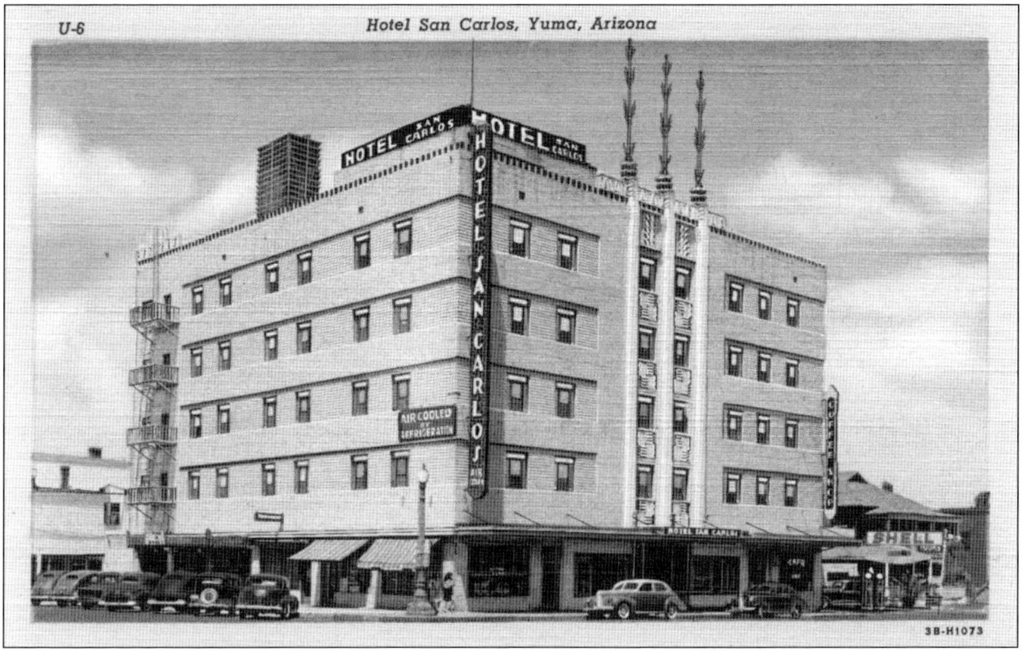

ABOVE, HOTEL SAN CARLOS, C. 1943 (CURT TEICH LINEN POSTCARD); BELOW, HOTEL SAN CARLOS, HAND DATED JULY 6, 1940 (REAL-PHOTO POSTCARD). This once-elegant hotel was used over the years by such stars as John Wayne, Marilyn Monroe, Jim Thorpe, Spencer Tracy, Herbert Hover, Ty Cobb, and many others. Constructed in 1929 in the modern Art Deco style, the San Carlos Hotel served as the hub of Yuma's social life well into the 1960s. In the lobby still sits a framed menu with autographs of celebrities who have stayed at the hotel. It is rumored that during a visit to Yuma, John Wayne boarded his horse on the roof of the hotel. Once the pride of Yuma, the San Carlos is now a low-income apartment complex for seniors. (Above, published by Lollesgard Specialty Co.; below, published by Artvue Post Card Co.)

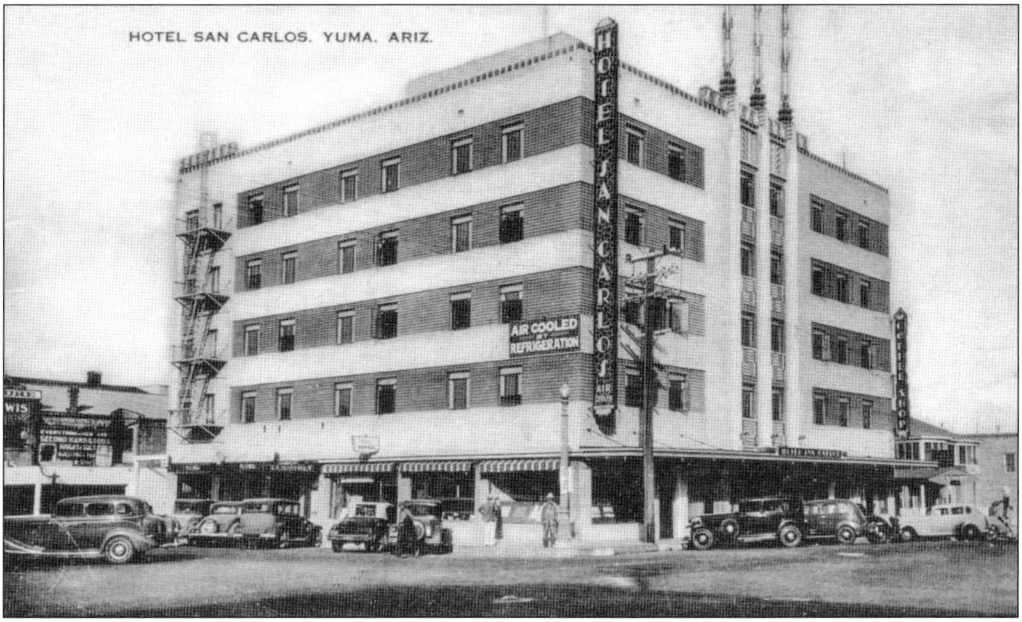

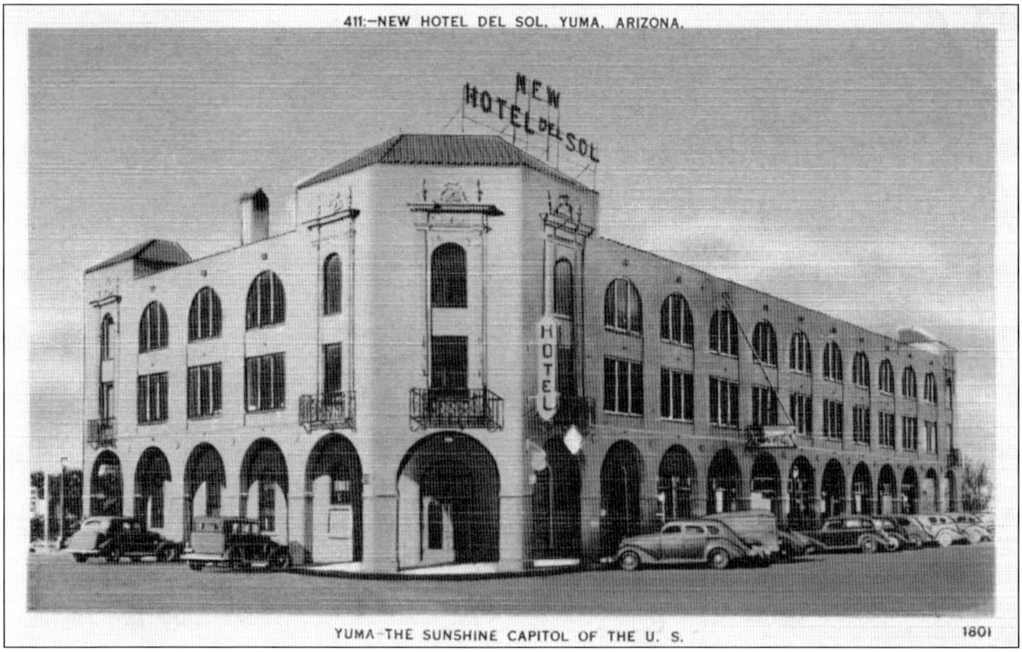

HOTEL DEL SOL, C. 1940S (LINEN ADVERTISING POSTCARD). Constructed in the Mission Revival style on the corner of Third and Gila Streets, the hotel opened for business in 1926. Originally, it was named the Hotel Del Ming after the owner, Frank S. Ming. Built directly across from the train station, the Del Sol was the first large hotel in Yuma, with 70 rooms. The hotel started to decline after World War II when rail traffic declined. It finally closed in the 1980s after passing through several owners. The City of Yuma purchased the empty and dilapidated hotel in 2006 and in 2015 received a federal grant of over $1 million for planning and designing the historic Hotel Del Sol Multimodal Transit Center. One of the last uses for the building was in the 1990s, when the movie *The Getaway*, starring Alec Baldwin and Kim Basinger, was filmed there. (Published by Herz Post Cards.)

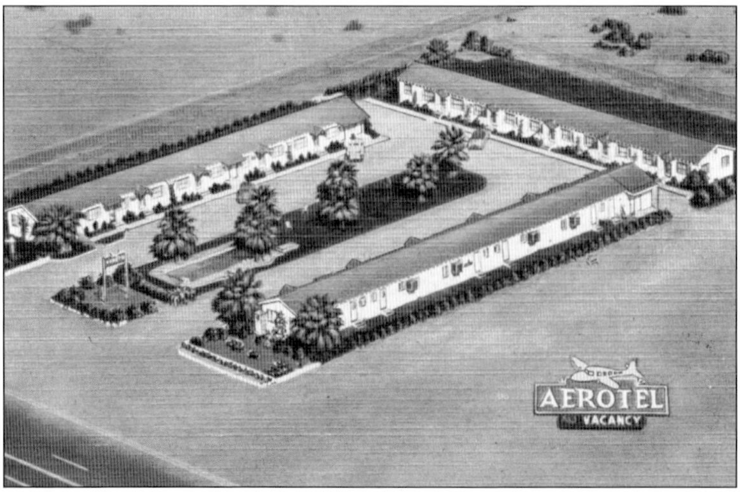

AEROTEL, C. 1940S (LINEN ADVERTISING POSTCARD). The back of the card reads, "Aerotel Tourist Court, 2115 Fourth Avenue, Yuma. 24 Modern units—kitchenettes and sleeping rooms—swimming pool—electric Heat—refrigerated and air conditioned—Children and pets welcome." (Published by Colourpicture.)

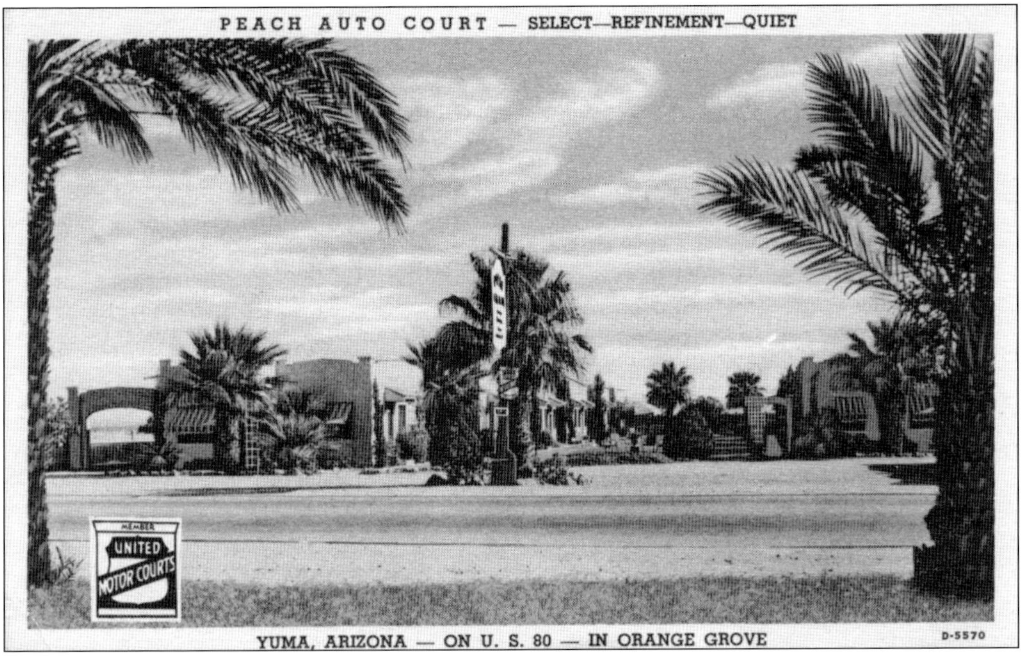

ABOVE, PEACH AUTO COURT, C. 1938 (ADVERTISING POSTCARD); BELOW, PEACH MOTOR COURT, C. 1940S (ADVERTISING POSTCARD). With lumber in short supply around Yuma in the 1930s, John and Mary Peach purchased the rights to the timbers from the old Southern Pacific Railroad Hotel that was located on Madison Avenue. On what was then Highway 80, they used this lumber to build the Peach Auto Court and opened in 1932. The auto court was torn down in 1979 and is now where WOW Electronics sits at 1881 South Fourth Avenue. (Above, published by Curteich; below, published by Associate Service.)

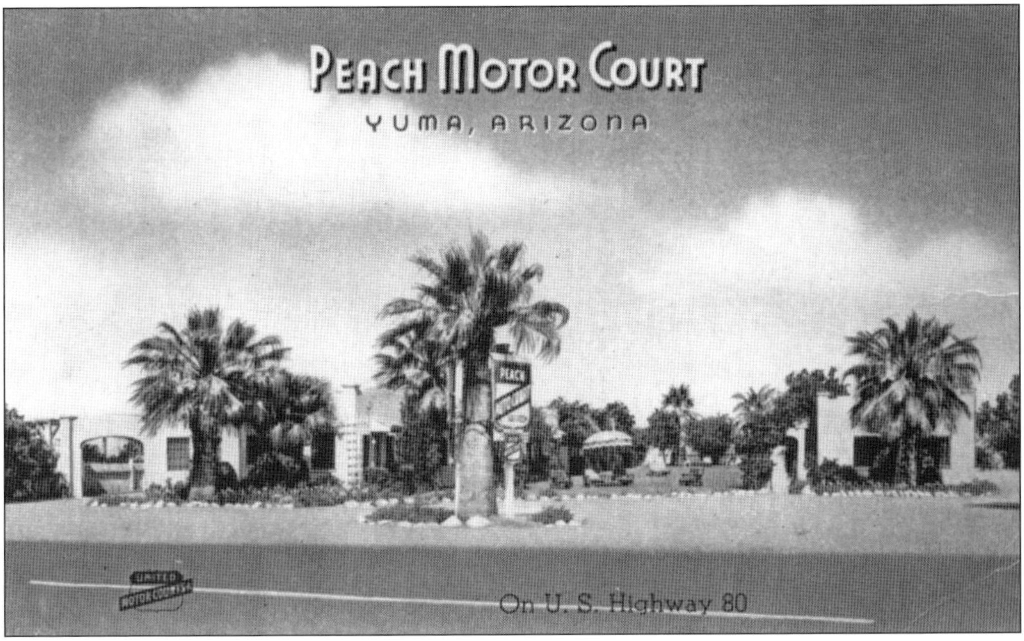

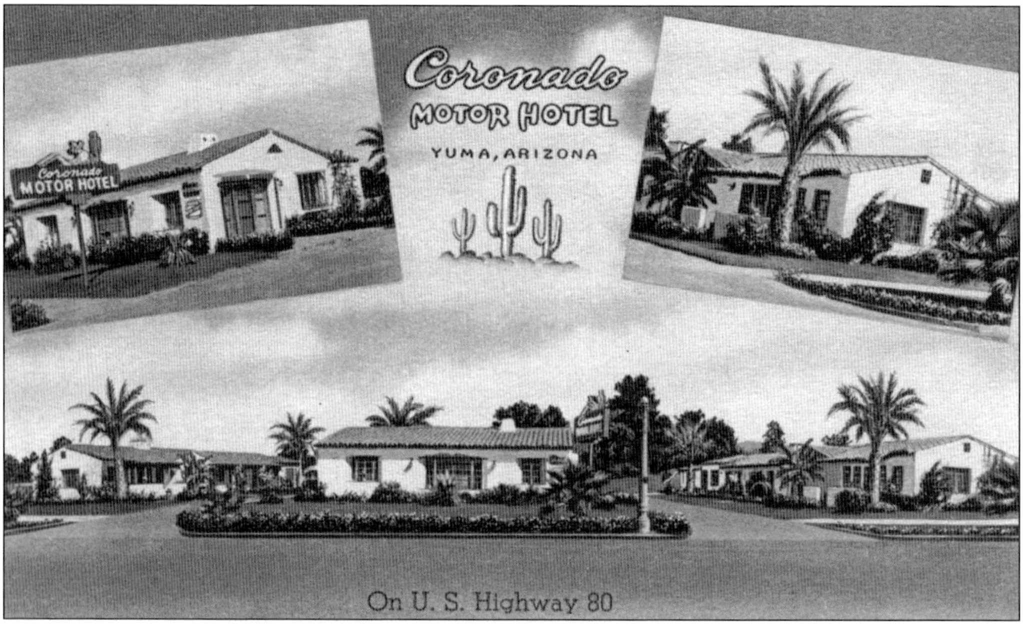

CORONADO MOTOR HOTEL, C. 1946 (ADVERTISING POSTCARD). An article from the February 3, 1963, issue of the *Yuma Daily Sun* reported, "Doing Well—John Peach a month after his new addition to the Coronado Hotel opened, is happily counting in the new customers. He added 14 new units, some of them kitchenettes, and a new office. Business is a little better this year than at the same time last year, Peach said." (Published by Associate Service.)

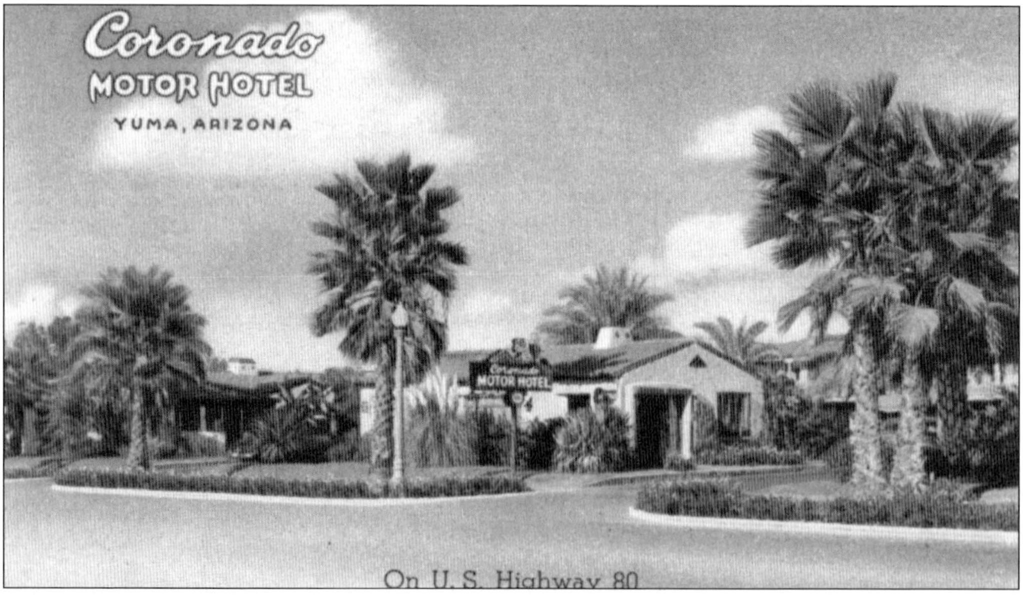

CORONADO MOTOR HOTEL, POSTMARKED FEBRUARY 14, 1950 (ADVERTISING POSTCARD). After the success of the Peach Auto Court, the Peaches decided to build a second hotel. A few years later, in 1938, the Coronado Motor Motel opened for business. It became one of what the April 6, 2014 *Yuma Sun* called the original "10 Best Western Hotels in the United States" in 1946. Over the years, the business stayed in the Peach family and grew from just 14 rooms to 127 rooms. (Published by Portraitone.)

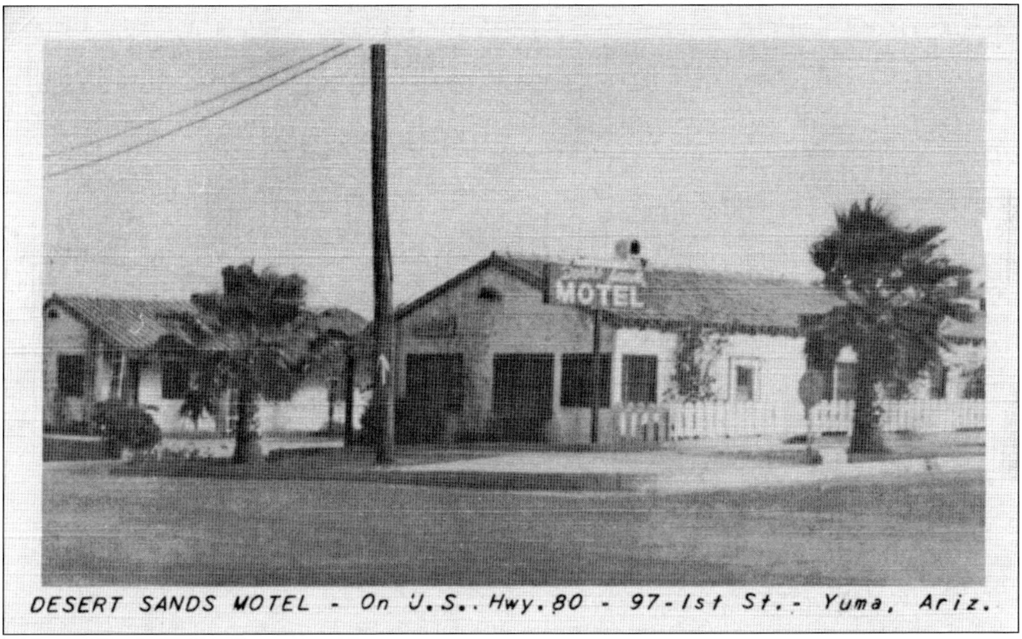

Desert Sands Motel, c. 1940s (Linen Advertising Postcard). The Desert Sands Motel would have been one of the first motels to be seen when entering Yuma from California on the old US Highway 80. The motel lasted well into the early 2000s, when it was used for lower-income housing. It was demolished around 2007, with the lot now sitting empty. (Published by National Press.)

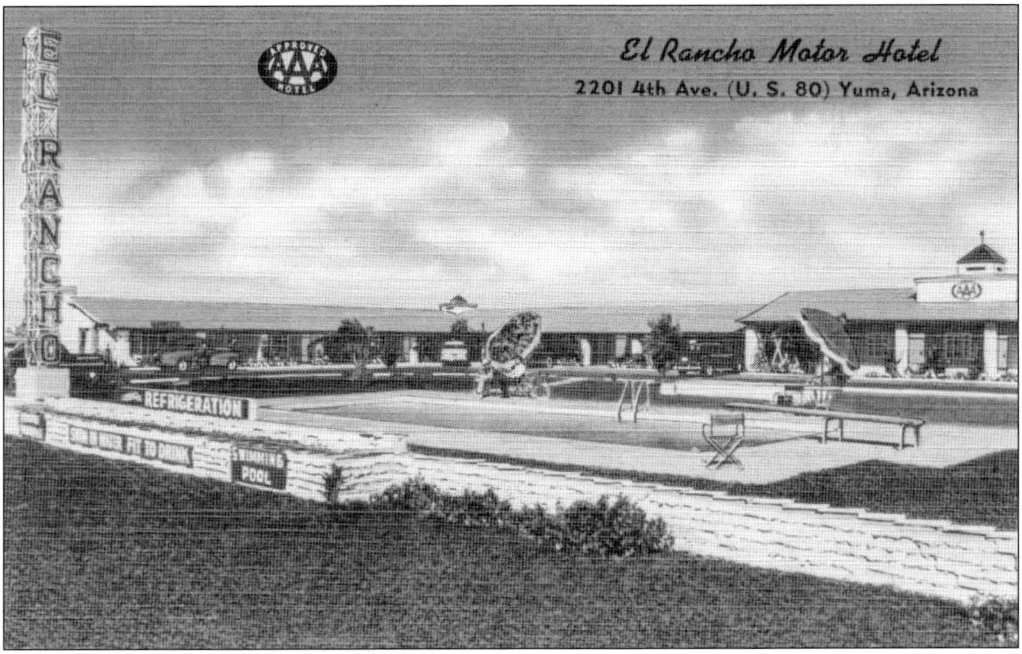

El Rancho Motor Hotel, c. 1940s (Linen Advertising Postcard). The El Rancho Motor Hotel is now known as the El Rancho Motel and appears remarkably as it did when this postcard was manufactured in the 1940s. (Published by Colourpicture Publication.)

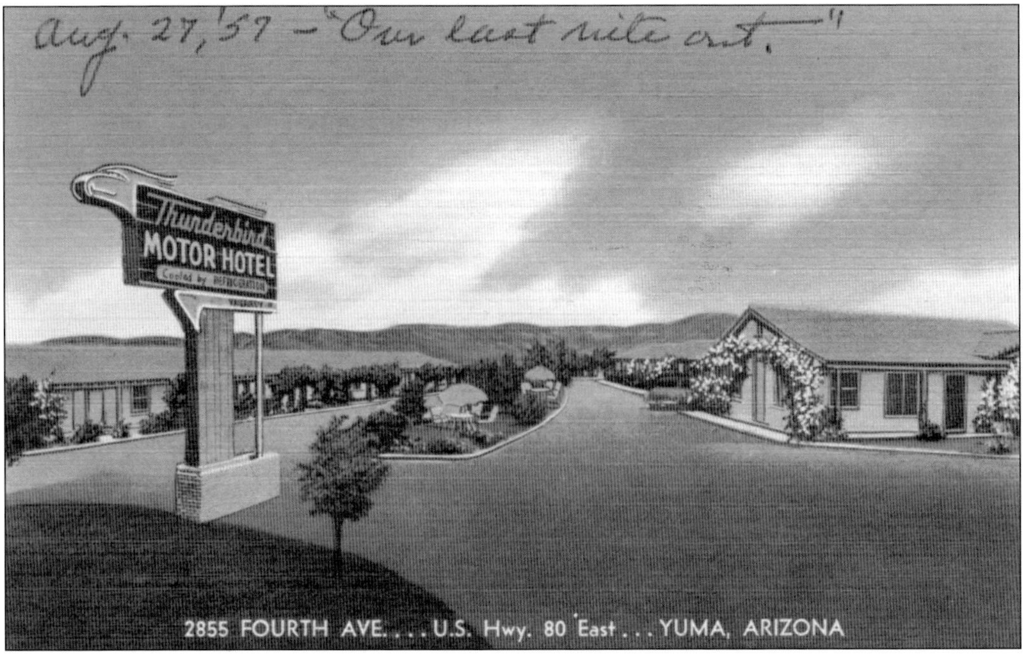

THUNDERBIRD MOTOR HOTEL, HAND DATED AUGUST 27, 1957 (LINEN ADVERTISING POSTCARD). Now known as the Thunderbird Plaza, the Thunderbird Motor Hotel has been converted into office space, along with a restaurant in the first building at right. One can still see the bird's head and tail on the Thunderbird Plaza sign. (Published by Douglas R. Smith Co.)

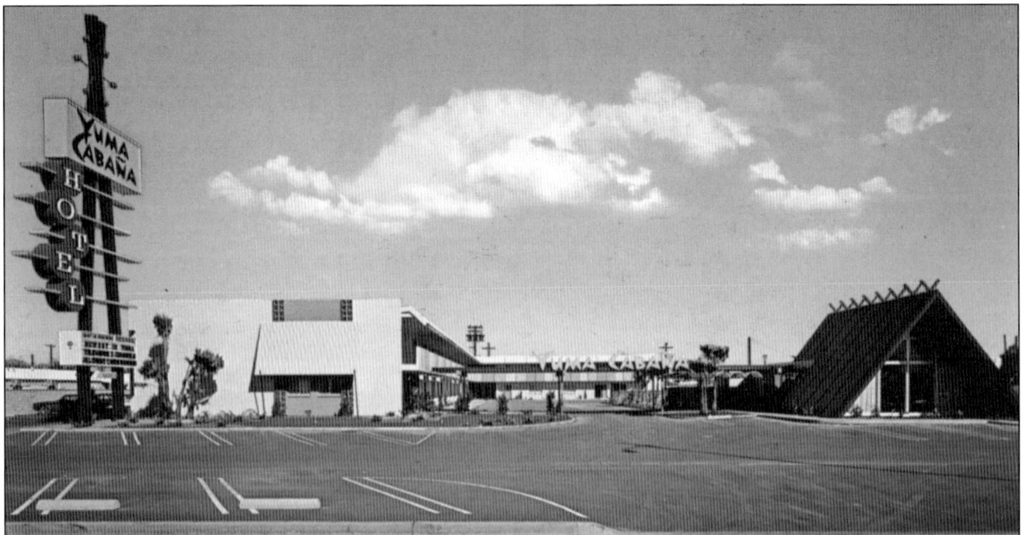

YUMA CABANA MOTOR HOTEL, C. 1960S (ADVERTISING POSTCARD). Built in the late 1950s or early 1960s, the Cabana Hotel is still in business at 2151 South Fourth Street with the same familiar old deco sign. The card reads, "Yuma Cabana Motor Hotel is located in Yuma, Arizona adjacent to Old Mexico and recreational areas of the Colorado River. Yuma Cabana has accommodations of all types for the traveler. All rooms are sound proof with central refrigeration and cabled T.V. Heated pool, suites, kitchenettes, Country Club privileges." (Published by George A. Douglas; photograph by George A. Douglas.)

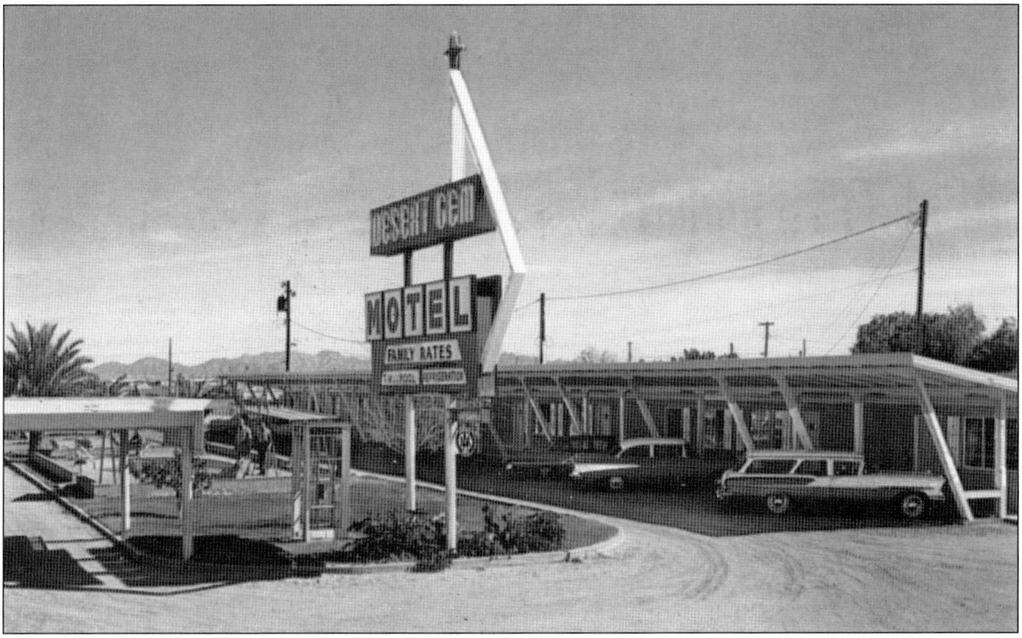

Desert Gem Motel, c. 1960s (Advertising Postcard). Built in 1956, when Highway 80 still went through downtown Yuma, the Desert Gem described itself as "a colorful oasis in the heart of the desert country. One of the best motels in this area. Carefully designed for your comfort with finest refrigeration and electric heating. Heated swimming pool—Television and wide sheltered carports at your door." (Published by Phoenix Specialty Advertising Co.)

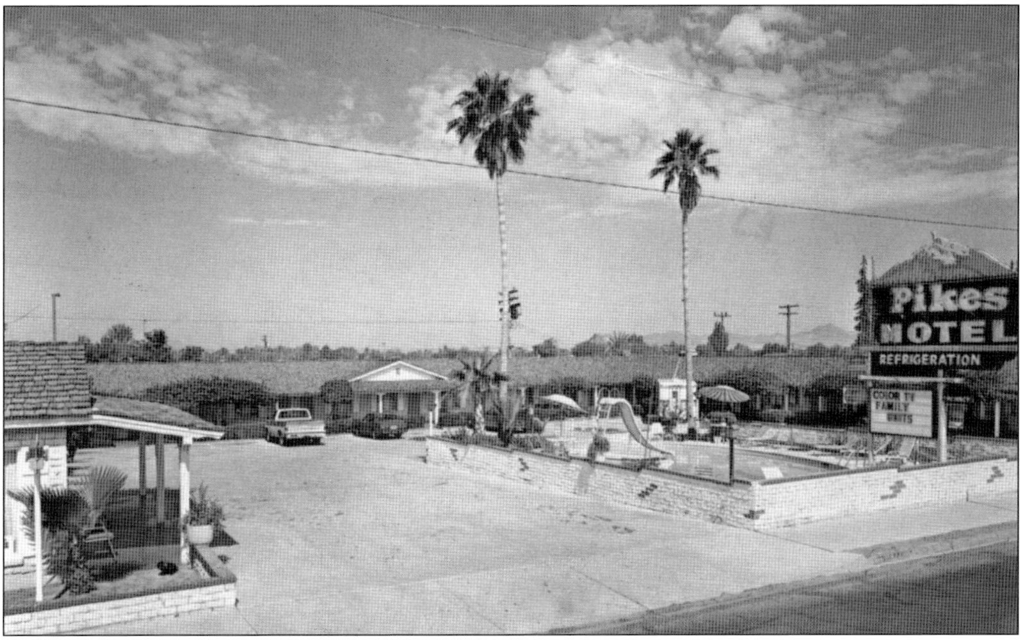

Pikes Motel, Postmarked October 27, 1978 (Advertising Postcard). Now part of the Coronado Hotel owned by the Peach family, Pikes Motel advertised on the back of the card: "26 units . . . 2 rm. family units available. Color Cable TV . . . Heated Pool . . . phones in room . . . Restaurant adjacent." (Published by Wild Country; photograph by Fred Baker.)

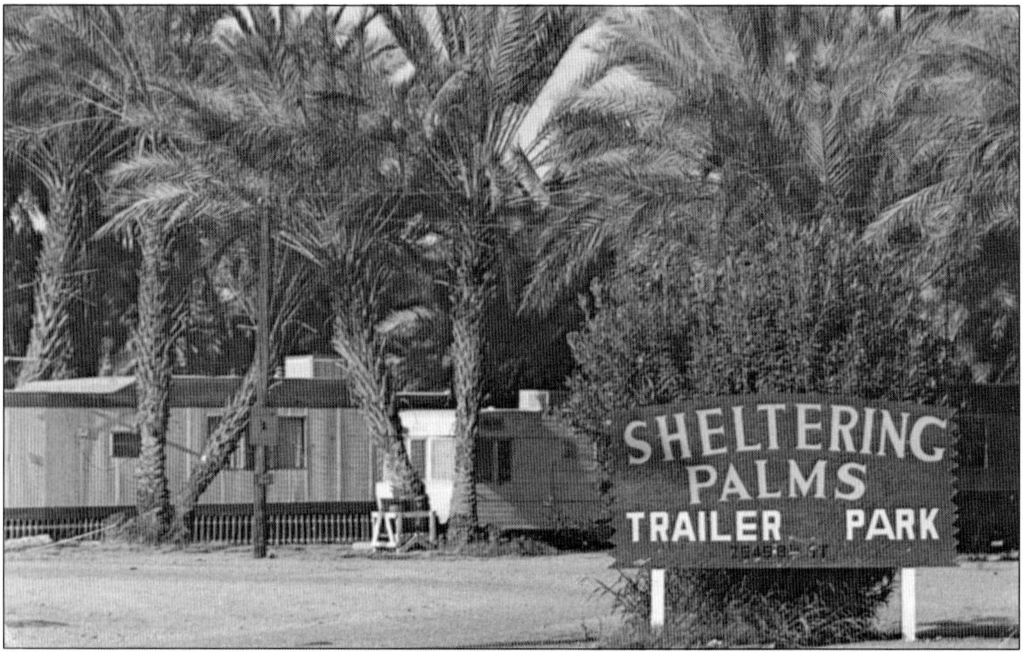

SHELTERING PALMS, POSTMARKED APRIL 10, 1973 (ADVERTISING POSTCARD). Opening for business around 1960 on Eighth Street at South Avenue B, the once-popular park experienced hard times and by 2007 fell into foreclosure. Cited by the city for blight issues, the park finally closed around 2010 and has since been torn down and replaced by a Walmart Neighborhood Market. (Published by Yuma Printing Co.)

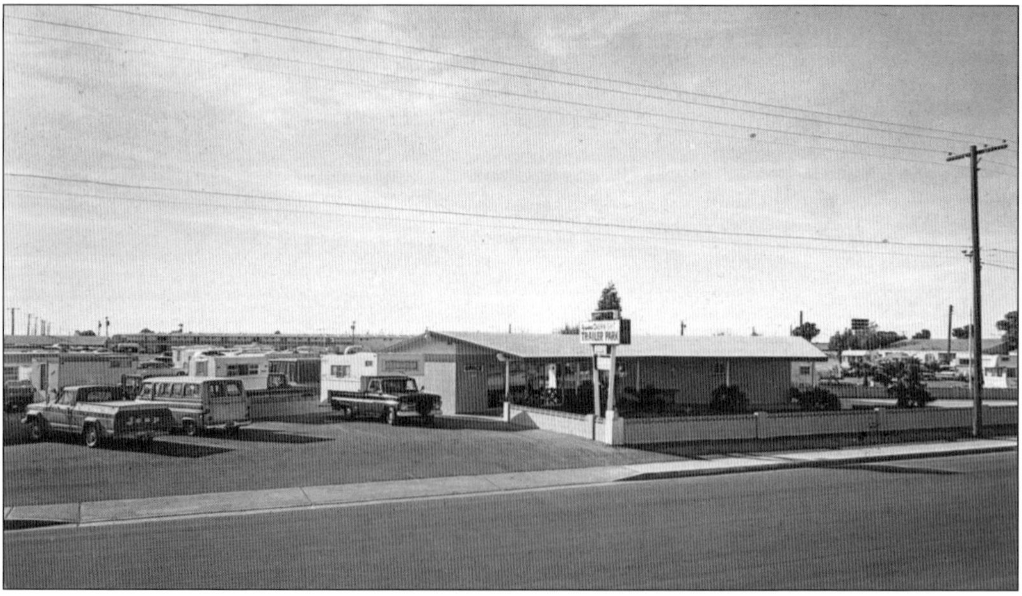

YUMA OVERNIGHT TRAILER PARK, C. 1970S (ADVERTISING POSTCARD). The Yuma Overnight Trailer Park was located at 201 West Twenty-Eighth Street. The back of the card reads, "Walking Distance to Supermarket, 56 Overnight Spaces—No Unhooking Necessary, Recreation Hall—Shuffleboard—Modern Laundry." The facility is now called Country Club Mobile Home Park. (Published by Tom and Bea Reed.)

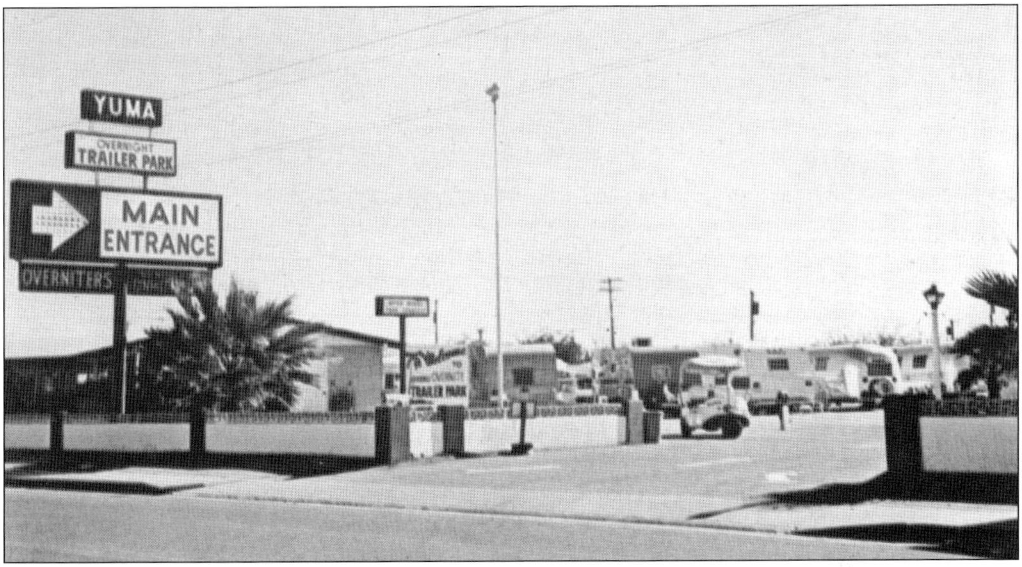

YUMA OVERNIGHT TRAILER PARK, HAND DATED JANUARY 1972 (ADVERTISING POSTCARD). In a newspaper article from the *Yuma Daily Sun* dated March 8, 1964, "Yuma First—The Yuma Overnight Trailer Park located just off of Fourth Avenue on 28th Street is the first such installation in Yuma, its builder, Ed Tunnell and Eldon Harvick claim. . . . The park offers nightly rates of $2.08 and weekly, $13, including utilities. It will only accommodate smaller travel trailers up to 40 feet. About 4000 persons have used it since the park opened last fall."

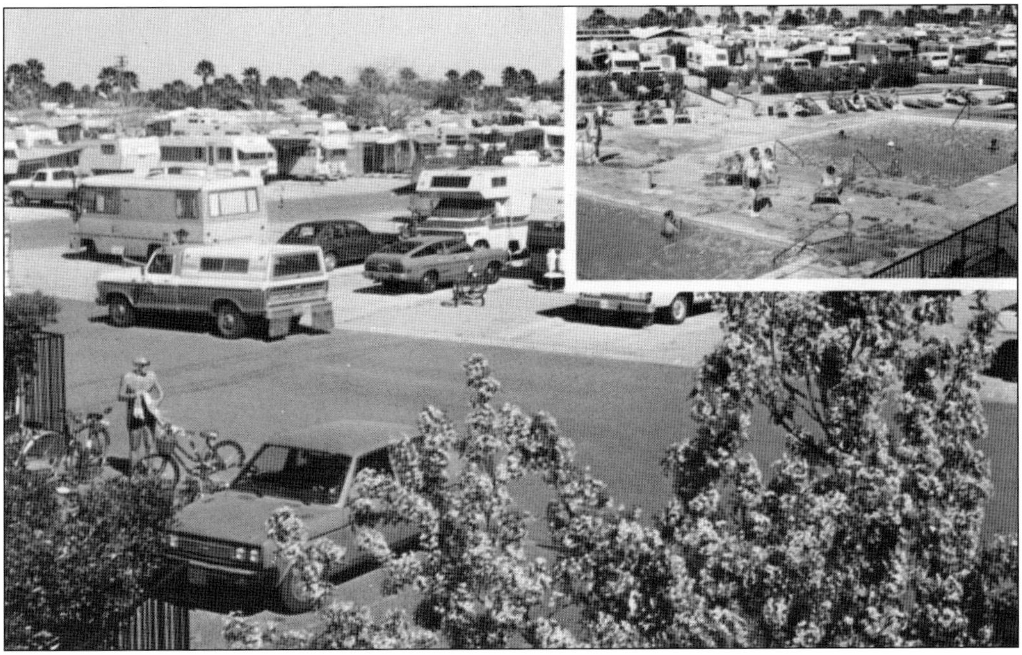

MESA VERDE TRAVEL TRAILER PARK, C. 1970S (ADVERTISING POSTCARD). Advertisements began appearing in the *Yuma Daily Sun* in the mid-1970s. The following advertisement is from October 4, 1974: "Mesa Verde Village Travel Trailer Park. For permanent travel trailers and temporary stay. Deluxe club house, 4 pools, laundry facilities, shower rooms. 3649 S. 4th Ave." (Published by Wild Country Photos.)

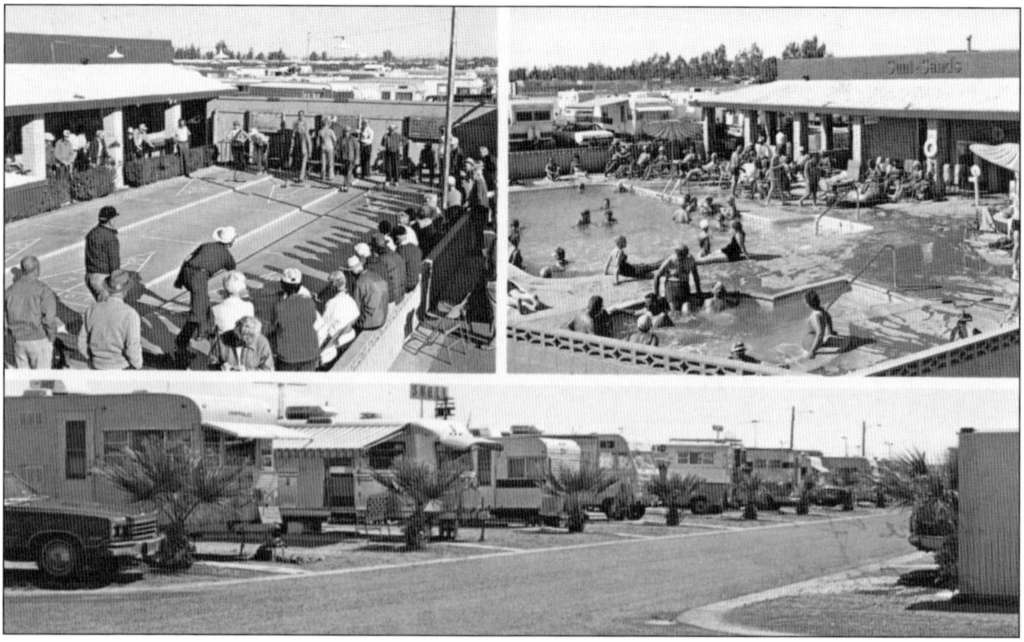

ABOVE, SUNI-SANDS TRAVEL TRAILER PARK, POSTMARKED DECEMBER 1979 (ADVERTISING POSTCARD); BELOW, SUNI-SANDS TRAVEL TRAILER PARK, C. 1970S (ADVERTISING POSTCARD). This travel park opened in the mid-1970s to capitalize on the growing number of people heading to the Southwest for the winter months. Located across from the Yuma airport, the park is still in operation today as the Suni Sands RV Resort. (Above, published by Karl R. Snyder; below, published by Kolor View.)

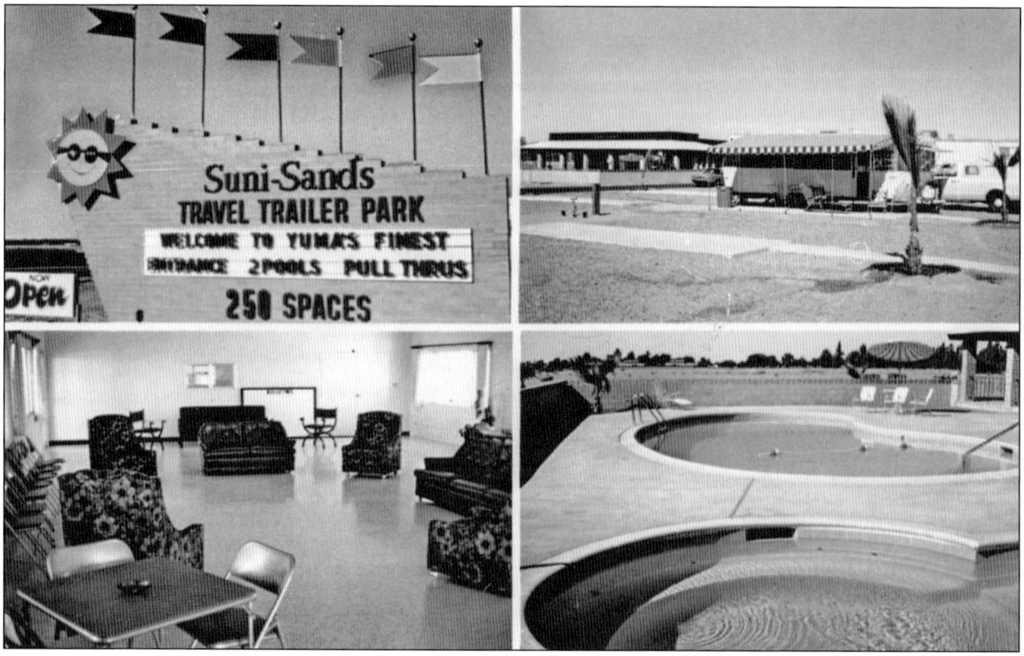

Three

Getting to Yuma
Riding the Rails and Roadways

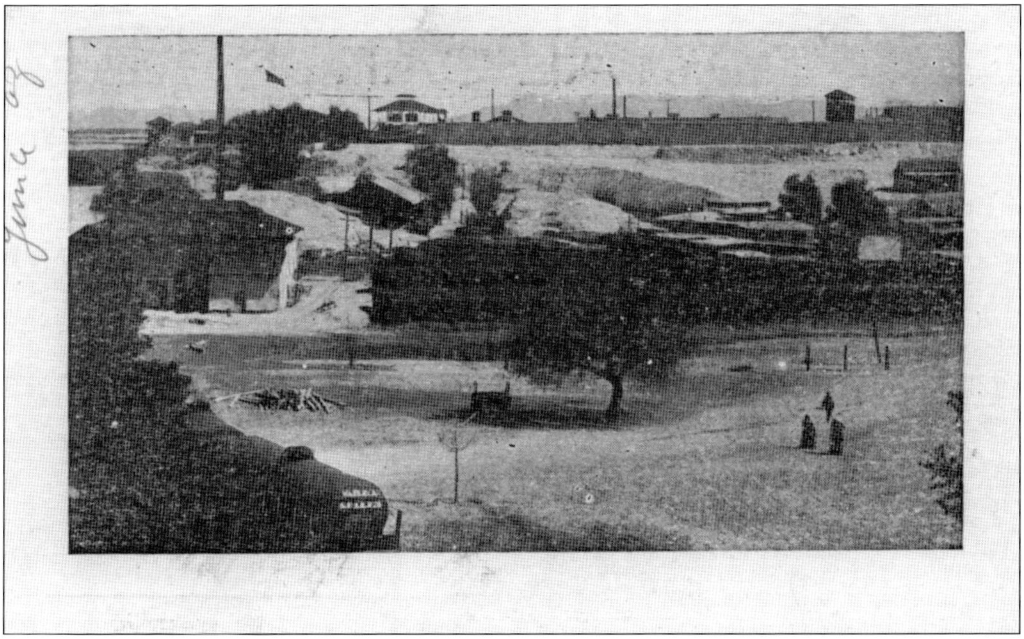

Railroad Yard, c. 1905 (Undivided Back Postcard). The *Arizona Sentinel* of September 30, 1908, stated, "Free View of Big Menagerie. A large number of people took advantage of a free view of the Barnum & Bailey menagerie in the railroad yards last Sunday, during the process of watering and feeding the animals. A big herd of camels and elephants were unloaded and given an airing, and most of the crowd also had a good view of the caged animals, which arrived in the morning on the first section."

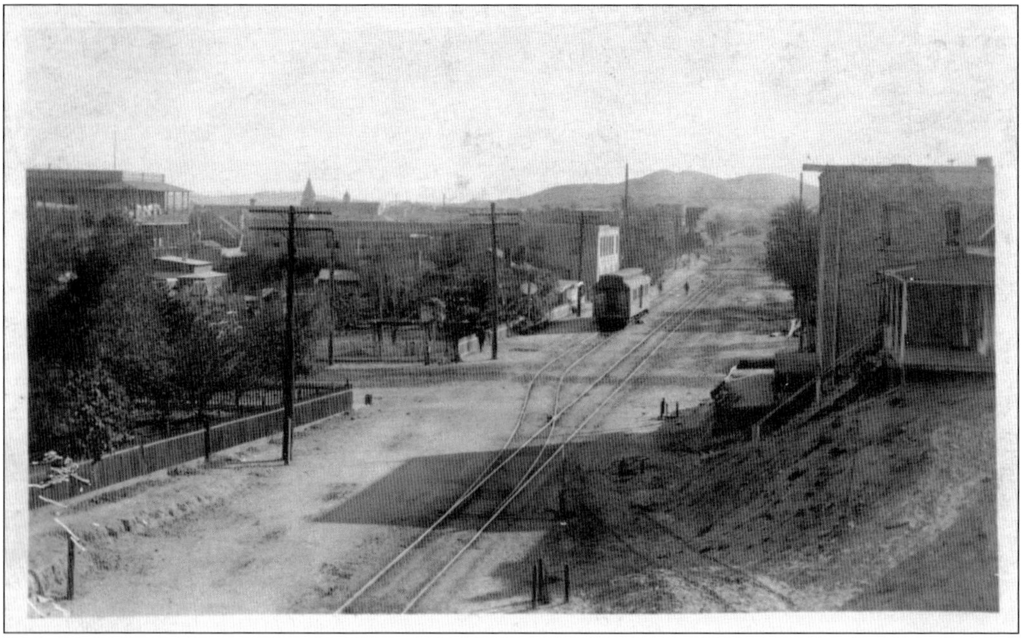

RAILROAD THROUGH YUMA, C. 1909 (REAL-PHOTO POSTCARD). The railroad originally crossed over the Colorado River onto Madison Avenue, about 1,300 feet downstream from the current bridge. This view is of Madison Avenue facing south, with the first intersection being First Street. The three-story Cotter Building at left, Yuma's first skyscraper, opened in 1897 and burned to the ground in 1923.

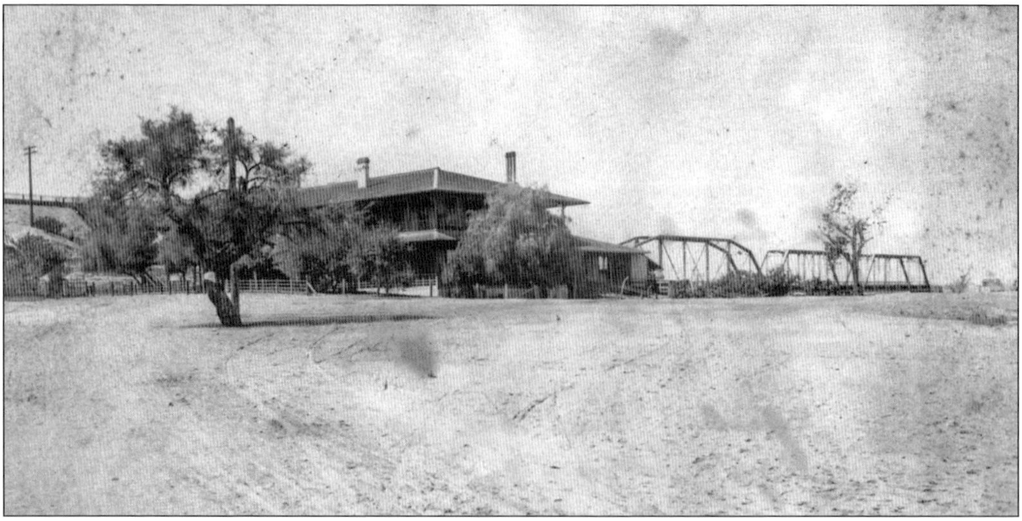

SOUTHERN PACIFIC HOTEL, POSTMARKED 1909 (REAL-PHOTO POSTCARD). Four years after the original bridge across the Colorado River was complete, the Southern Pacific Hotel opened for business. An advertisement from the *Arizona Sentinel* newspaper dated June 25, 1881, read, "The Southern Pacific Railroad Hotel—Yuma A.T.—is now complete. Parties traveling through desiring to stop over a few days, weeks, or months, can at this hotel receive all accommodations desired by the most fastidious. Hot and cold water baths, Barber Shop, Private Dining and Wine Rooms. One of the finest Bars on the Pacific Coast where can be had the choicest of Wines, Brandies, Ales, Porter, Liquors and Cigars. Prices moderate."

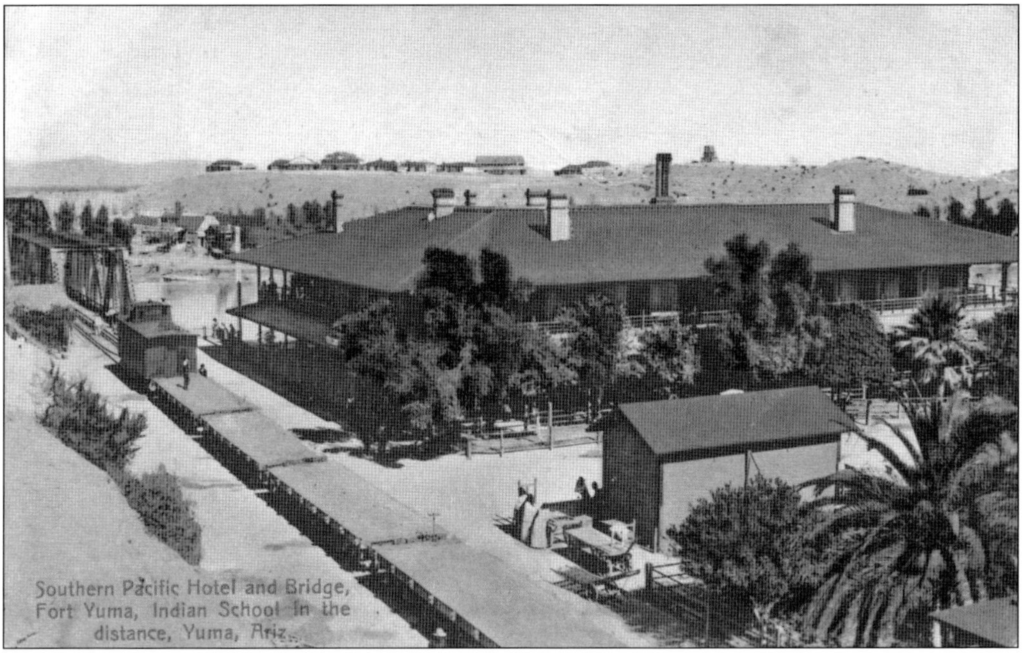

ABOVE, SOUTHERN PACIFIC HOTEL AND BRIDGE, POSTMARKED JULY 1908 (HAND-COLORED POSTCARD); BELOW, SOUTHERN PACIFIC HOTEL AND BRIDGE, C. 1915 (DIVIDED BACK POSTCARD). The back of the card below reads, "View of railroad station at Yuma, Arizona, on the eastern bank of the Colorado River, where the Southern Pacific crosses into California. The Laguna Dam is located at this point. This dam, together with a great inverted siphon that carries the waters of a main canal under the Colorado River, forms a vast government irrigation system which is rapidly developing the Yuma Region." (Above, published by the *Yuma Examiner.*)

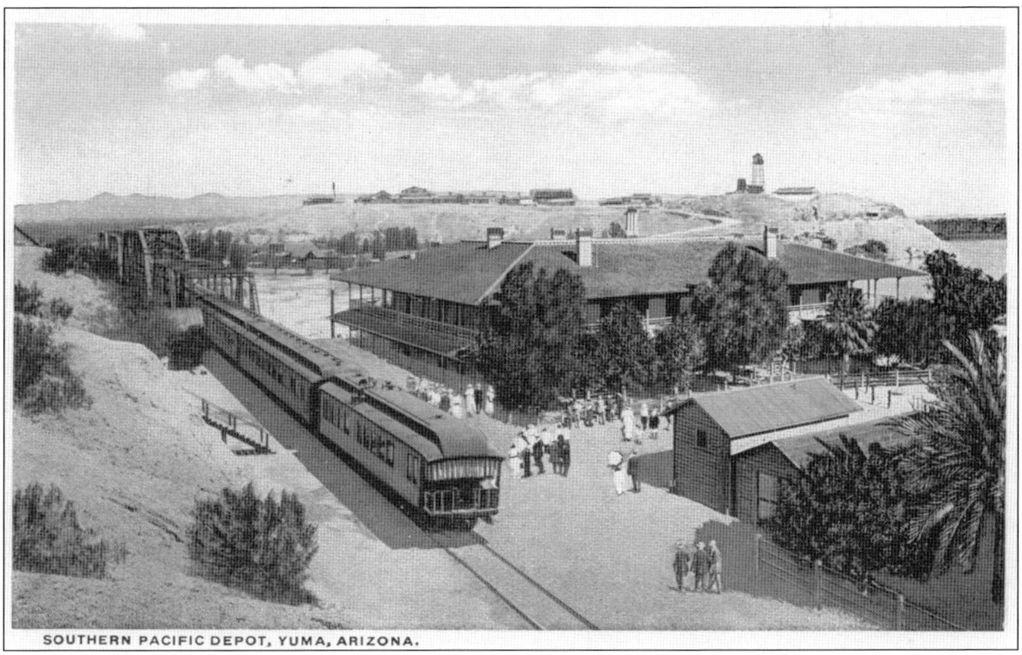

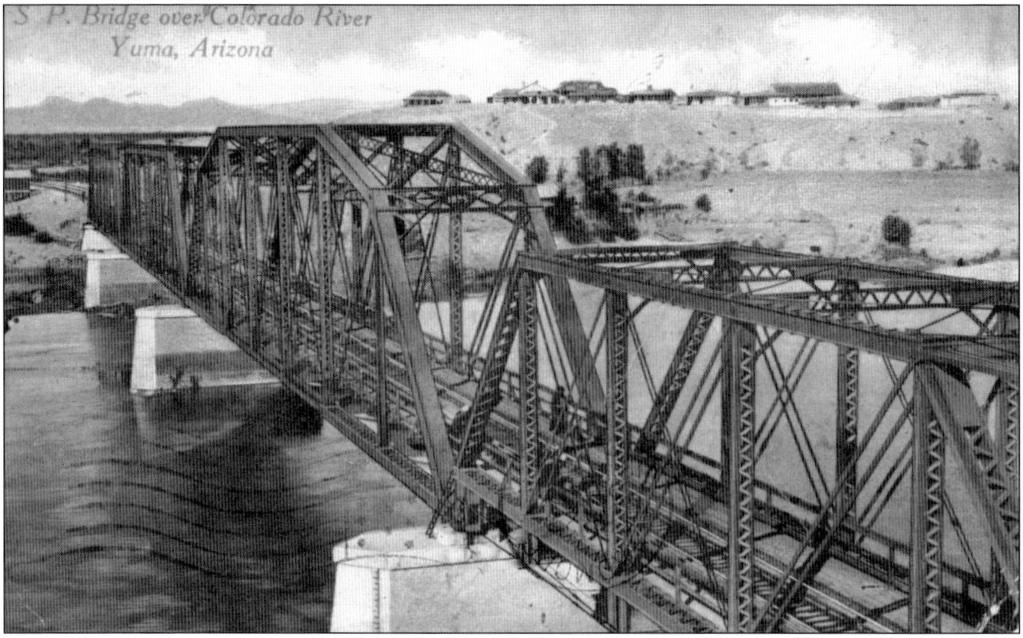

Above, S.P. Bridge over Colorado River, Postmarked September 24, 1912 (Hand-Colored Postcard); Below, S.P. Bridge over Colorado River, Hand Dated December 9, 1921 (Divided Pack Postcard). The first bridge, built in 1877 by the Southern Pacific Railroad, was a wooden structure that was damaged by the flood of July 1884. A new bridge was completed later that same year, but it burned in 1885. The third bridge, completed in 1886 and also made of wood, was replaced by 1899 with the steel bridge pictured in these postcards. (Above, published by Souvenir Publishing Co.; below, published by Newman Post Card Co.)

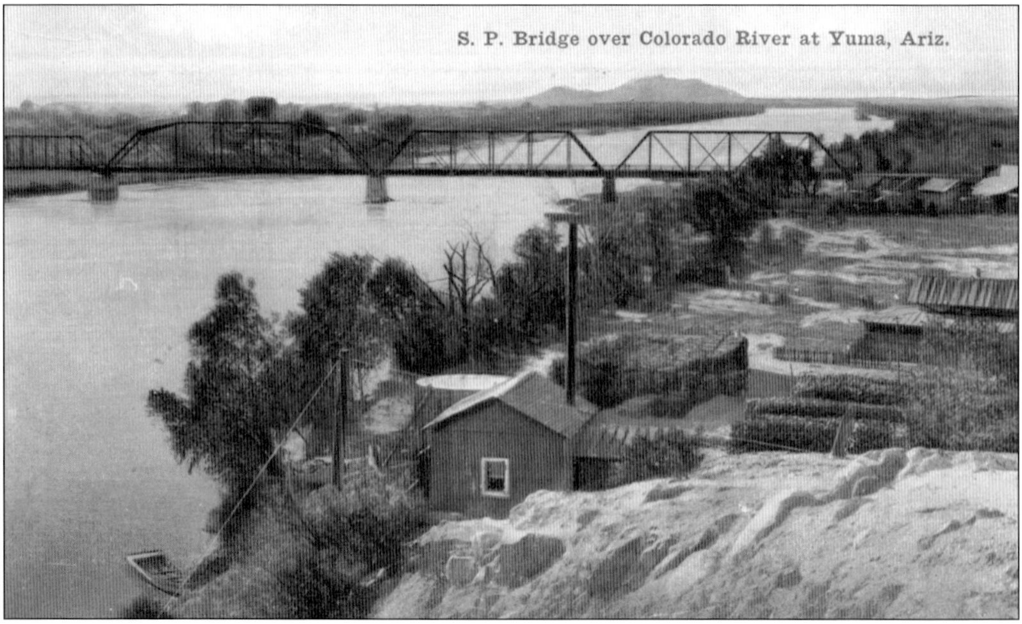

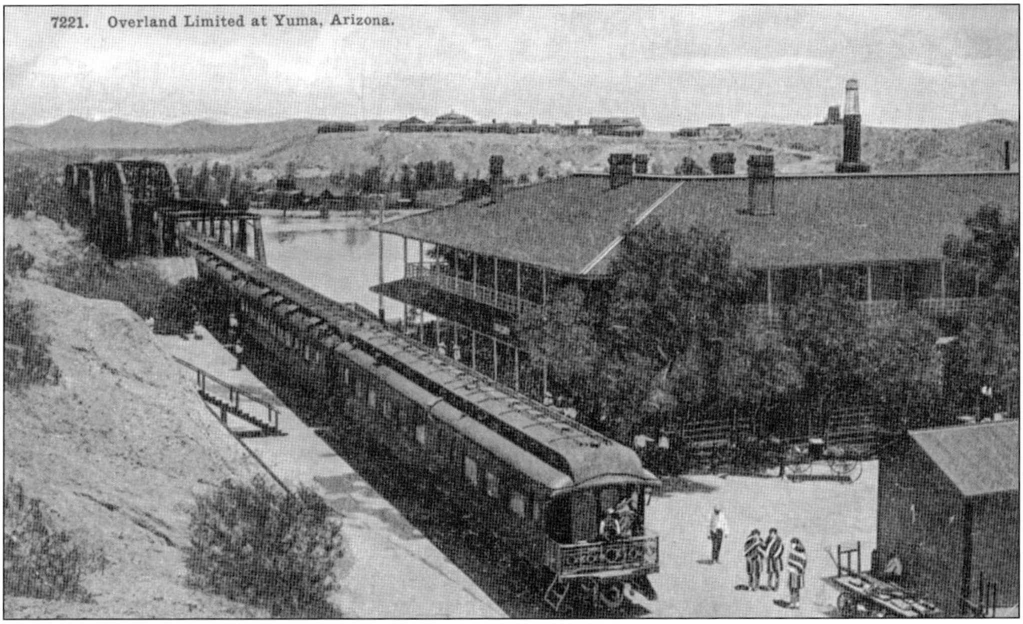

***OVERLAND LIMITED*, C. 1910S (HAND-COLORED POSTCARD).** The *Overland Limited* has had a variety of names over the years, including *Overland Flyer*, *San Francisco Overland Limited*, *San Francisco Overland*, or just the *Overland*. It ran passenger service from Chicago to San Francisco and involved three railroads, the Southern Pacific, the Union Pacific, and lastly the Chicago & North Western Railway. The last time the name was used was January 2, 1964.

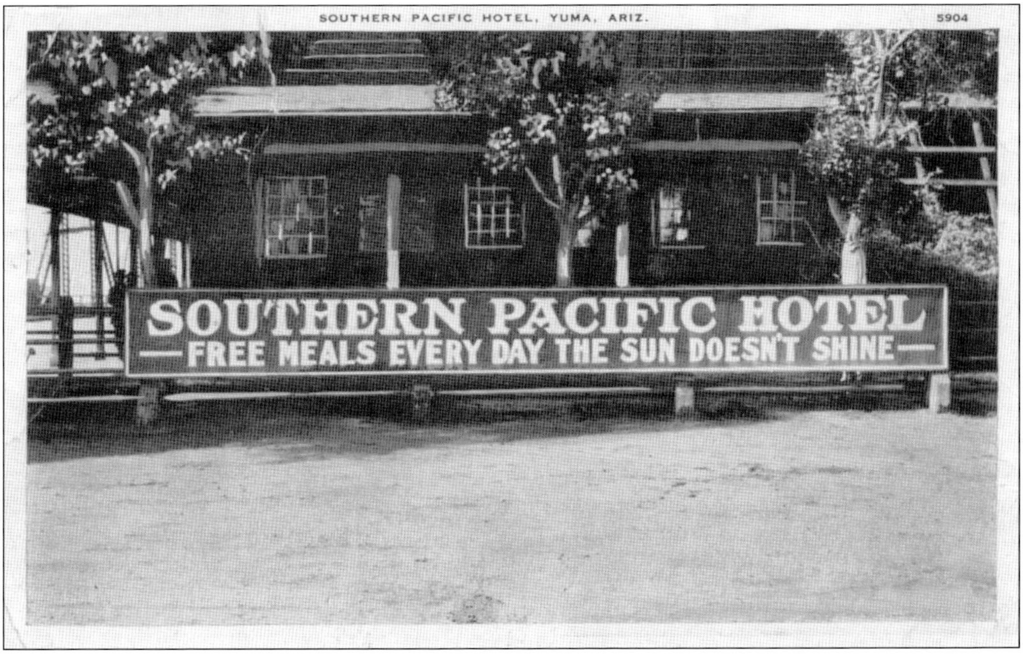

SOUTHERN PACIFIC HOTEL, POSTMARKED JULY 20, 1925 (REAL-PHOTO POSTCARD). On the back of the card, a visitor to the hotel writes, "Howdy Slim, I am spending the weekend in Yuma, great town. I wanted to get some free meals but don't seem like I will get them. I'm going back to Tucson tomorrow." (Published by Dean's News Depot.)

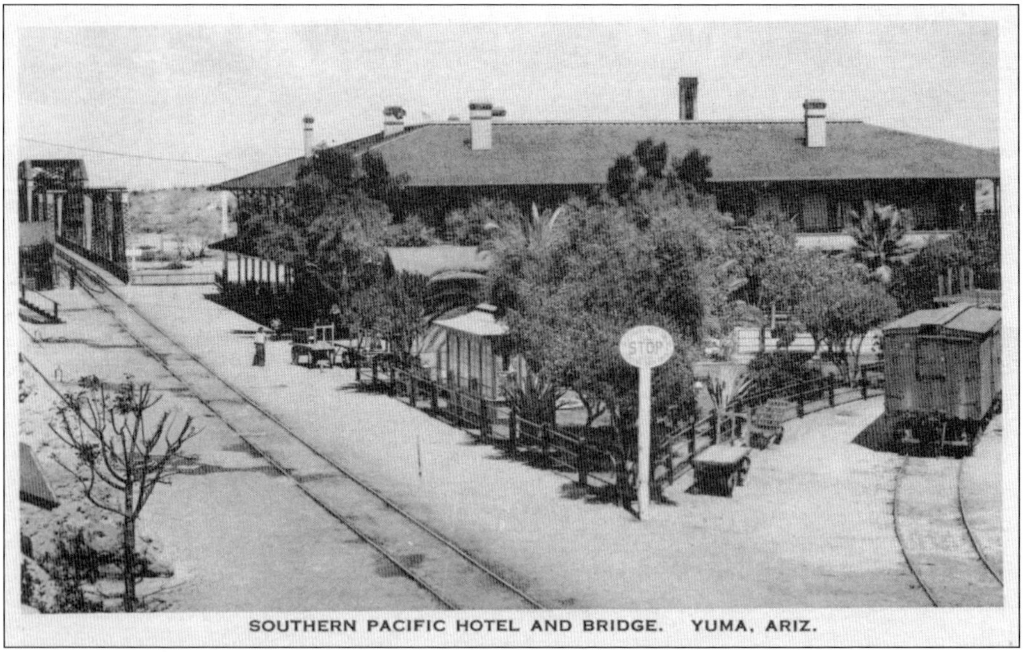

SOUTHERN PACIFIC HOTEL AND BRIDGE, C. 1920 (ALBERTYPE POSTCARDS). Constructed in the 1920s, the Southern Pacific Depot was built in the Spanish Colonial Revival style. Southern Pacific ceased passenger service when Amtrak took over in 1971. The depot served as the Yuma Fine Arts Museum for many years until 1993, when a devastating fire ripped through the building, which led to it being demolished in 1994. (Both, published by A. Homer Smith.)

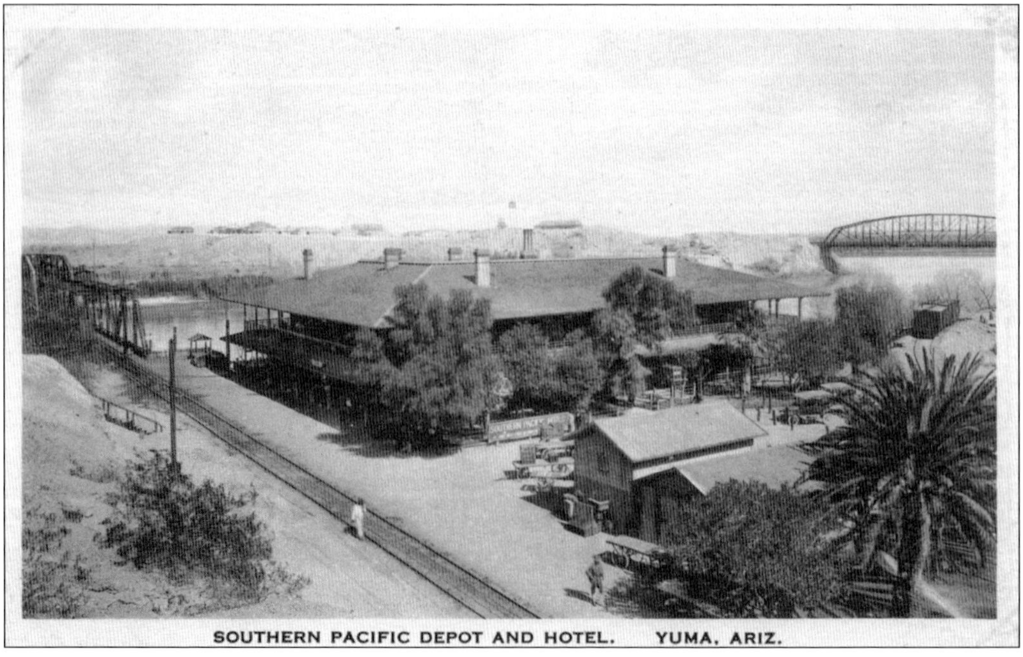

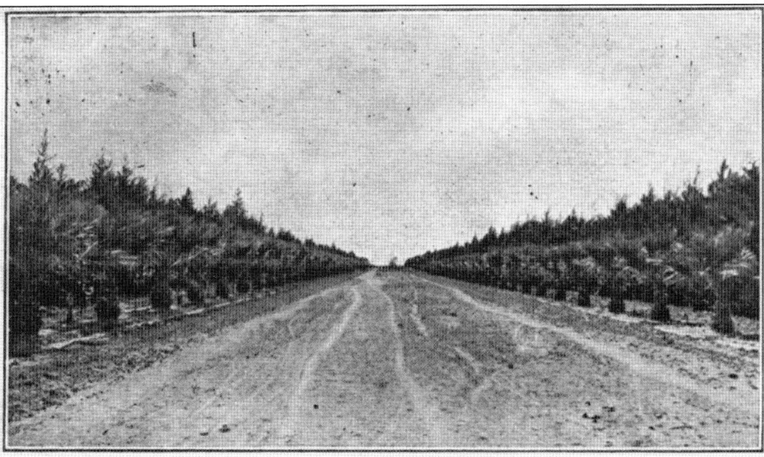

PALM DRIVE--YUMA, ARIZONA

ABOVE, PALM DRIVE, POSTMARKED APRIL 1907 (UNDIVIDED POSTCARD); BELOW, ENTERING YUMA, 1938 (REAL-PHOTO POSTCARD). Highway 80 east of Yuma was once lined with palm trees and orange groves. As the town expanded east, the trees were replaced with wider roads, stores, and homes. Highway 80 was once known as the Old Spanish Trail Highway and was part of the Ocean to Ocean Highway spanning eight states. (Below, published by Frashers Fotos.)

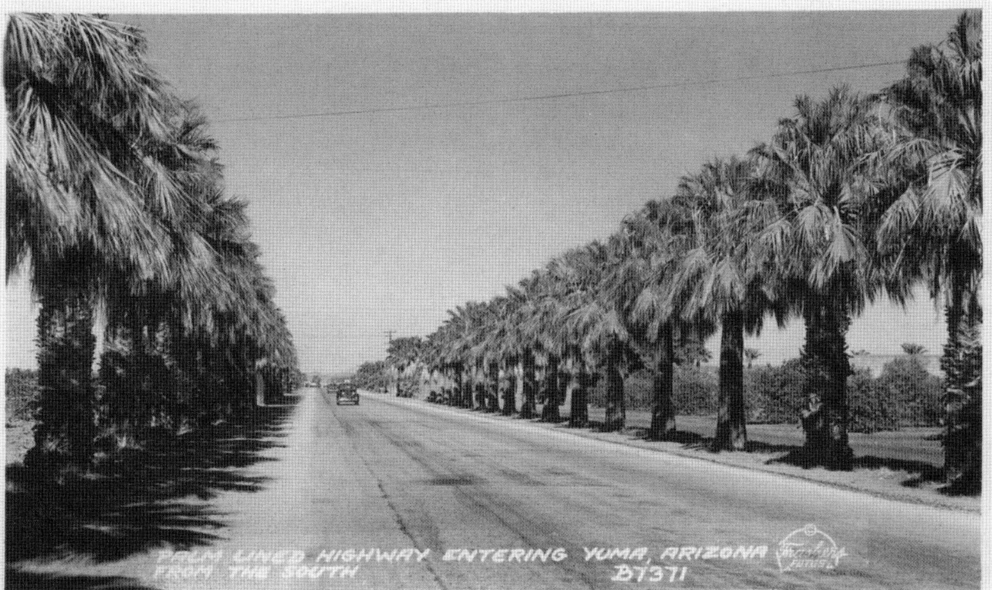

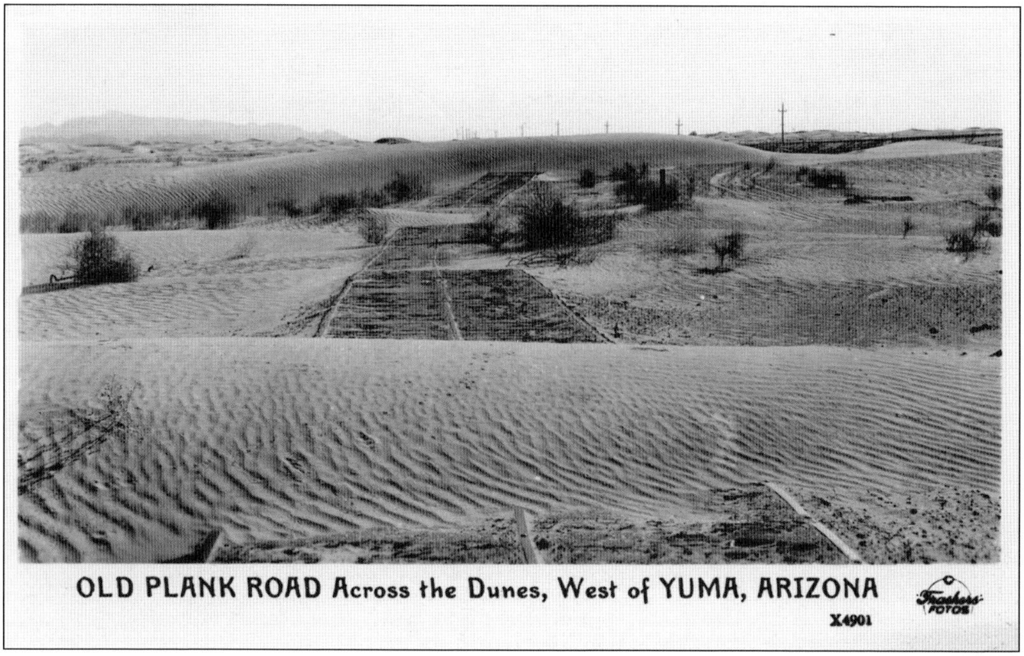

Above, Old Plank Road across the Dunes, c. 1930s (Real-Photo Postcard); Below, New and Old Highway, Postmarked April 15, 1938 (Real-Photo Postcard). The first six and a half miles of the plank road over the Algodones Dunes were set in 1915. The roadbed consisted of 13,000 25-inch-wide wooden planks secured to wooden crosspieces, which were laid underneath. (Both, published by Frashers Fotos.)

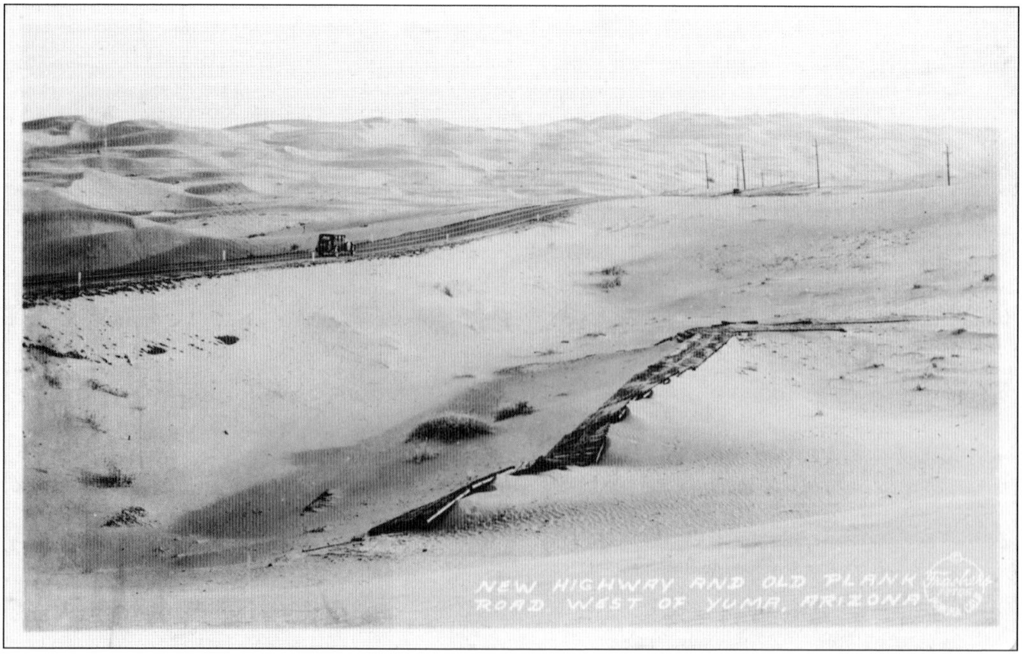

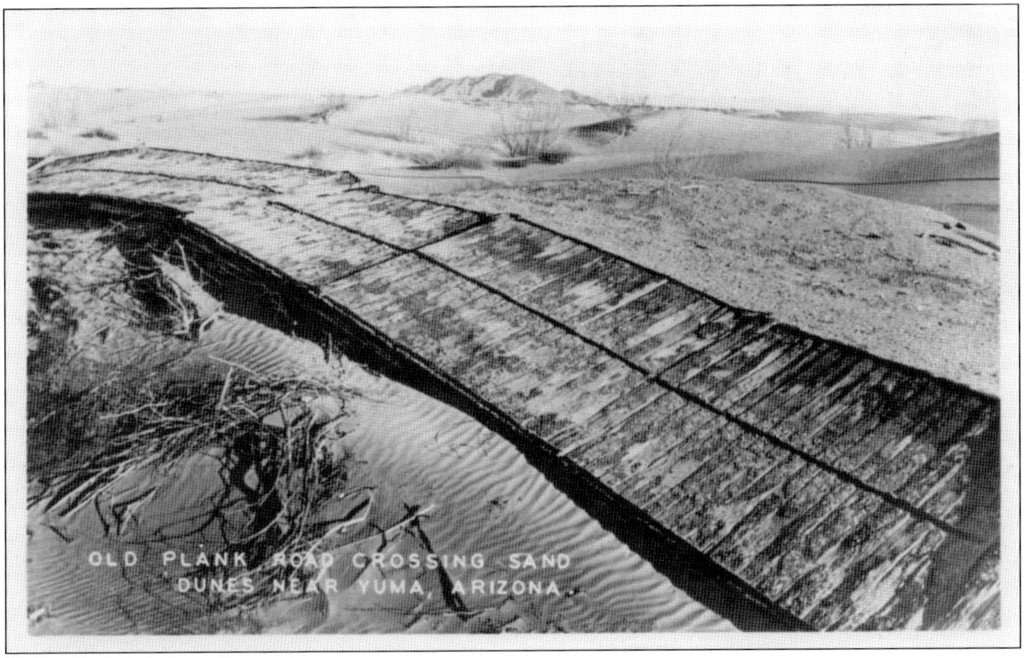

ABOVE, OLD PLANK ROAD, C. 1940S (REAL-PHOTO POSTCARD); BELOW, US HIGHWAY 80, POSTMARKED FEBRUARY 10, 1951 (CURT TEICH LINEN POSTCARD). In 1916, construction on a second road was started using prefabricated sections that were eight feet wide with double-wide turnouts every 1,000 feet. Ten years later, in 1926, a 20-foot-wide asphalt road replaced the plank road. The same roadway eventually became Highway 80, which was replaced with the designation of Highway 8 years later. An article from the *Morning Sun* newspaper dated November 8, 1925, read as follows: "Travelers arriving in Calexico from Yuma have complained of the plank road over the sand hills between this point and the Arizona Town. They declare that the heavy traffic over the road is rapidly making the thoroughfare impassible." Within a year of this article's printing, a paved highway was started across the desert to Yuma. (Below, published by Lollesgard Specialty Co.)

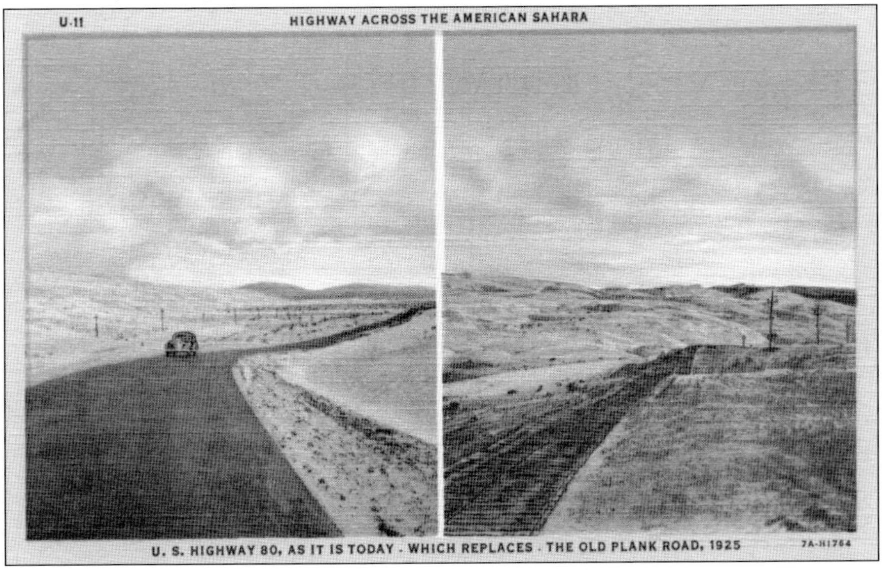

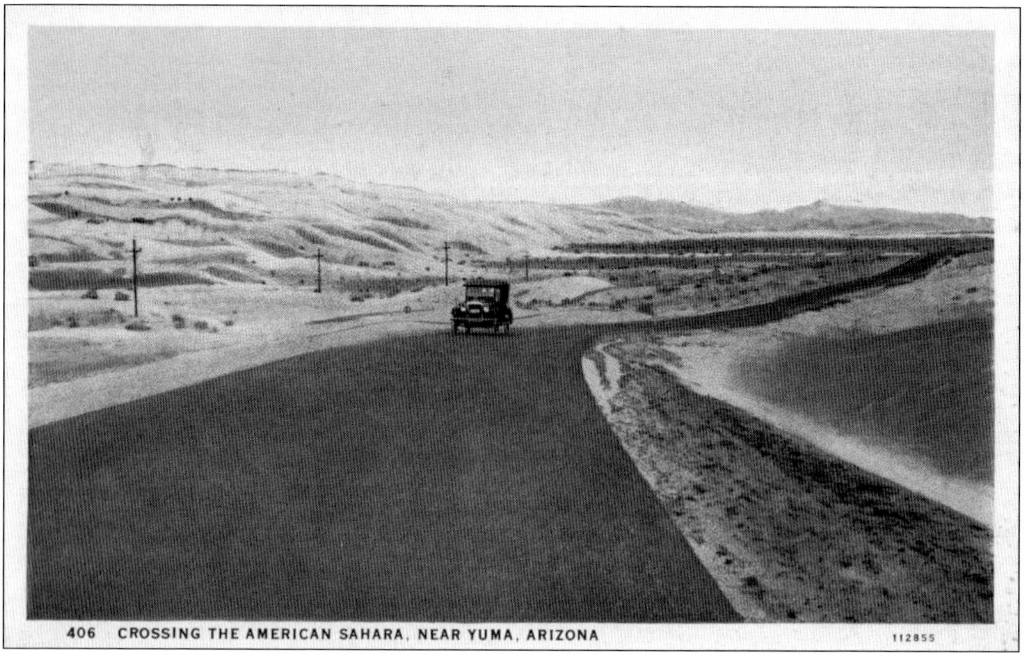

ABOVE, CROSSING THE AMERICAN SAHARA, POSTMARKED MARCH 9, 1932 (CURT TEICH POSTCARD); BELOW, OCEAN TO OCEAN HIGHWAY, POSTMARKED JUNE 14, 1939 (CURT TEICH POSTCARD). Conceived in 1914 by the Automobile Club of Savannah, the Dixie Overland Highway was established from Savannah, Georgia, to San Diego, California, between 1917 and 1919. By 1939, the entire Arizona portion of the highway was paved except for a section between Florence and Oracle Junction, which was completed in 1949. (Both, published by Harry Herz.)

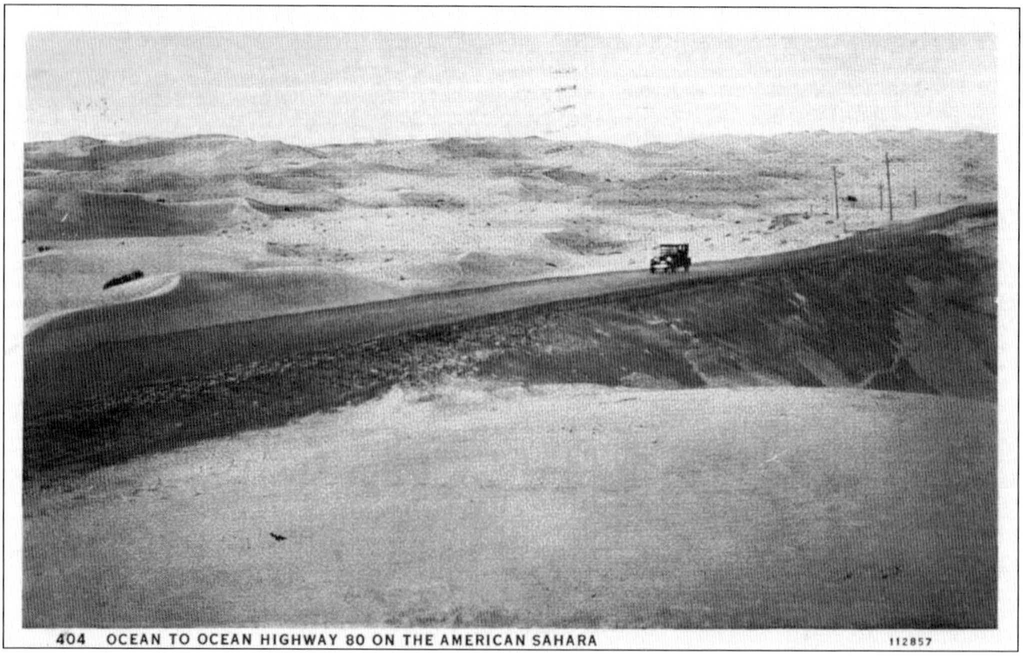

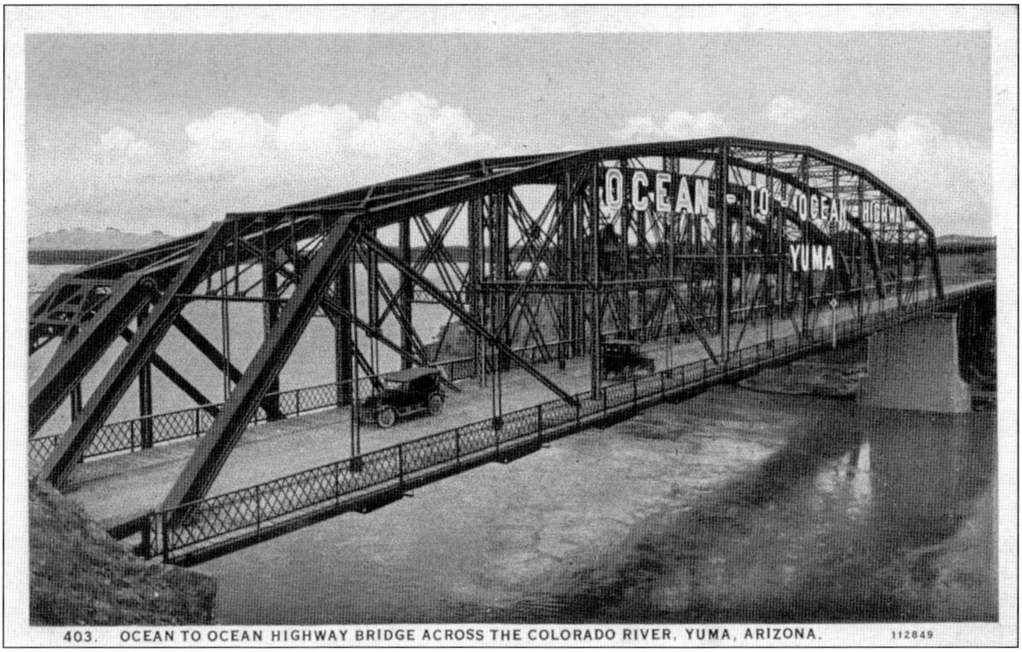

Ocean to Ocean Highway Bridge, c. 1926 (Above, Curt Teich Postcard) and c. 1942 (Below, Curt Teich Linen Postcard). The Ocean to Ocean Highway Bridge opened to traffic with great fanfare on May 22, 1915. The bridge spanned 336 feet across the Colorado River and erased the problem of crossing the river via a ferry or detouring hundreds of miles upriver. The bridge closed to vehicle traffic in 1988, and after a $2-million renovation, it reopened to vehicles in 2002. (Above, published by Harry Herz; below, published by Lollesgard Specialty Co.)

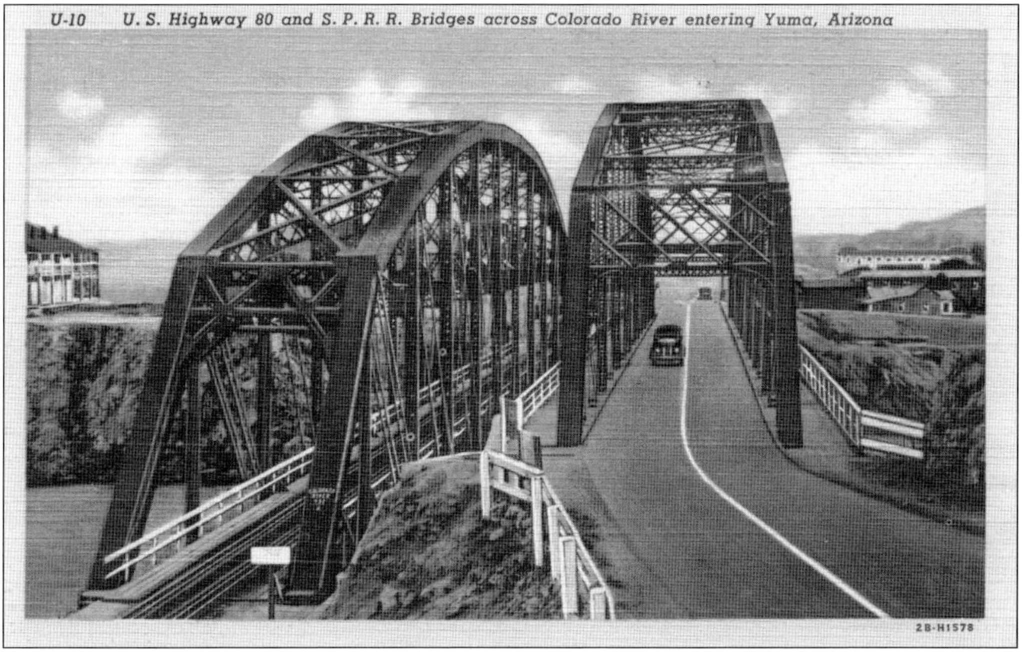

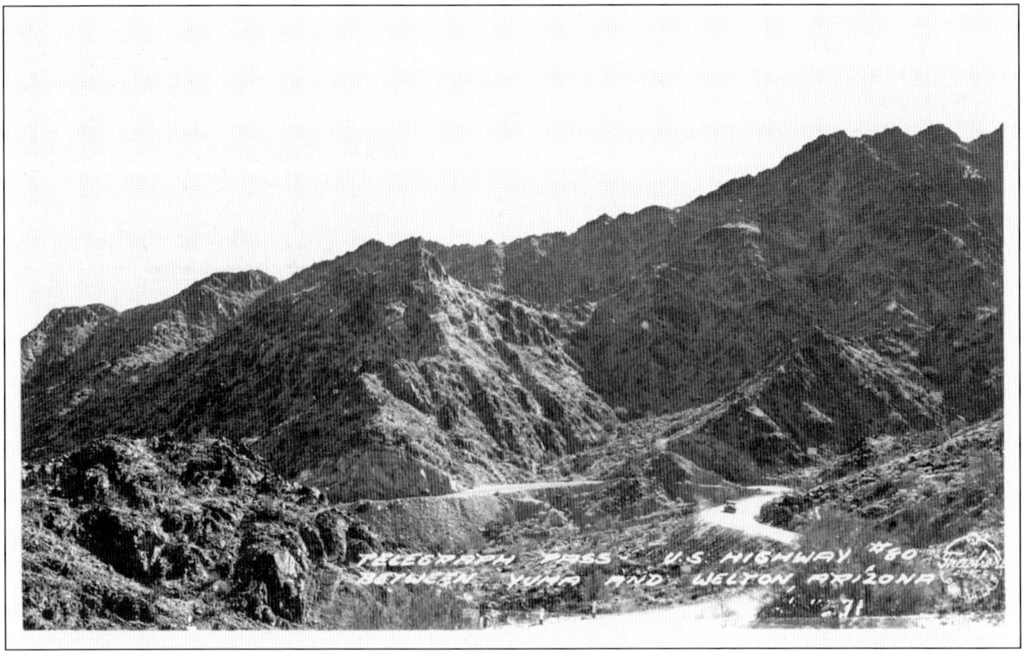

Telegraph Pass, c. 1940s (Real-Photo Postcards). Highway 80 was part of the Ocean to Ocean Highway that crossed the country from San Diego, California, in the west to Savannah, Georgia, in the east. The original section between Yuma and Wellton followed the Southern Pacific Railroad tracks north around the Gila Mountains and through Dome until the cutoff through Telegraph Pass was completed in 1928. For the first four years of its existence, the highway was mostly dirt, and it was not until 1931 that the entire stretch of Telegraph Pass was paved. (Both, published by Frashers Fotos.)

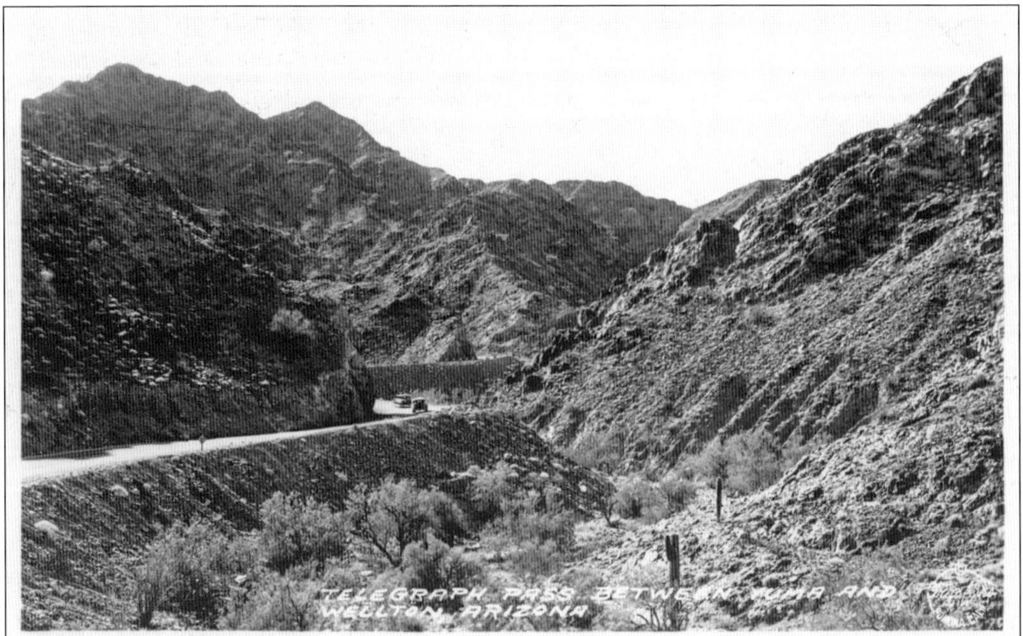

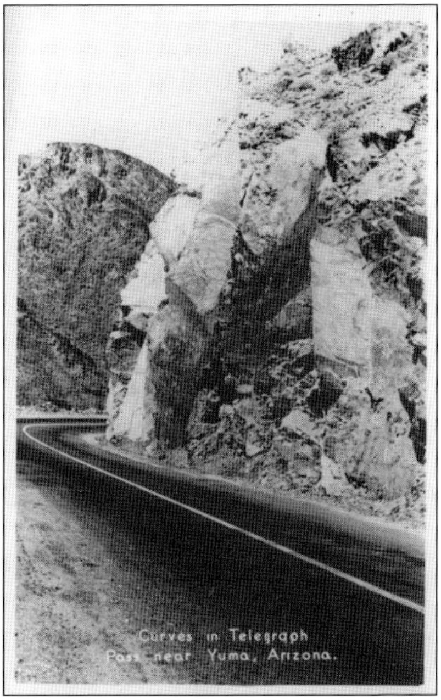

Curves in Telegraph Pass, c. 1940s (Real-Photo Postcard). Not far from Telegraph Pass, according to Old West lore, a large cache of coins and jewelry known as "The Lost Treasure of Telegraph Pass," worth about $50,000, was buried in an iron pot at a campsite near a small butte, on the east end of Estrella Mountains. This treasure was supposedly buried during the early 1870s.

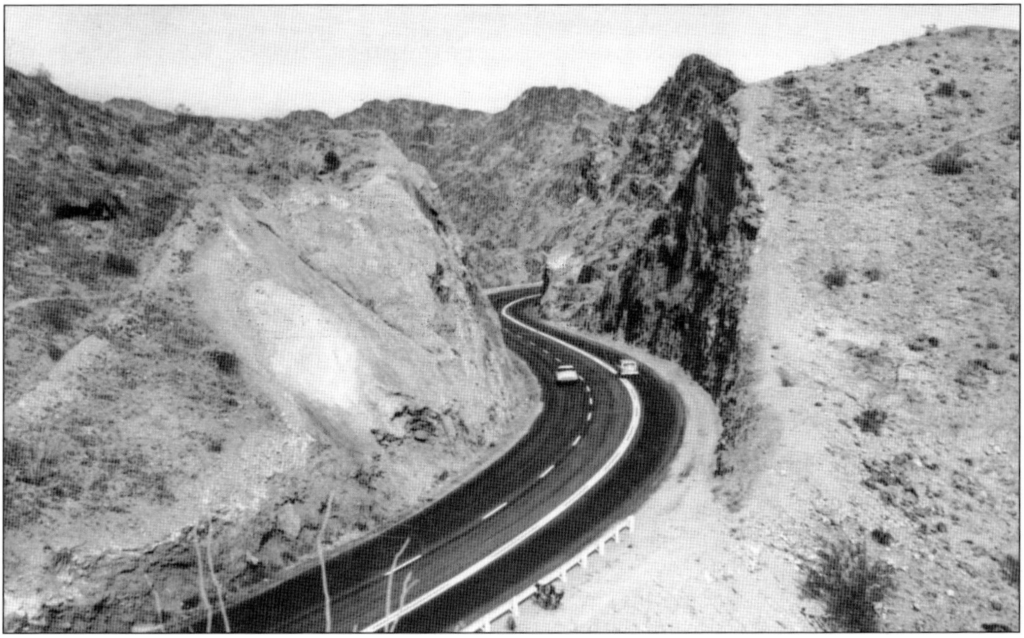

US Highway 80 through Telegraph Pass, Postmarked May 9, 1961 (Kodachrome Postcard). In the early 1960s, numerous plans were being made to widen the highway through Telegraph Pass. In the *Yuma Daily Sun* newspaper of January 24, 1961, three of the plans were being discussed. "All three routes would come through Telegraph Pass and the entire route would be a four-lane divided highway. . . . Route A would be 47.9 miles long. . . . It would follow very close to the present Highway 80. . . . Route B would be 47.9 miles long. . . . This would swing south of Highway 80 and be south of the railroad tracks. Route C was 49.2 miles. . . . This one swings further south and completely bypasses the Wellton-Mohawk Irrigation and Drainage District." (Published by Petley Studios; photograph by Ray Foster.)

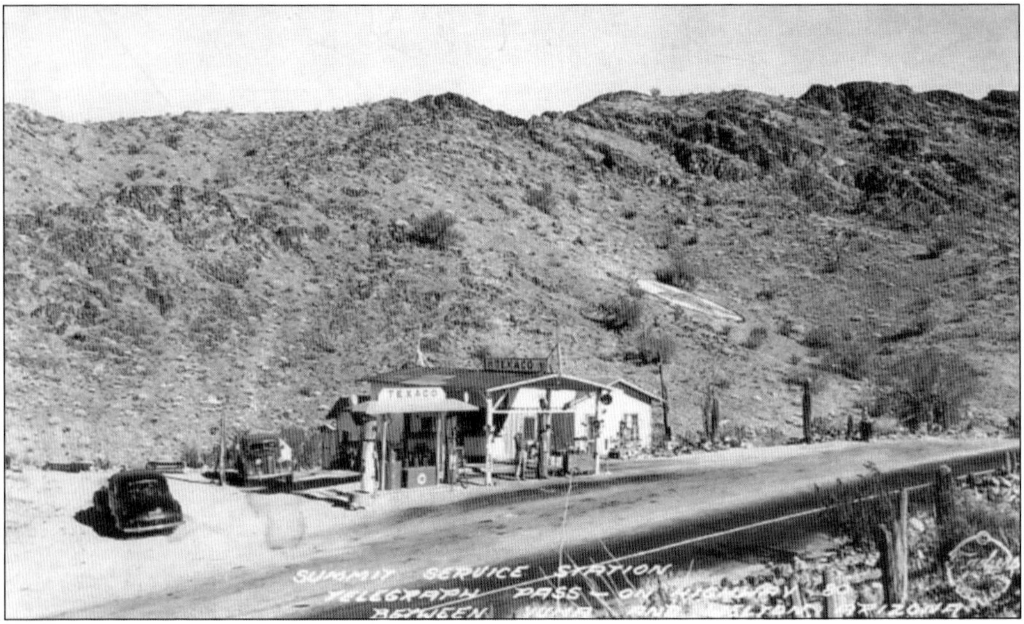

SUMMIT SERVICE STATION, C. 1940 (REAL-PHOTO POSTCARD). The Summit Service Station was located on Highway 80 on Telegraph Pass between Yuma and Wellton. Note the large Texaco star painted on the hill over the station. (Published by Frashers Fotos; courtesy of Mike Hawk.)

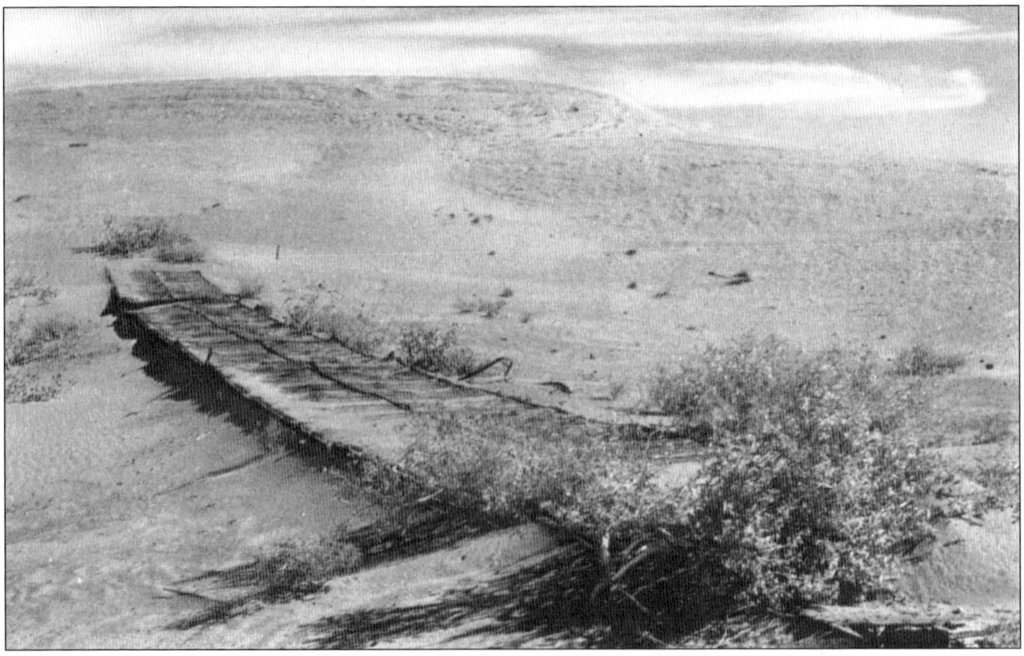

OLD PLANK ROAD, C. 1970S (KODACHROME POSTCARD). Using some of the existing fragments of the old road, a 1,500-foot-long replica was built in the 1970s. The fenced-in section can be seen off Interstate 8 near Grays Well Road. (Published by Union Oil Co.)

Four

Yuma County Communities
Towns Past and Present

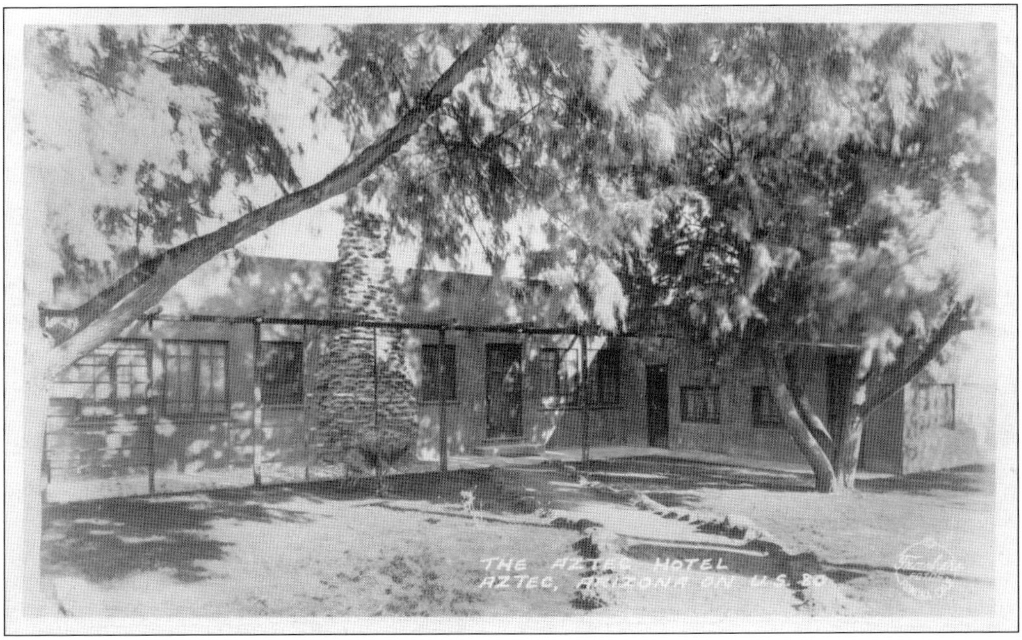

Aztec, Aztec Hotel, c. 1930s (Real-Photo Postcard). Not much is left of Aztec today but a few dilapidated buildings, foundations, and a railroad water tank. Aztec was once a stop along the Southern Pacific Railroad between Phoenix and Yuma. Located about 80 miles east of Yuma on Interstate 8, Aztec established a post office on September 12, 1889. (Published by Frashers Fotos.)

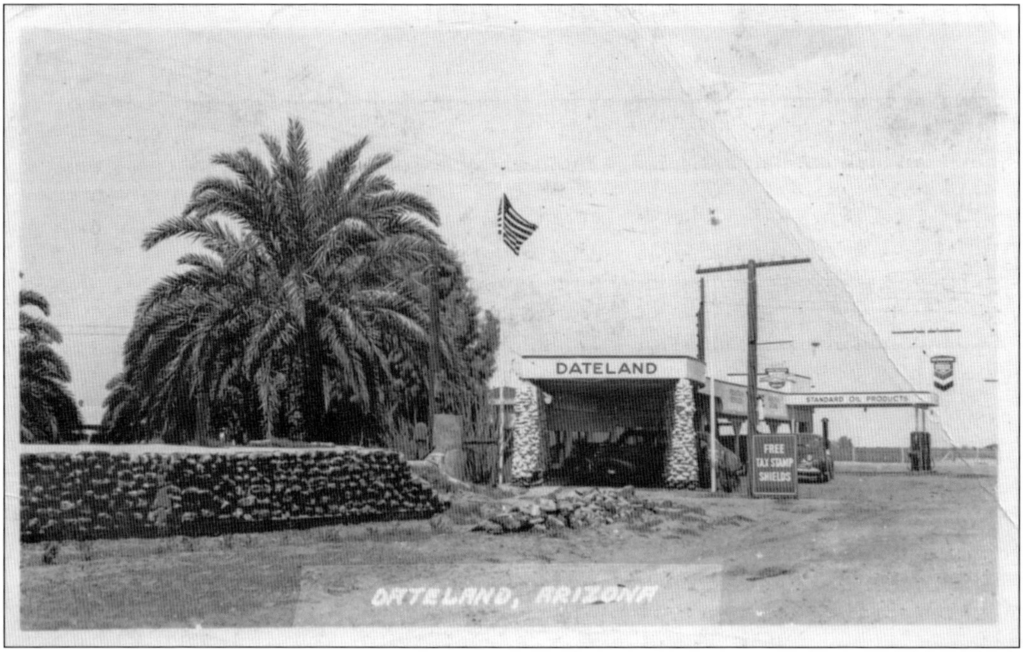

Above, Dateland, Service Station, c. 1940s (Real-Photo Postcard); Below, Dateland, Service Station, Hand Dated December 1949 (Real-Photo Postcard). Located on Highway 8 between Yuma and Gila Bend, Dateland started out as a watering stop for the Southern Pacific Railroad. In 1965, when Highway 80 was replaced by Interstate 8, the highway relocated about a quarter-mile north, dooming the small town. (Above, published by Frashers, Inc.)

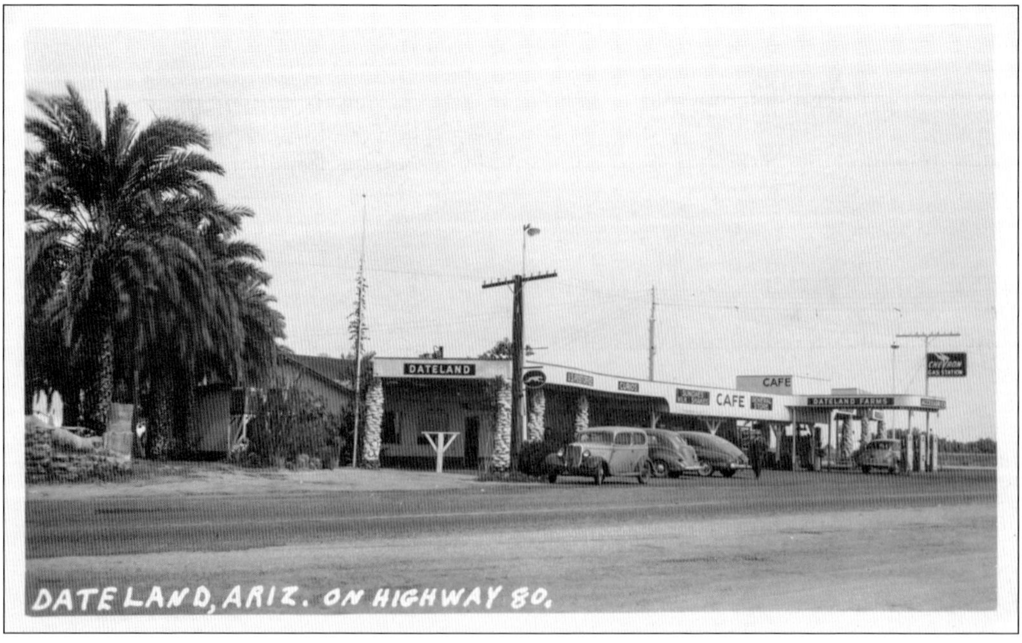

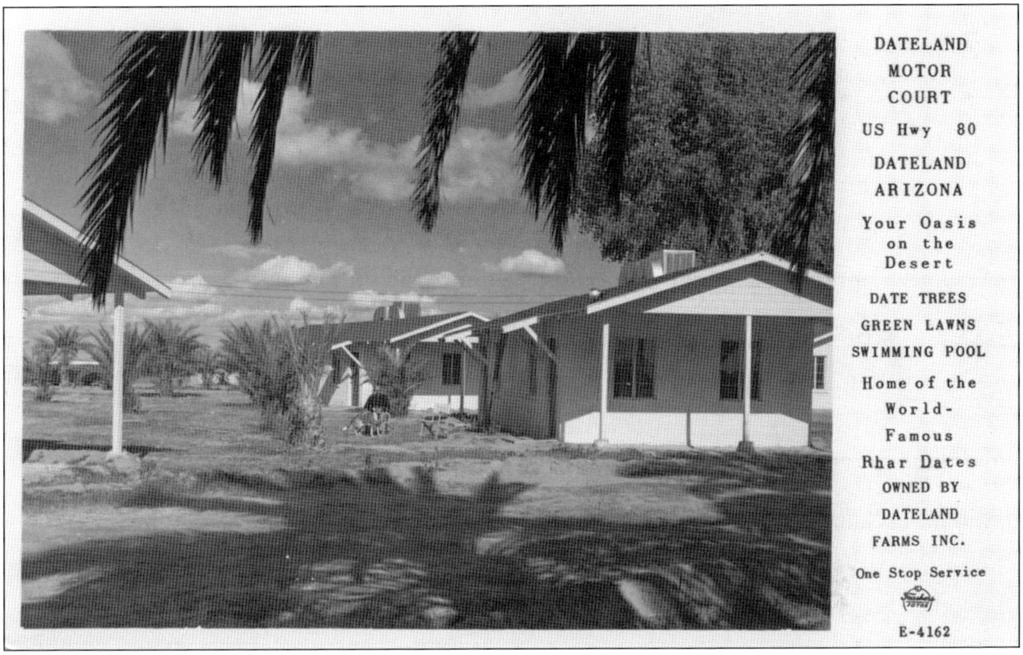

ABOVE, DATELAND, DATELAND MOTOR COURT, C. 1940S (REAL-PHOTO POSTCARD); BELOW, DATELAND, SWIMMING POOL, C. 1940S (REAL-PHOTO POSTCARD). In the 1940s, Gen. George Patton built two desert training camps near Dateland. Camp Horn was located 10 miles north of Dateland along the Southern Pacific Railroad, while Camp Hyder trained as many as one million troops to fight Field Marshal Erwin Rommel and the Nazis in Africa. In 1942, three airstrips were constructed to train B-25 bomber pilots for battle. The buildings are long gone, but the airstrip and foundations are still clearly visible. (Both, published by Frashers.)

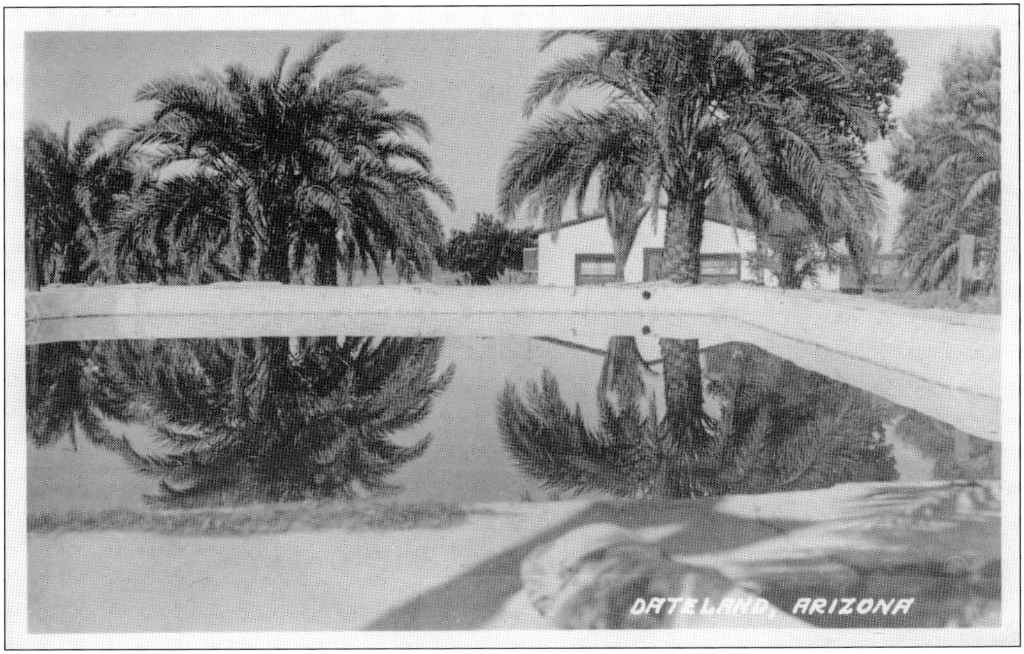

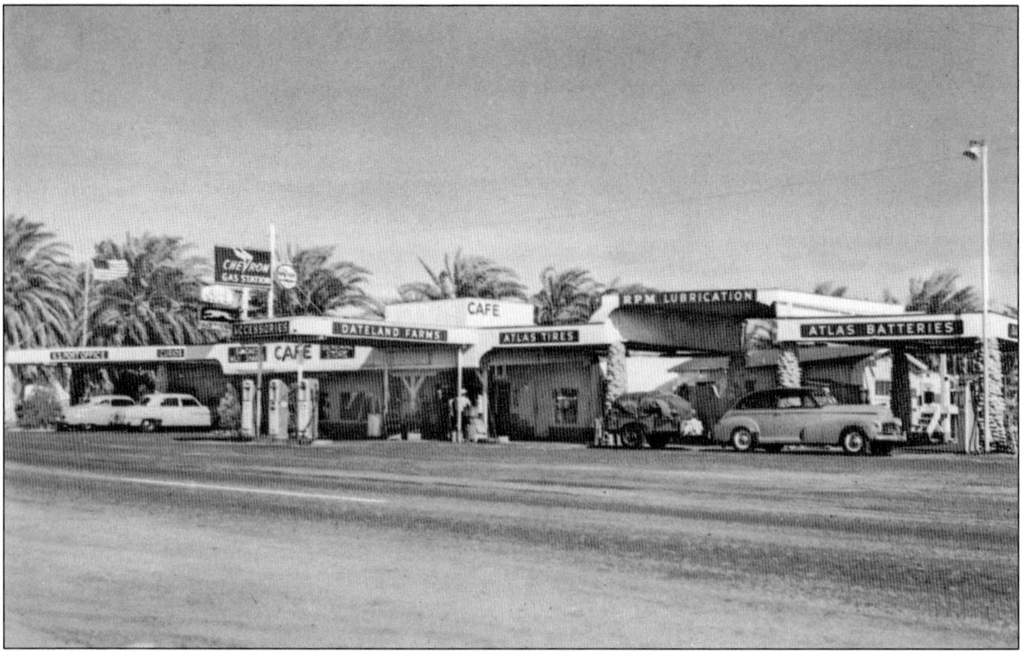

DATELAND, SERVICE STATION, C. 1950S (REAL-PHOTO POSTCARDS). Years after the airfield closed, the surrounding area was subdivided and made into individual homesites. Since the 1970s, the small town has shown its resilience to survive and has grown to a population near 1,000 people. The buildings of the old motor court are still in use today. Portions of the old pool are still visible to the passerby. (Both, published by Petley Studios.)

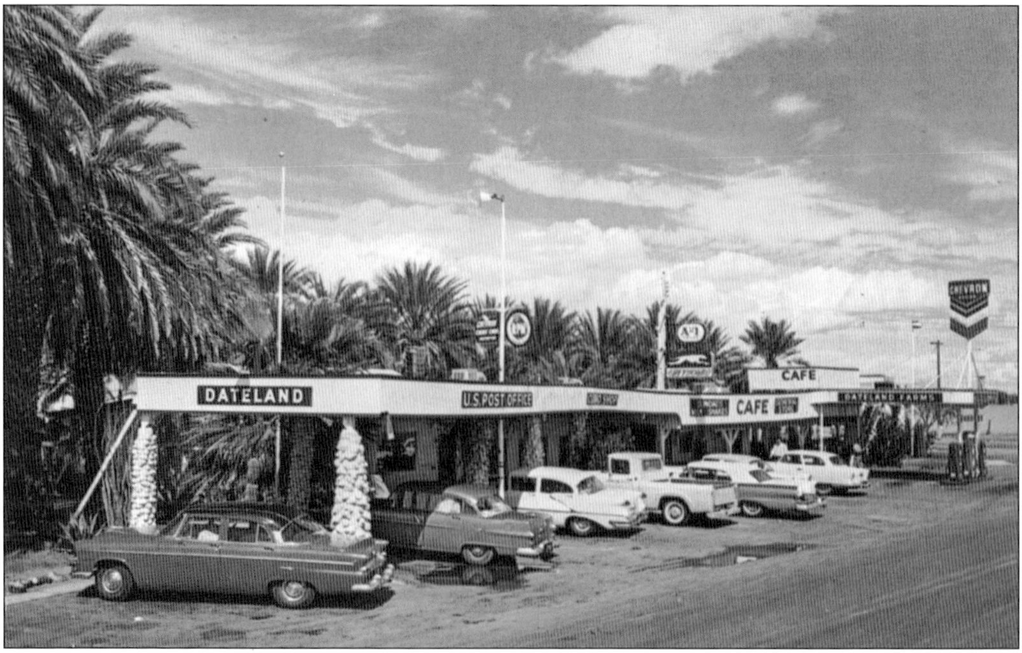

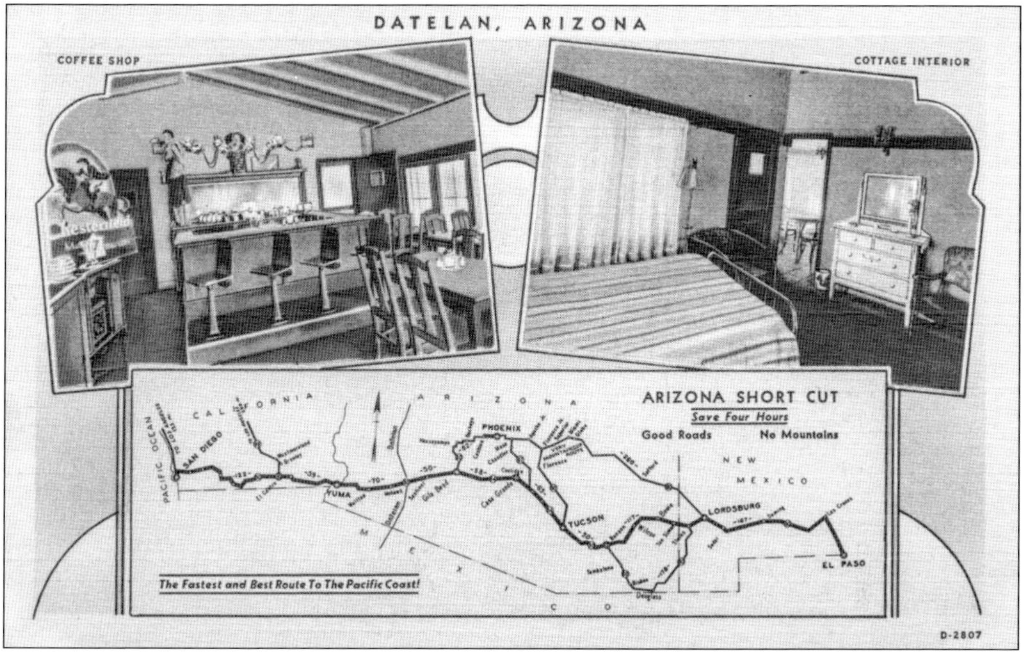

ABOVE, DATELAND, COFFEE SHOP, C. 1933 (ADVERTISING POSTCARD); BELOW, DATELAND, COFFEE SHOP AND STORE, C. 1940S (REAL-PHOTO POSTCARD). After the highway relocated in 1965, the gas station and business hung on for a few years before closing. The building was torn down in 1997, but the motor court buildings, RV park, and remnants of the old swimming pool remain. (Above, published by Curt Teich; below, published by Lollesgard Specialty Co.)

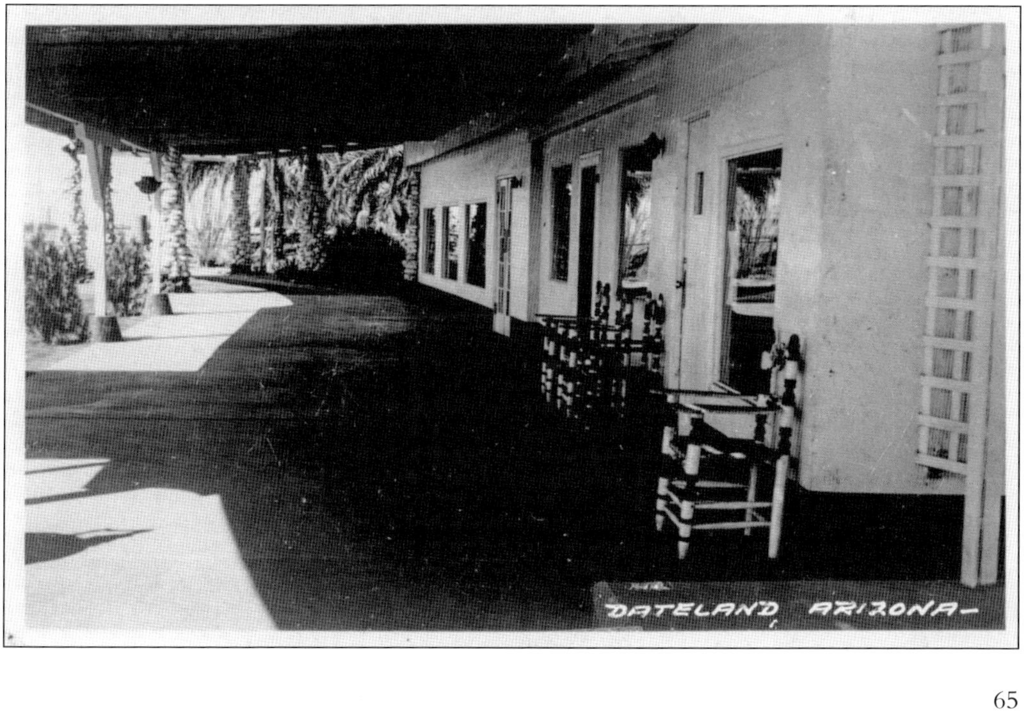

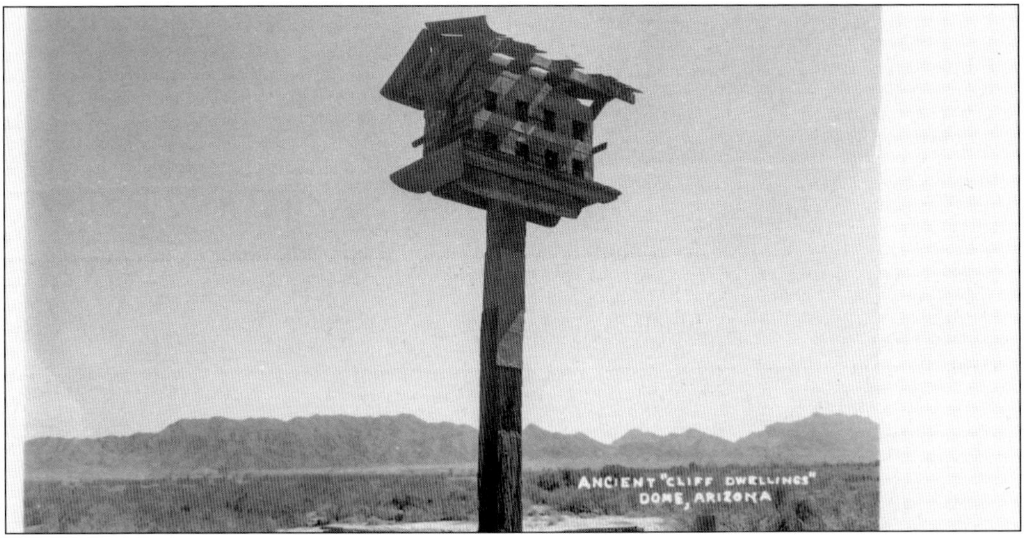

DOME, ANCIENT CLIFF DWELLING, C. 1950 (REAL-PHOTO POSTCARD). Not to be confused with Castle Dome, the town of Dome is now a ghost town located on the old route of the Butterfield stage about 20 miles east of Yuma. A post office was first established in 1858 under the name of Swiveler's Station. The post office was closed shortly after. Large-scale mining in the area began in early 1890s, and a new post office was established in 1892 as Dome. The mines opened and closed many times in the ensuing years, finally closing in 1940 for good.

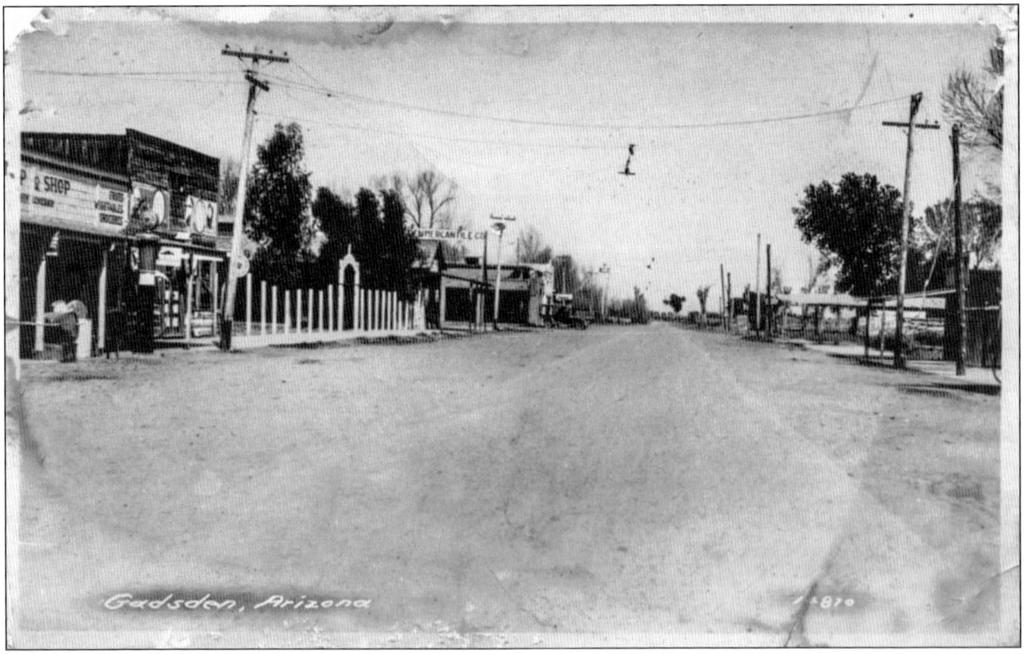

GADSDEN, MAIN STREET, C. 1920S (REAL-PHOTO POSTCARD). Established in 1915, Gadsden was known for its cotton production and was once home to four cotton gins. The town was named after either the Gadsden Purchase or James Gadsden, who was the secretary of state at the time. The town's main street no longer resembles its past, as it once consisted of two banks, a movie house, pool hall, two service stations, a mercantile, a butcher shop, a restaurant, and a barbershop. (Courtesy of Louie Gradias.)

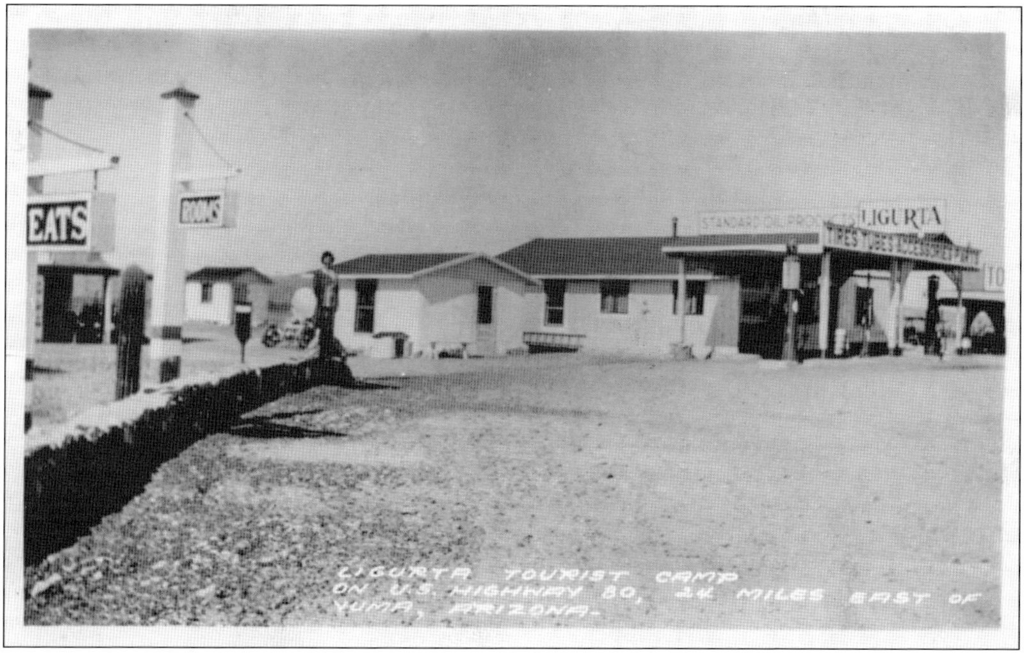

LIGURTA, TOURIST CAMP, C. 1930S (REAL-PHOTO POSTCARD). The origins of the name Ligurta are lost in history. Some speculate the name is derived from the Spanish word *lagarto,* meaning lizard. Ligurta was established around 1880 as a railroad station for the Southern Pacific Railroad.

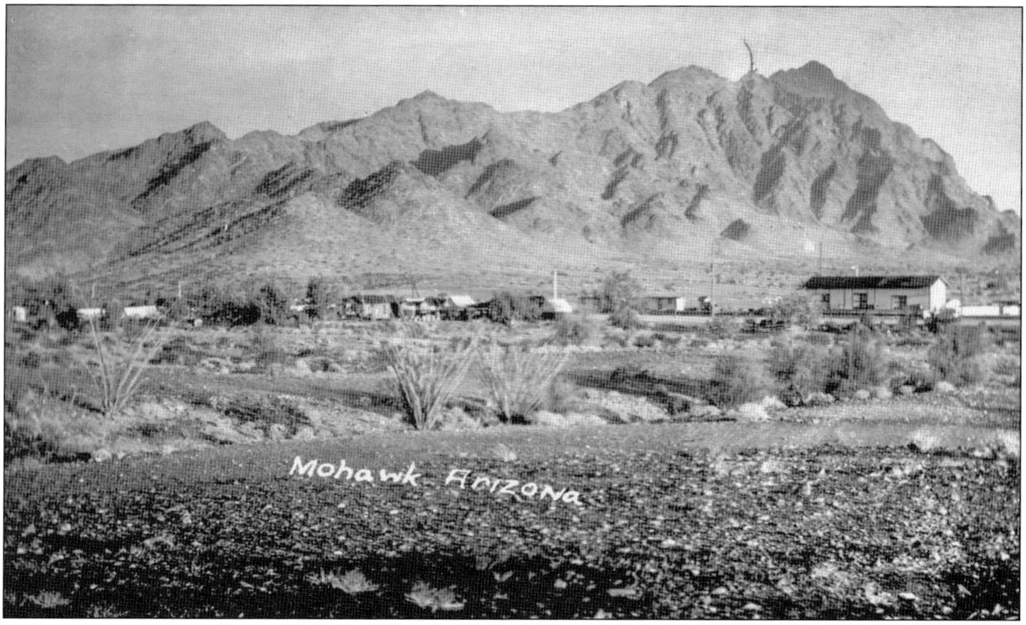

MOHAWK, TOWN VIEW, C. 1910S (REAL-PHOTO POSTCARD). According to the September 10, 1900, issue of the *Arizona Republican* newspaper, Mohawk was described as "quite a bustling town." Also noted in the newspaper was that the Southern Pacific Railroad station was relocated from Texas Hill to Mohawk to meet the increasing demand for shipping from the King of Arizona Mine.

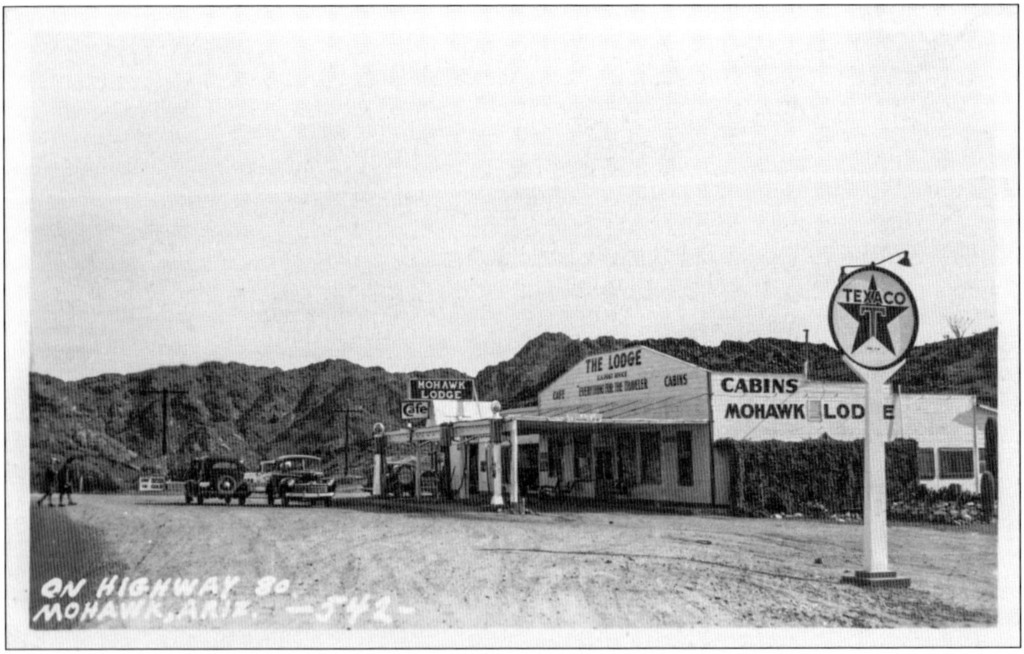

Above, Mohawk, the Lodge, c. 1940s (Real-Photo Postcards). Mohawk is located about 50 miles east of Yuma on the old US Highway 80. The only remnant left is the foundation of the old gas station and lodge. The town of Mohawk once was home to about 300 people. (Below, published by Frashers Fotos.)

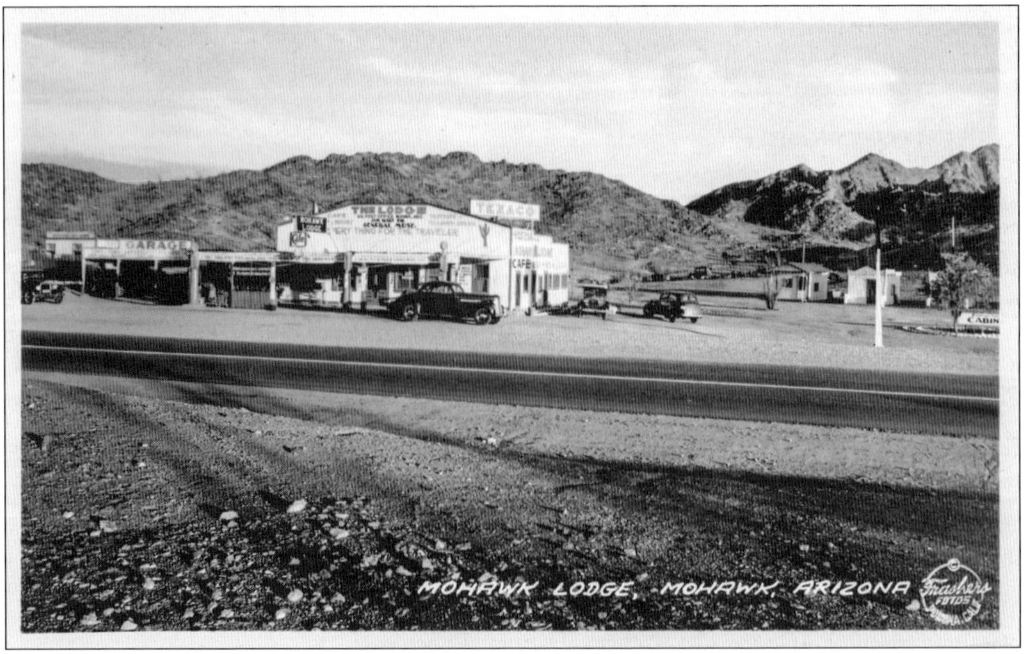

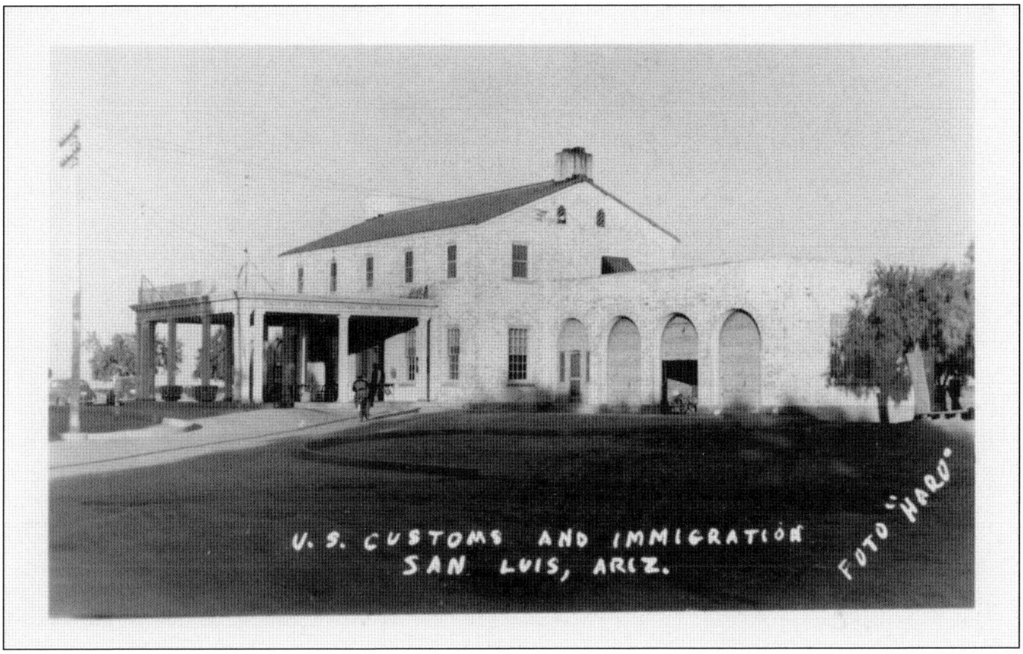

SAN LUIS, US CUSTOMS AND IMMIGRATION, C. 1940 (REAL-PHOTO POSTCARD). The city of San Luis was established in 1930 with the border crossing station opening between the city of San Luis Rio Colorado in Mexico and the United States. Civil rights activist and labor leader Cesar Chavez, born in Yuma in 1927, died in San Luis on April 23, 1993, while visiting longtime friend Dofia Maria Hau. (Published by Haro.)

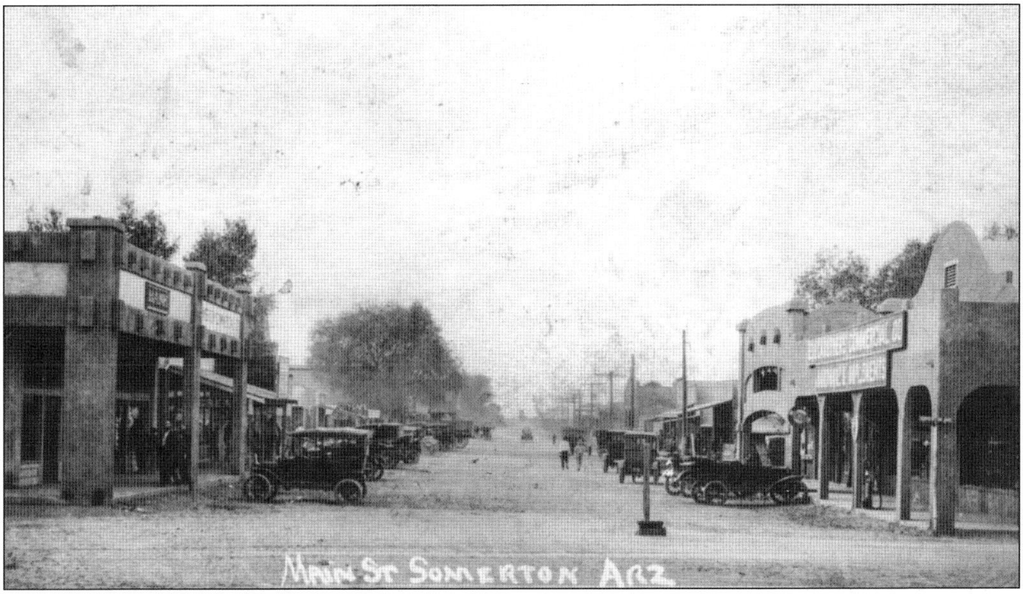

SOMERTON, MAIN STREET, C. 1910S (REAL-PHOTO POSTCARD). Somerton, located about 12 miles south of Yuma, was established in 1898 and incorporated in 1918. Local farmers named it after the hometown of one of the town's founders, Capt. A.D. Yocum. Somerton's economy is primarily dependent on agriculture, but industry and tourism are also important elements to the town's welfare. (Courtesy of Arizona Historical Society.)

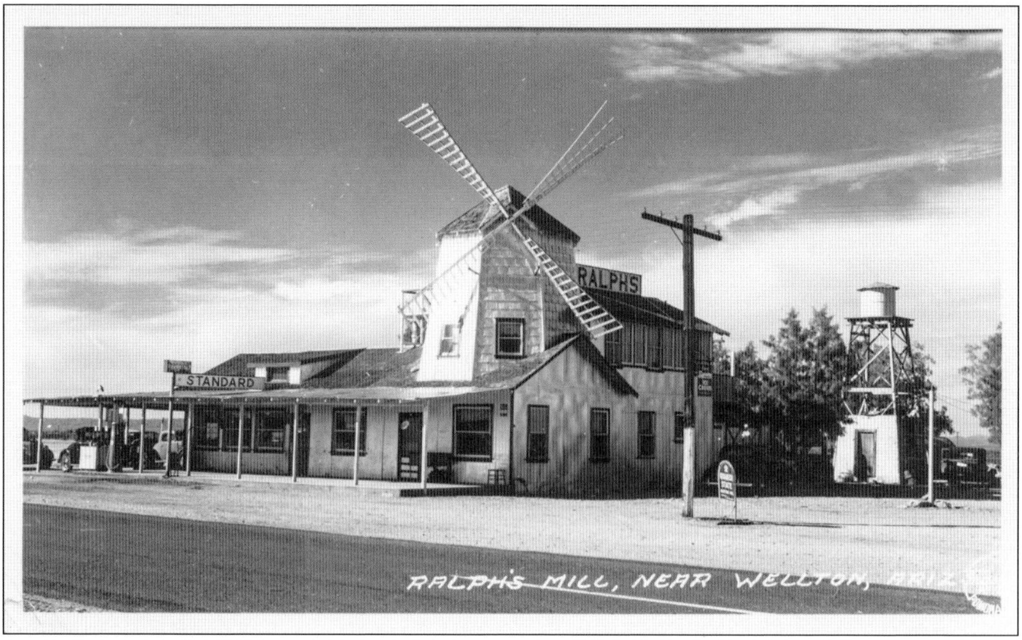

Above, Ralph's Mill, c. 1940 (Real-Photo Postcard); Below, Ralph's Mill, c. 1930s (Advertising Postcard). Located about 30 miles east of Yuma on Highway 8, Wellton was originally named Well Town after the water wells that were drilled to service the Southern Pacific Railroad. Wellton, with a population near 3,000, was founded in 1878 and incorporated in 1970. (Above, published by Frashers.)

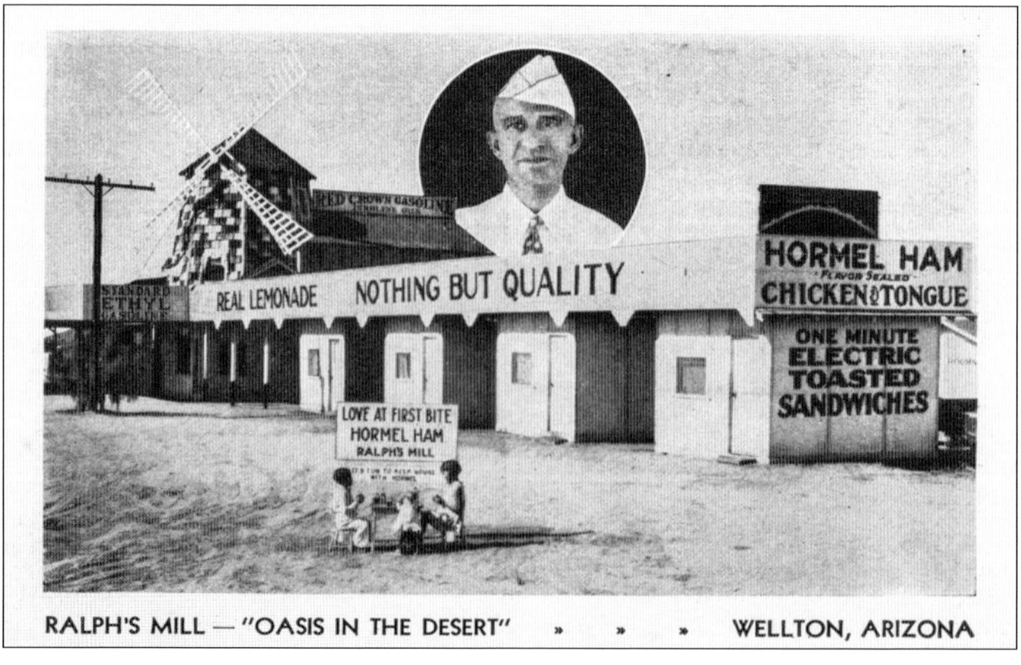

Five

Military and Prison

Serving Your Country and Serving Time

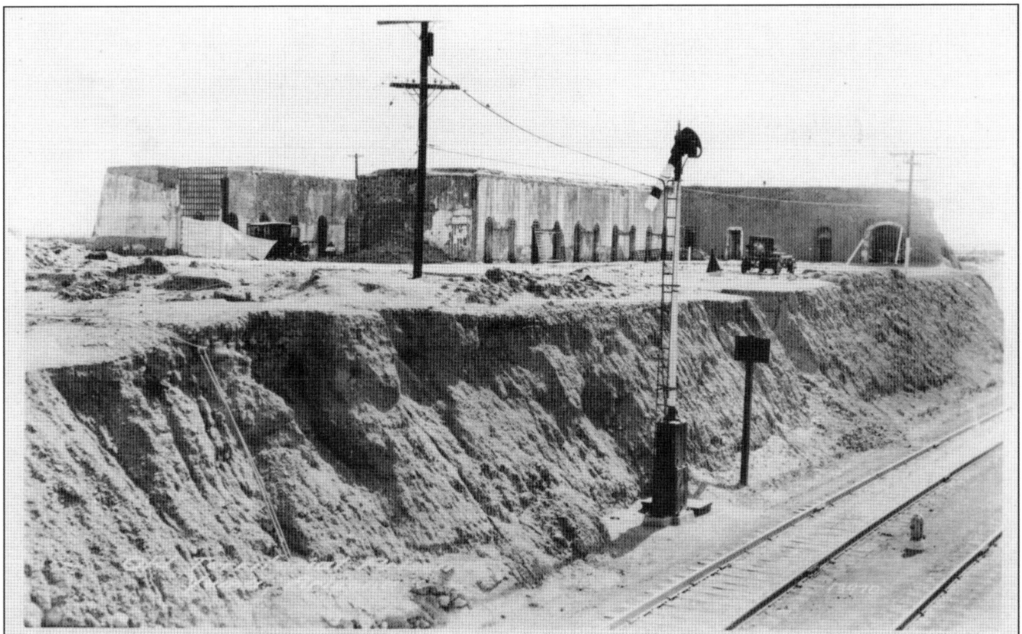

Old Territorial Prison, c. 1920s (Real-Photo Postcard). In 1923, the Southern Pacific Railroad demolished one-third of the prison to make way for new tracks. The Southern Pacific Railroad was allowed the right-of-way to cut 40 feet into Prison Hill, making it easier to build a bridge across the Colorado River.

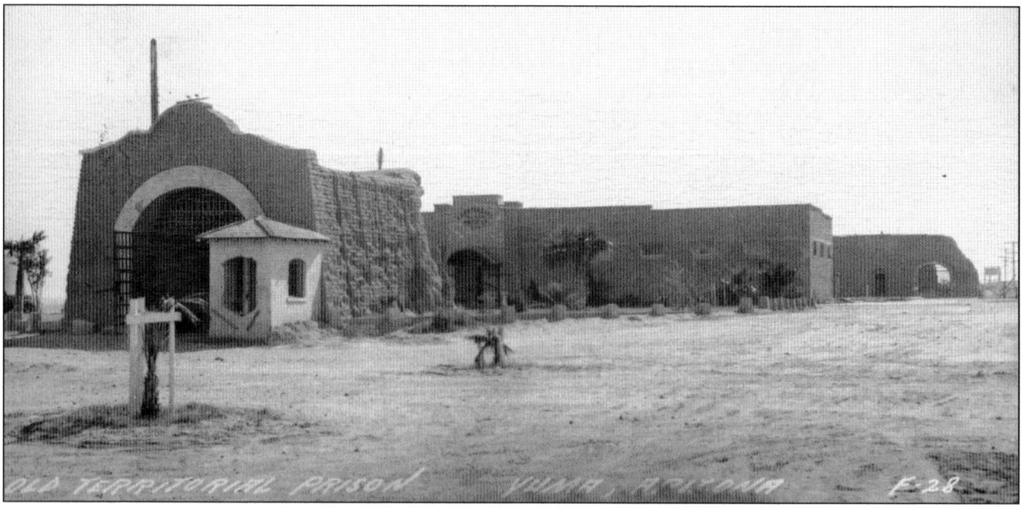

OLD TERRITORIAL PRISON, POSTMARKED APRIL 30, 1943 (REAL-PHOTO POSTCARD). The prison has been a favorite of Hollywood since 1914, when the silent movie *Life in a Western Penitentiary* was filmed there. Other silent films include *The Honor System* (1917) and *Brothers Divided* (1919). Talking motion pictures that were also filmed there include *The Three Musketeers* (1933), starring John Wayne; *Red River Valley* (1936), starring Gene Autry; *The Badlanders* (1958), starring Alan Ladd and Ernest Borgnine; *Riot* (1969), starring Gene Hackman and Jim Brown; and *To Kill a Memory* (2012), starring Kix Brooks. The most famous movies about the prison, *3:10 to Yuma* (1957 and 2007), were made without a single scene at the prison. (Published by L.L. Cook Co.)

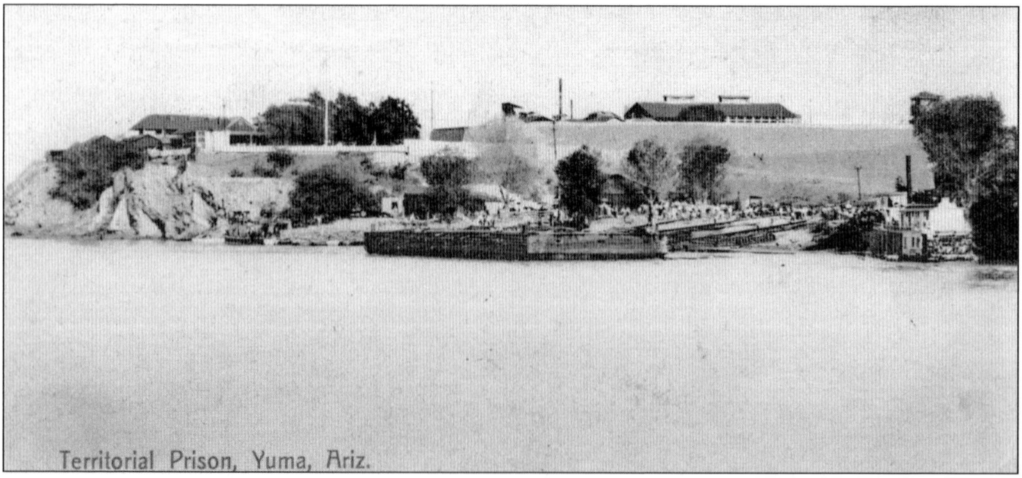

YUMA TERRITORIAL PRISON, POSTMARKED DECEMBER 30, 1909 (HAND-PAINTED POSTCARD). Some of the more infamous prisoners included Ricardo Flores Magon, a Mexican revolutionary who was imprisoned in 1906, and William Jordan Flake, who served six months in 1877 for polygamy. Pearl Hart, the "Bandit Queen," was sentenced to five years for robbing the Globe-to-Florence stage. Elene Estrada was known as the "Heartbreaker" and was sentenced to seven years for killing her unfaithful lover. "Buckskin" Frank Leslie, who worked for Wyatt Earp in Tombstone for a time, was sent to Yuma for killing his girlfriend during a drunken rage. Barney K. Riggs was serving a life sentence for killing a man who was involved with his girlfriend. He was later pardoned by Gov. C. Meyer Zulick when he rescued Superintendent Thomas Gates during the prison's "Gates Riots." (Published by the *Yuma Examiner*.)

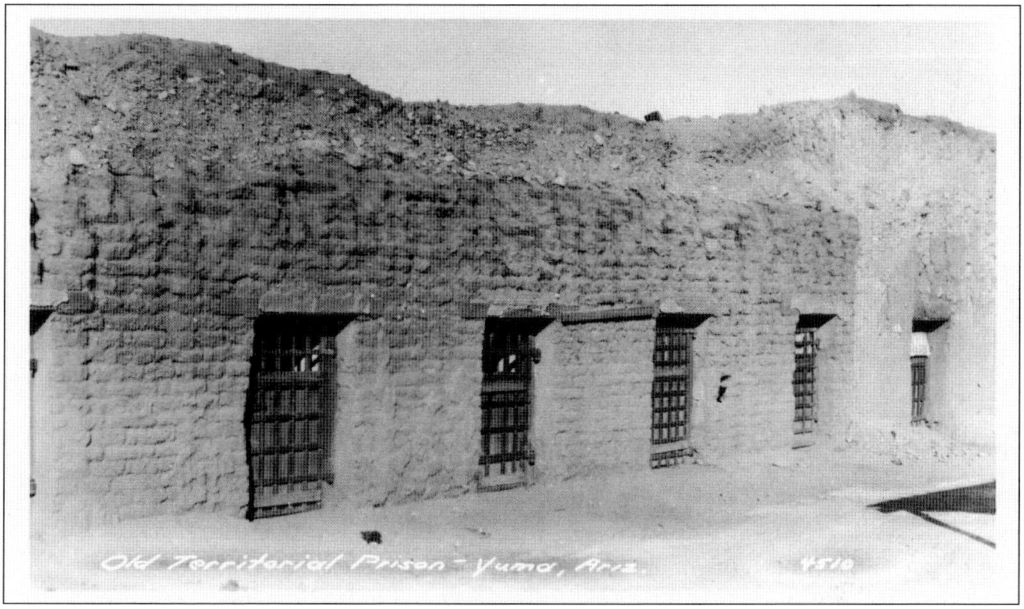

Old Territorial Prison, c. 1920s (Real-Photo Postcard). An article in the *Arizona Sentinel* of September 16, 1909, reads in part: "Pen Almost Deserted—With the outgoing of fifty nine prisoners from the penitentiary Sunday night the evacuation of the old prison, which for thirty four years has held the territory's convicts, is almost complete. The last bunch of prisoners, who are all trusties, will be taken to Florence by the remaining guards, and travel as ordinary passengers."

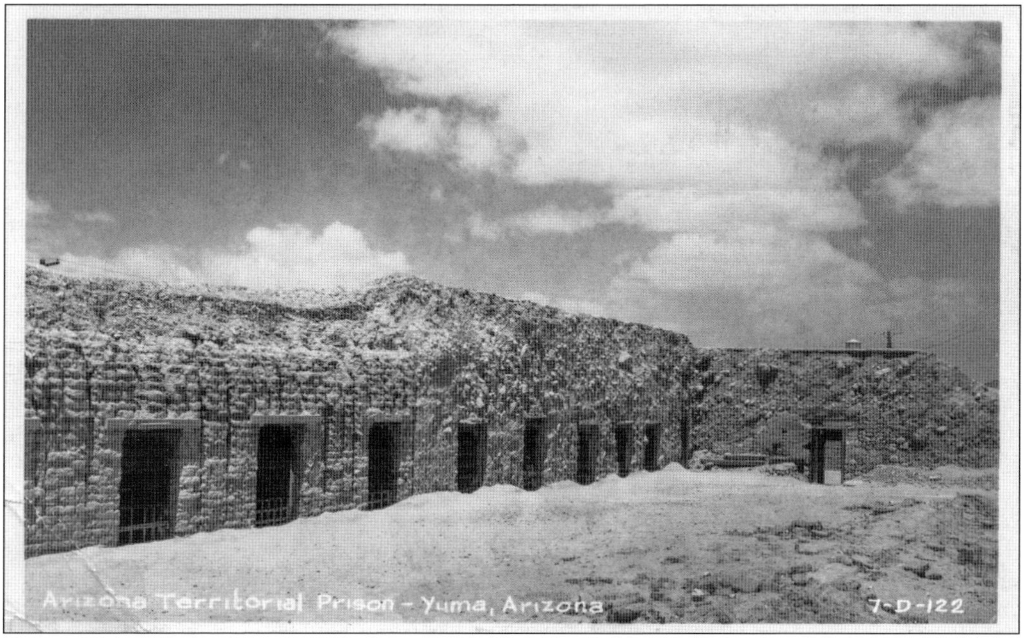

Old Territorial Prison, c. 1950 (Real-Photo Postcard). Prison life was not as bad as Hollywood made it out to be. Many of the prisoners attended school, where they learned to read and write. The prison also housed one of the first public libraries in the territory. It had its own power-generating plant, one of the first in the West, which supplied the prison with lighting and ran the ventilation systems for the cells.

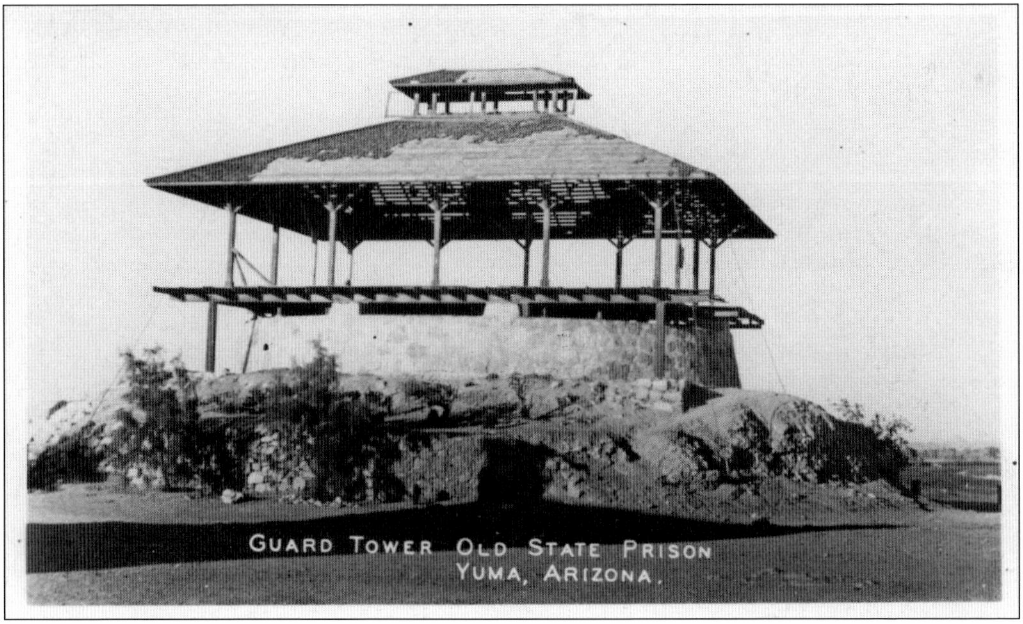

GUARD TOWER, C. 1940S (REAL-PHOTO POSTCARD). During the early part of the 1930s, the citizens of Yuma started to raise funds to rebuild the guard tower and construct a museum on the site where the mess hall once stood. The large main tower sits atop the prison's water reservoir near the entrance to the prison. There were as many as six other towers, each situated on a corner of the prison wall.

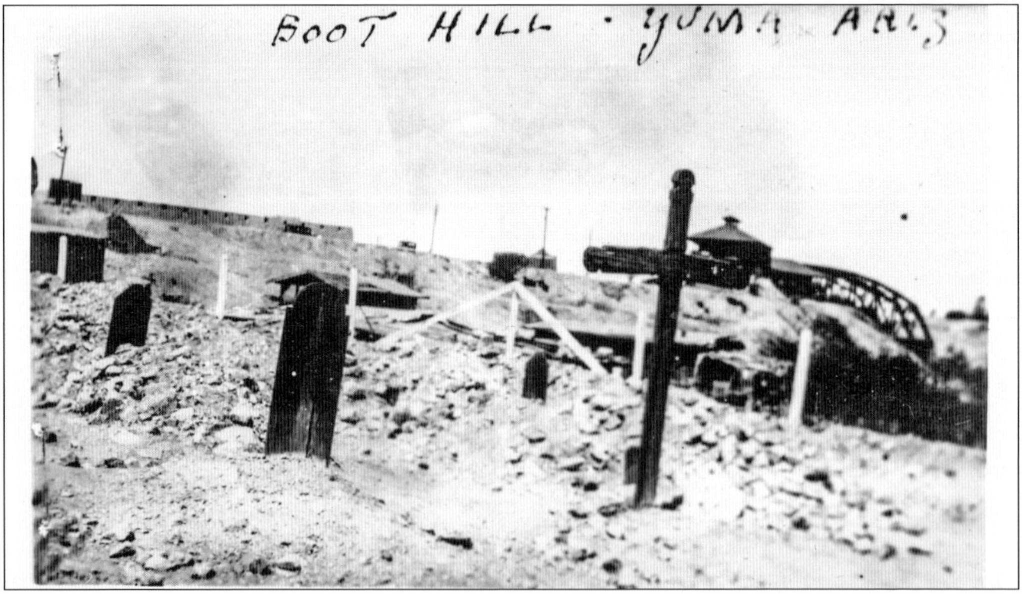

GRAVEYARD, C. 1930S (REAL-PHOTO POSTCARD). During its brief 33 years of housing the worst of the worst, Yuma Prison saw only 112 deaths. Half were contributed to tuberculosis, with 33 percent to other natural causes. Eight were shot dead trying to escape, six died of suicide, five died from work-related accidents, and two were murdered by other inmates. Of the 112 deaths, 104 were buried in the prison's cemetery. The first recorded death was that of Richard Russell, who died on November 1, 1882. The last death was Angel Otero, who died of consumption on July 20, 1909.

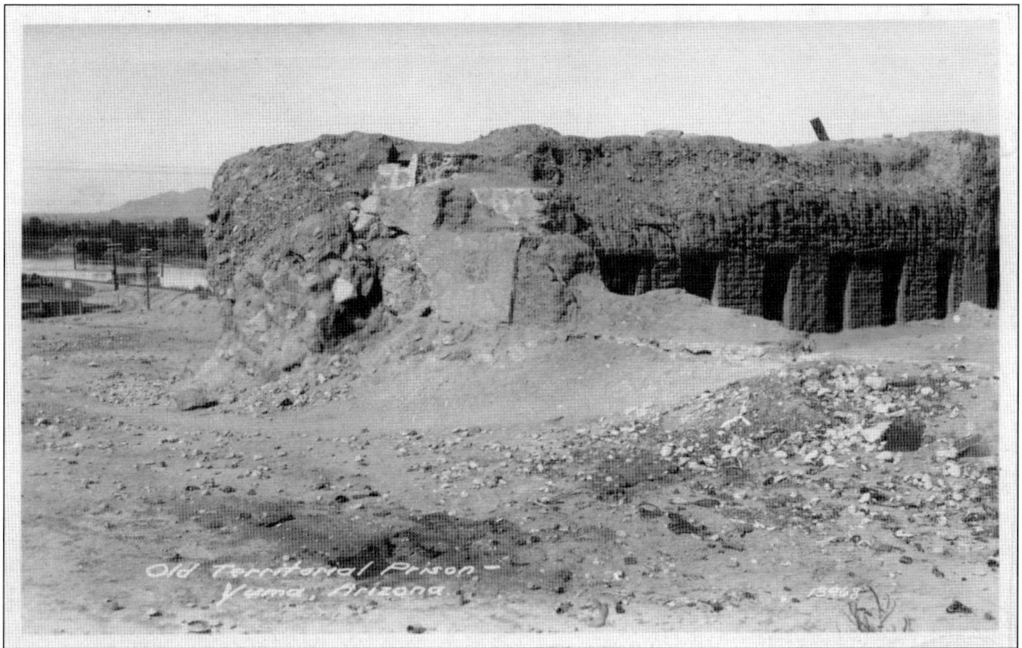

Old Territorial Prison, c. 1930 (Above) and c. 1940 (Below) (Real-Photo Postcards). With a $25,000 budget, ground was broken on April 28, 1876, by inmates who would eventually be housed at the prison. On July 1, 1876, the first seven inmates were imprisoned in the Yuma Territorial Prison. After the prison closed in 1909, Yuma High School used some of the buildings for classrooms from 1910 to 1914.

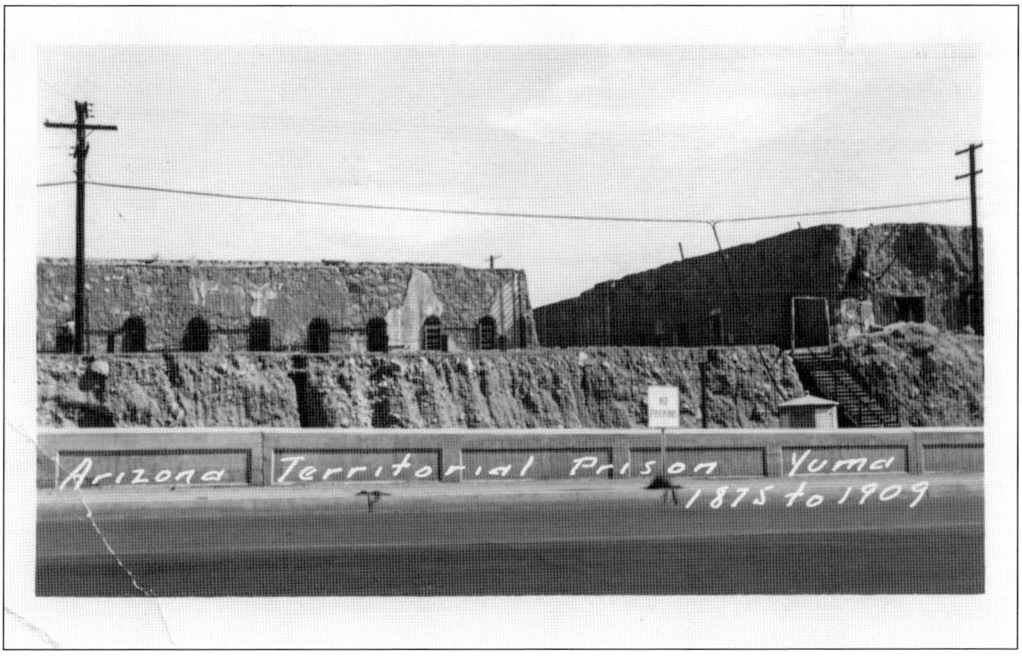

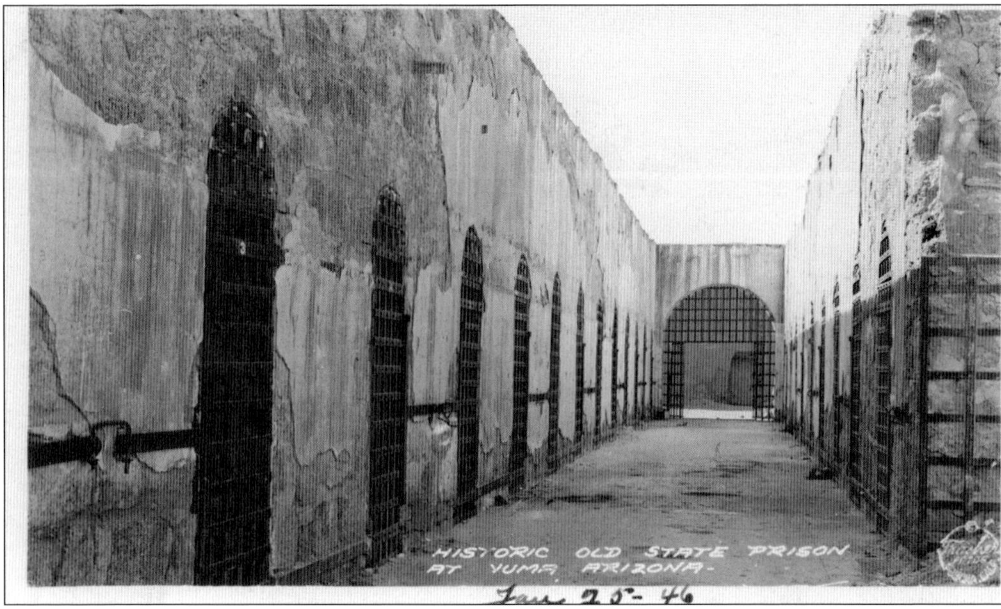

PRISON CELLS, HAND DATED JANUARY 25, 1946 (REAL-PHOTO POSTCARD). A total of 3,069 prisoners, including 29 women, lived in these cells during the prison's 33 years of operation. Of all the prisoners who attempted their escape, only 26 were successful, and an additional eight died from gunshot wounds during an escape. Many of these prisoners were buried in the prison's cemetery. (Published by Frashers Fotos.)

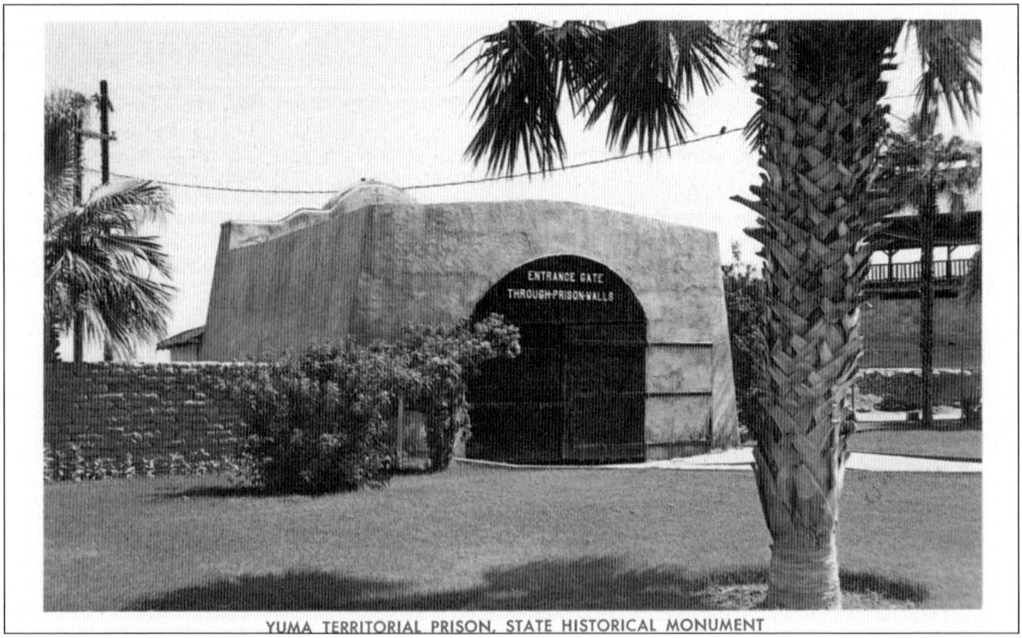

FRONT GATE, POSTMARKED FEBRUARY 5, 1965 (CURT TEICH POSTCARD FOLDER). The prison's front gate, which also went by the name sally port, is the last of the original adobe structures remaining at the prison. More than 3,000 convicts walked through these gates between 1876 and 1909, when the prison closed. The prison is now an Arizona state park and open year-round. (Published by Yuma Color Cards.)

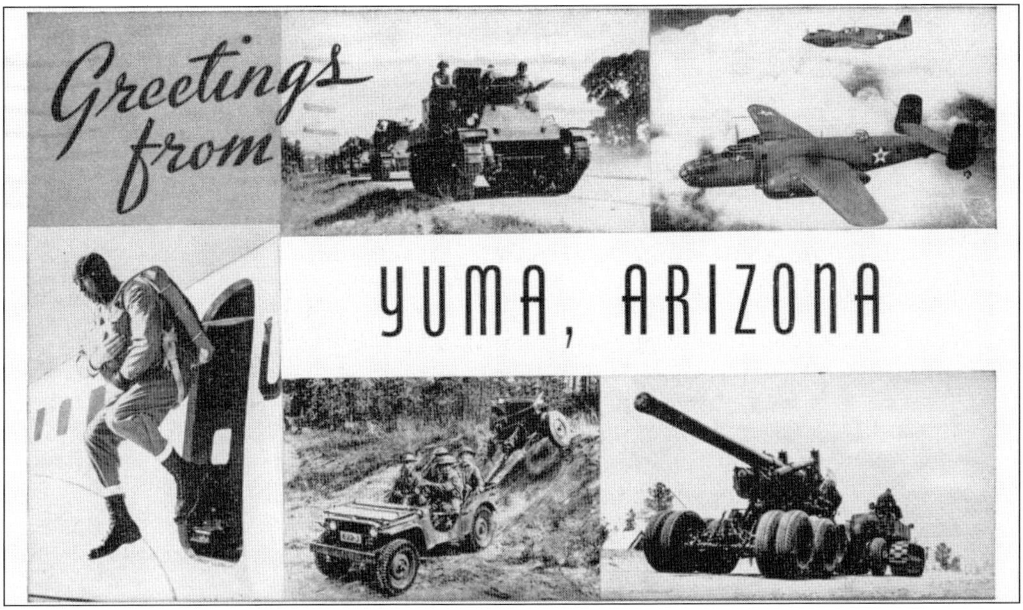

US MILITARY, POSTMARKED AUGUST 9, 1946 (MILITARY POSTCARD). The US Army Yuma Proving Grounds encompasses almost 1,300 square miles and is one of the largest military installations in the world. The site is large enough that it can train and hold over 100 tests and exercises simultaneously. The Yuma Proving Grounds is Yuma County's largest employer. (Published by Graycraft Card Co.; photograph by the US Army and Marine Corps.)

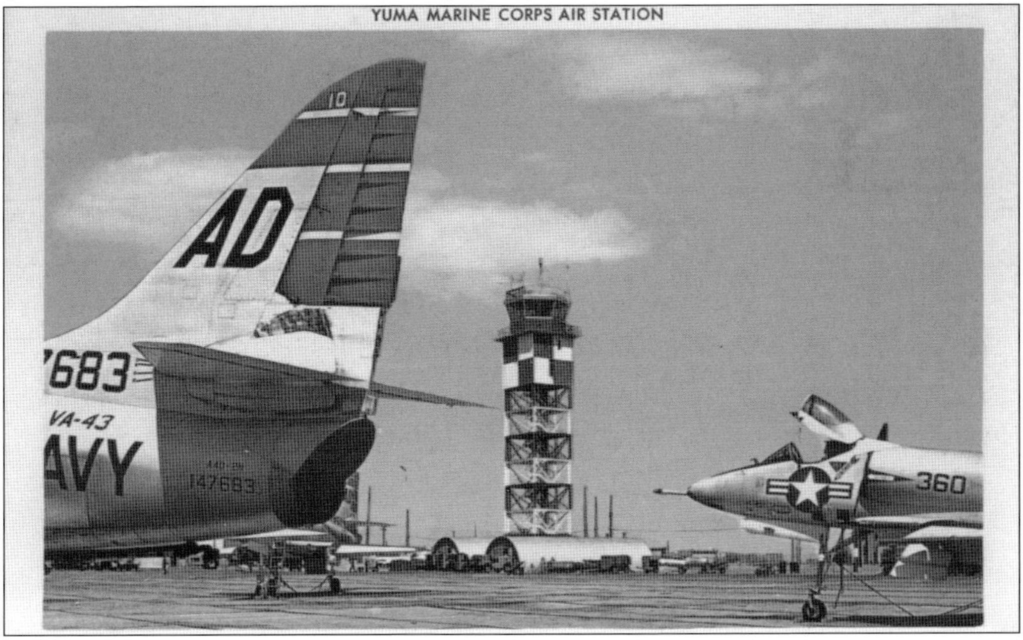

MARINE CORPS AIR STATION YUMA, POSTMARKED FEBRUARY 5, 1965 (CURT TEICH POSTCARD FOLDER). The jet fighters pictured here are A-4 Skyhawks, developed for the Navy and Marine Corps as a single-seat subsonic aircraft in the 1950s. Built by McDonnell-Douglas, the fighters had a maximum speed of 670 miles per hour and carried a bomb load equal to a World War II B-17. (Published by Yuma Color Cards.)

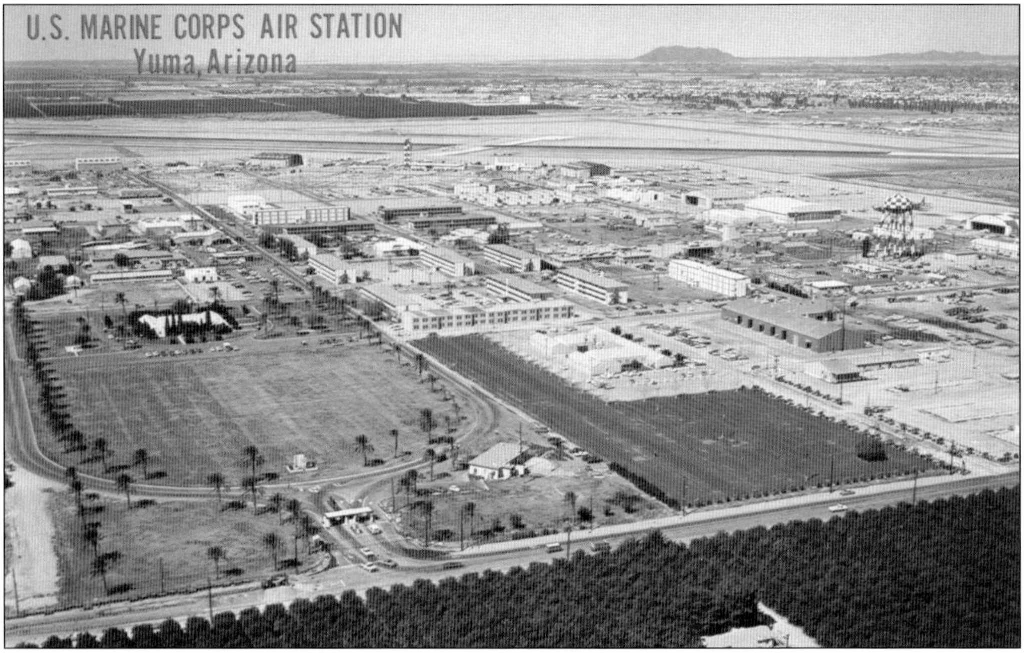

MARINE CORPS AIR STATION, C. 1970S (KODACHROME POSTCARD). Much has changed since this photograph was taken. The orange grove is long gone, with a strip mall now located across the street from the main gate. To the left of the main gate, historic jets and helicopters are on display. The grass area right of the gate is almost gone; part is now set aside for K-9 training, while most is a parking lot. (Published by Petley Studios.)

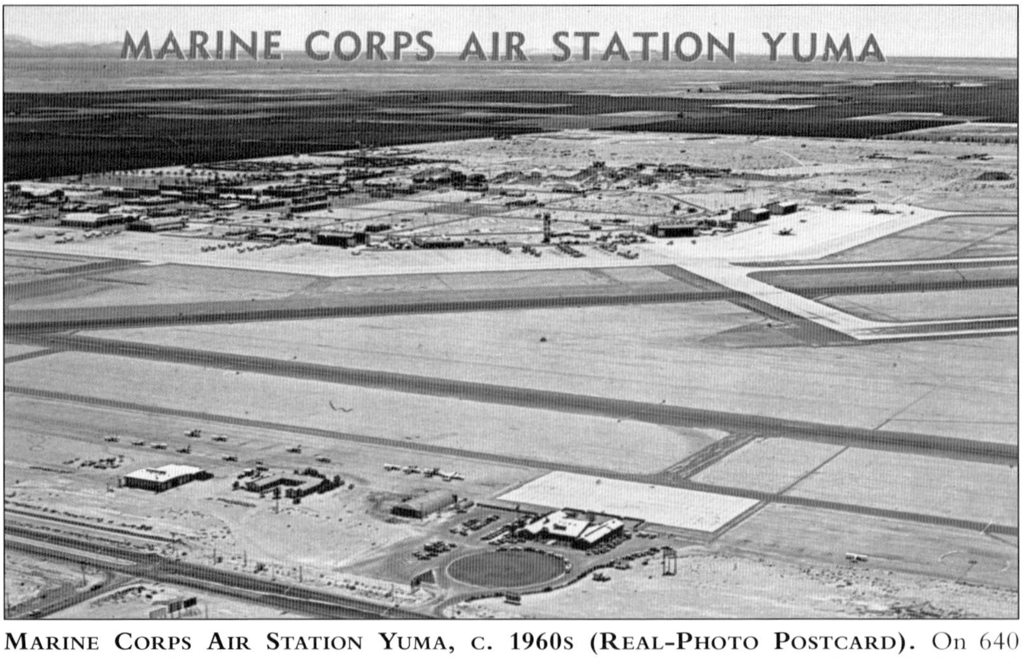

MARINE CORPS AIR STATION YUMA, C. 1960S (REAL-PHOTO POSTCARD). On 640 acres purchased by the government in 1928, an airport was constructed for both civilian and military use. The dirt runway airport was originally named Fly Field, after Col. Benjamin F. Fly. (Published by Bob Petley; photograph by Bob Petley.)

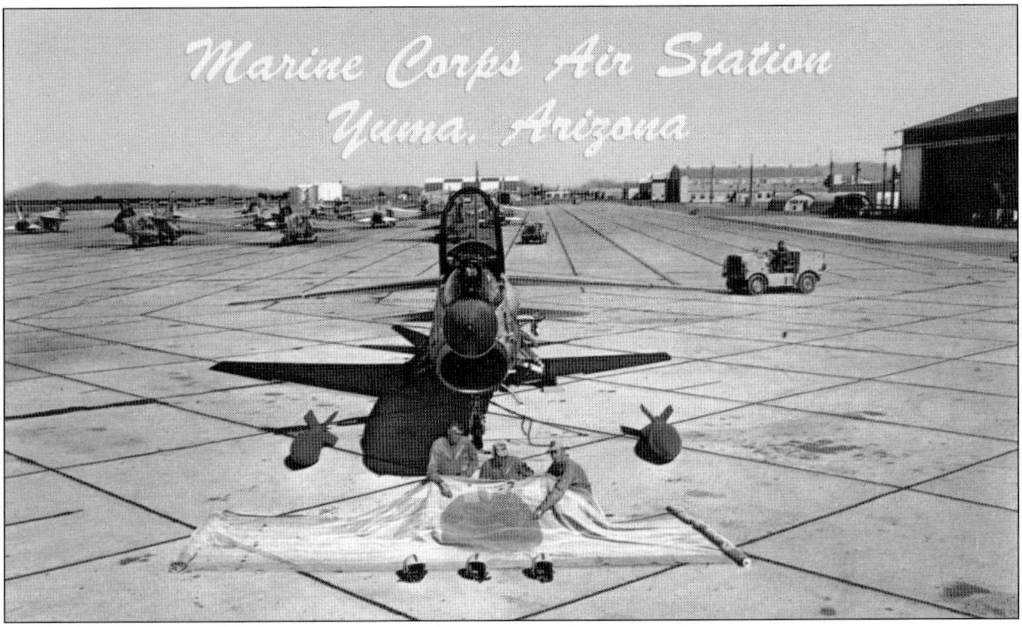

Marine Corps Air Station, c. 1960s (Curt Teich Postcard). The back of the card states, "Marine and Navy pilots from land and carrier based squadrons sharpen their eye on the vast desert gunnery and bombing ranges of the Marine Corps Air Station, Yuma. The pilot of this F8A checks hits on a tow target after a gunnery run." (Published by Yuma Distributing Service.)

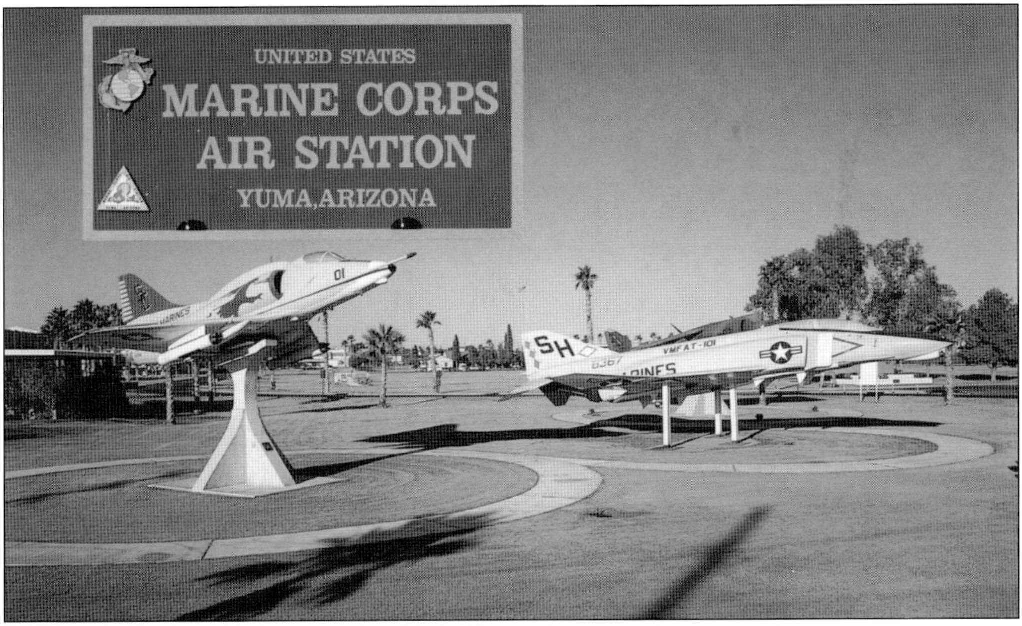

Marine Corps Air Station, c. 1980s (Real-Photo Postcard). The back of the card states, "Marine Corps Air Station Yuma, Arizona. The A-4 (foreground) and F-4 fighter aircraft at the main gate represent the pilot training, tactics, and top gun schooling taught here." There are now four aircraft at the base's front gate. In addition to the A-4L Skyhawk and F-4 Phantom II, there are an AV-8A Harrier and a US Navy HH-1N Iroquois helicopter. (Published by Smith-Southwestern, Inc.; photograph by Finchum.)

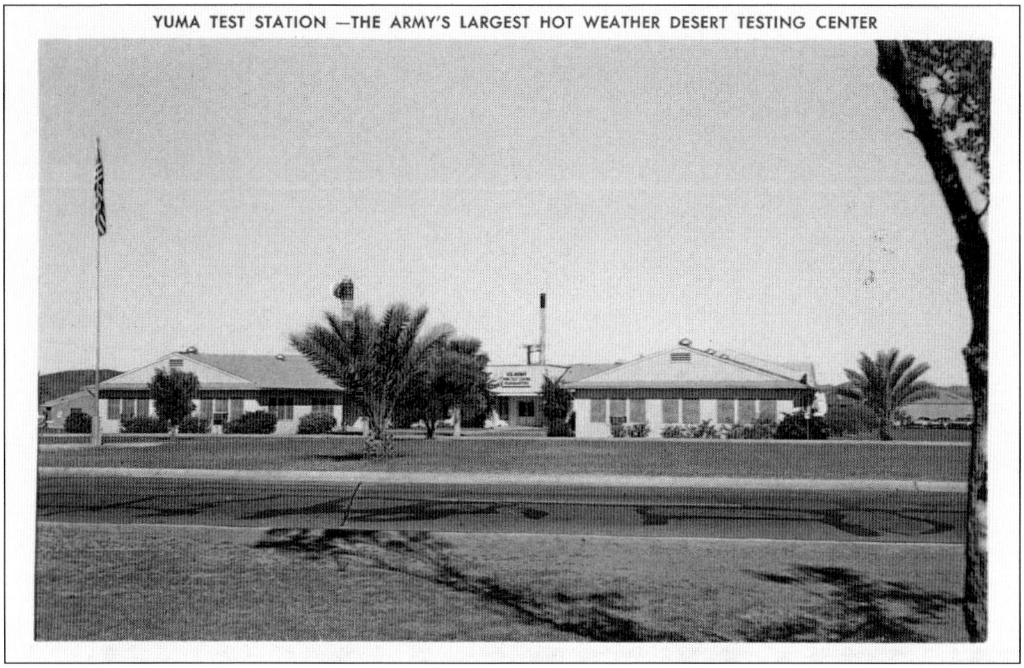

Above, Yuma Test Station, Postmarked February 5, 1965 (Curt Teich Postcard Folder); Below, Yuma Test Station, c. 1970s (Real-Photo Postcard). Equipment and aircraft testing by the US Army at the Yuma Proving Grounds goes back to 1943, when the site was known as the Yuma Test Branch. In the 1950s, the name was changed to the Yuma Test Station, and in 1963, it was renamed the Yuma Proving Grounds. (Above, published by Yuma Color Cards; below, published by Kendall Photography.)

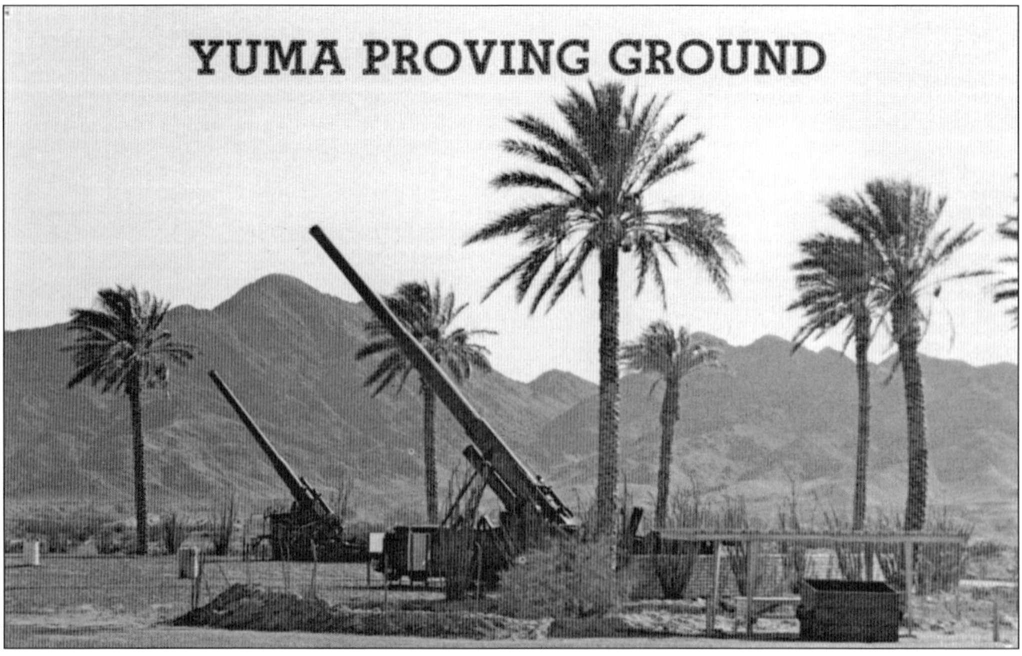

Six

Wedding Chapels
Get'n Hitched

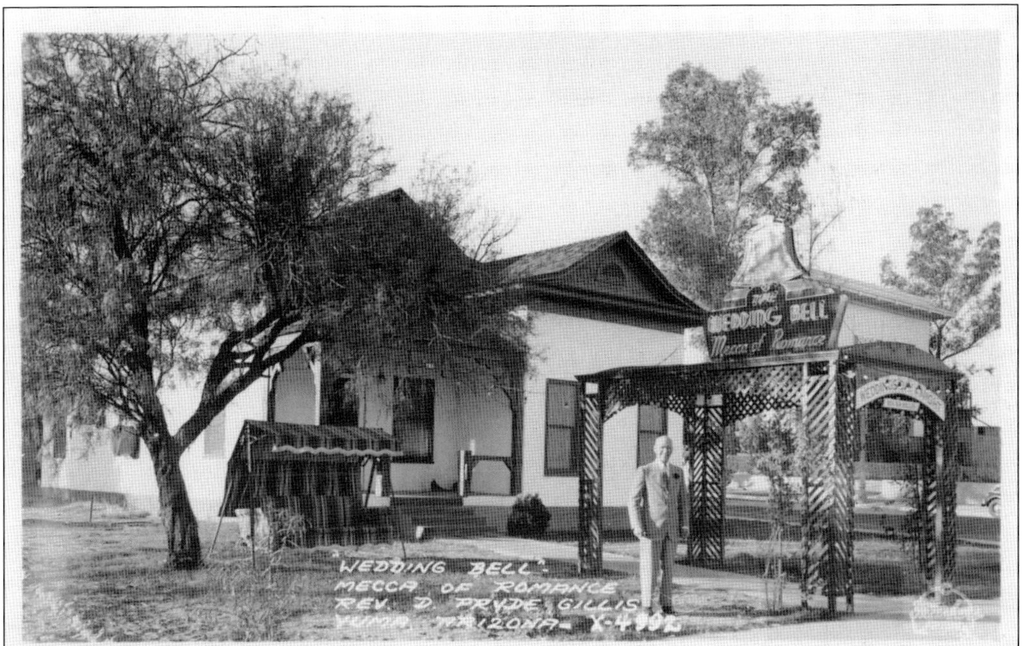

Mecca of Romance, c. 1940s (Real-Photo Postcard). An advertisement in the April 10, 1942, edition of the *Chula Vista Star* newspaper in San Diego County reads, "The Wedding Bell, Information Regarding Age, Race, Licenses, Drive Through and Save Time. Rev. D. Pryde Gillis, Highway 80 at Second Ave. Yuma, Arizona Reasonable Rates, Dressing Rooms, Open Day and Night." (Published by Frashers Fotos.)

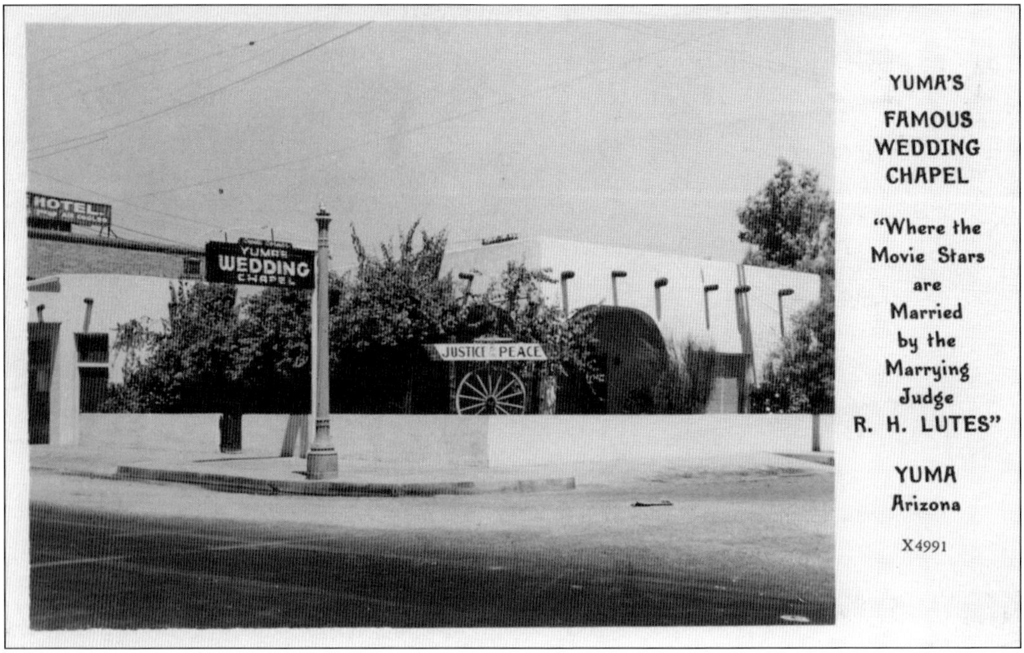

Above, Yuma Wedding Chapel, c. 1940s (Photo Postcard); Below, Yuma Wedding Chapel, c. 1960s (Advertising Postcard). Robert Henry Lutes was a justice of the peace in Yuma for over 40 years, marrying thousands of people. Many of Hollywood's elite, such as Tom Mix, Paul Kelly, Constance Bennett, Gilbert Roland, Franchot Tone, Victor Mature, Joe Louis, and Stan Laurel were married at Lutes's chapel. (Above, published by Lollesgard Specialty Co.; below, published by Bob Petley.)

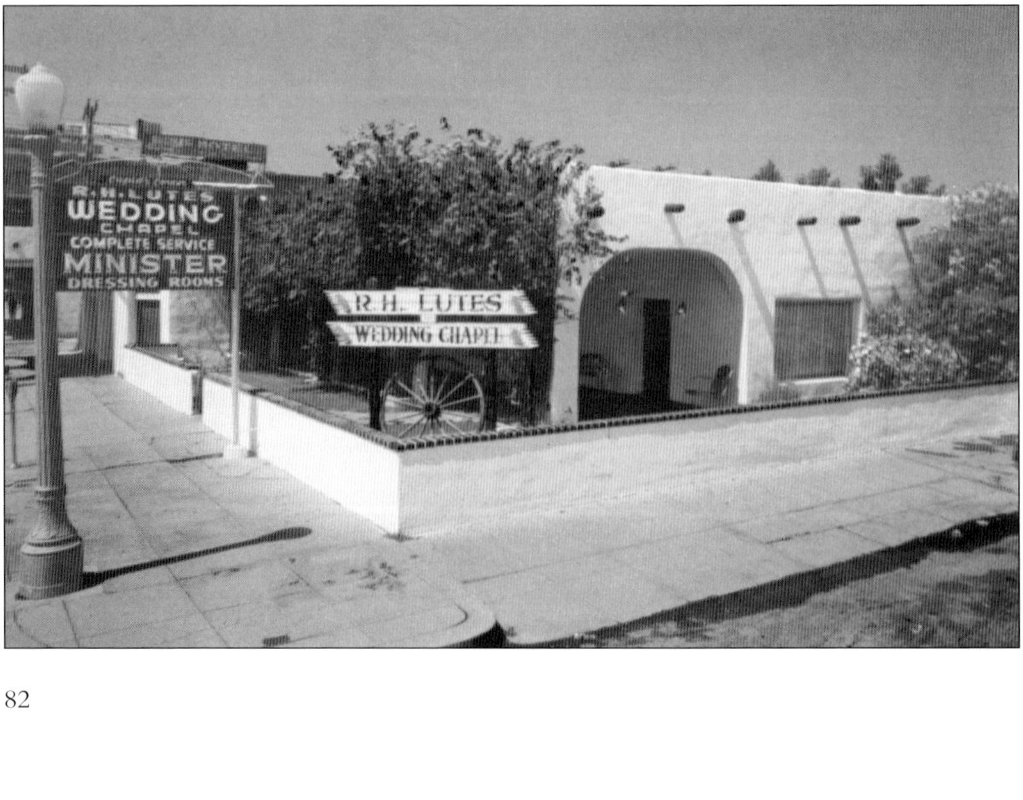

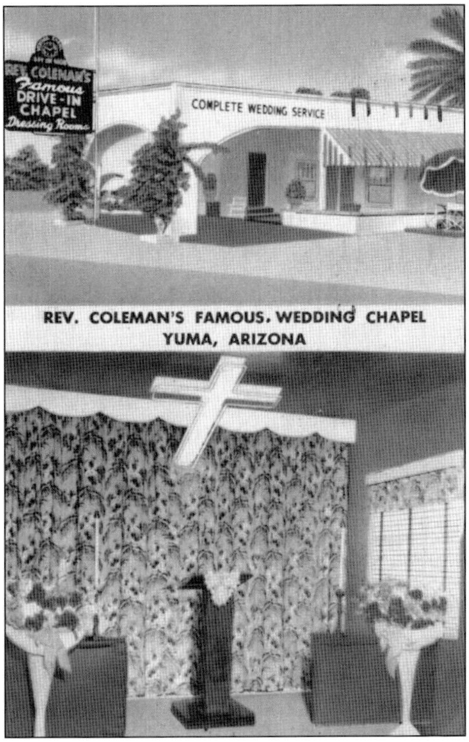

REVEREND COLEMAN'S FAMOUS WEDDING CHAPEL, POSTMARKED JULY 14, 1952 (ADVERTISING POSTCARD). Written on the back of the card is the following: "Dear Sister, Just a card to let you know that this chapel is where Florence and I got married." Long before it became a famous wedding location, it was Rich's Super Service Station and the first building seen as one entered Arizona from California. (Published by M.W.K. Co.)

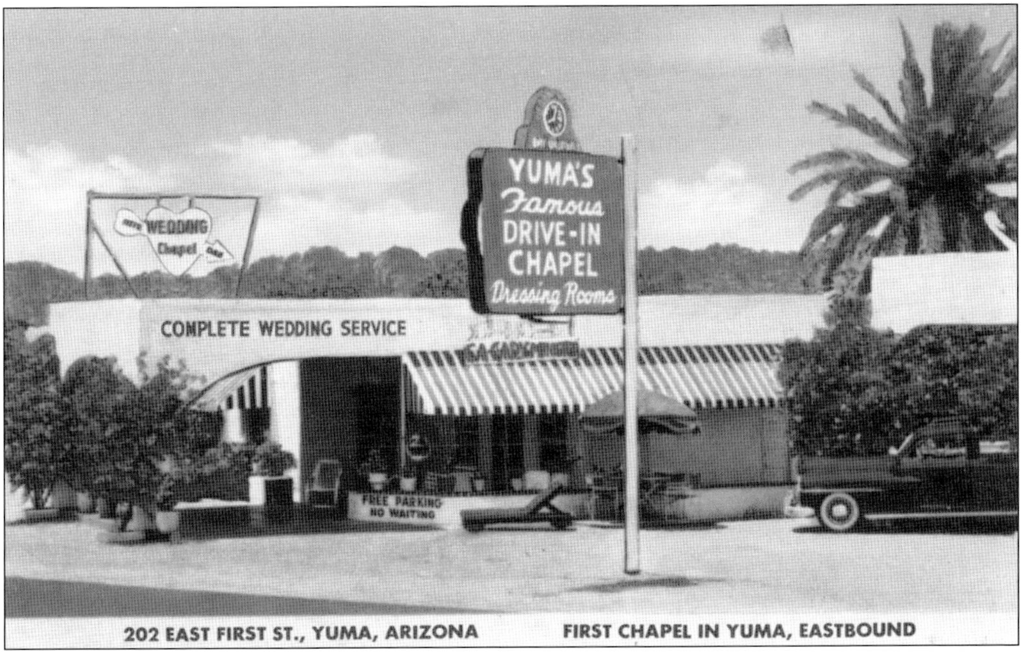

FAMOUS DRIVE-IN CHAPEL, C. 1950S (ADVERTISING POSTCARD). The back of the card states, "Yuma's Famous Drive-In Chapel Is Unique in being the only Drive-In Wedding Chapel in the U.S. Located on Highway 80, on the right as you enter Arizona from California. All wedding details arranged and marriage services performed day and night." (Published by Emils' Studio.)

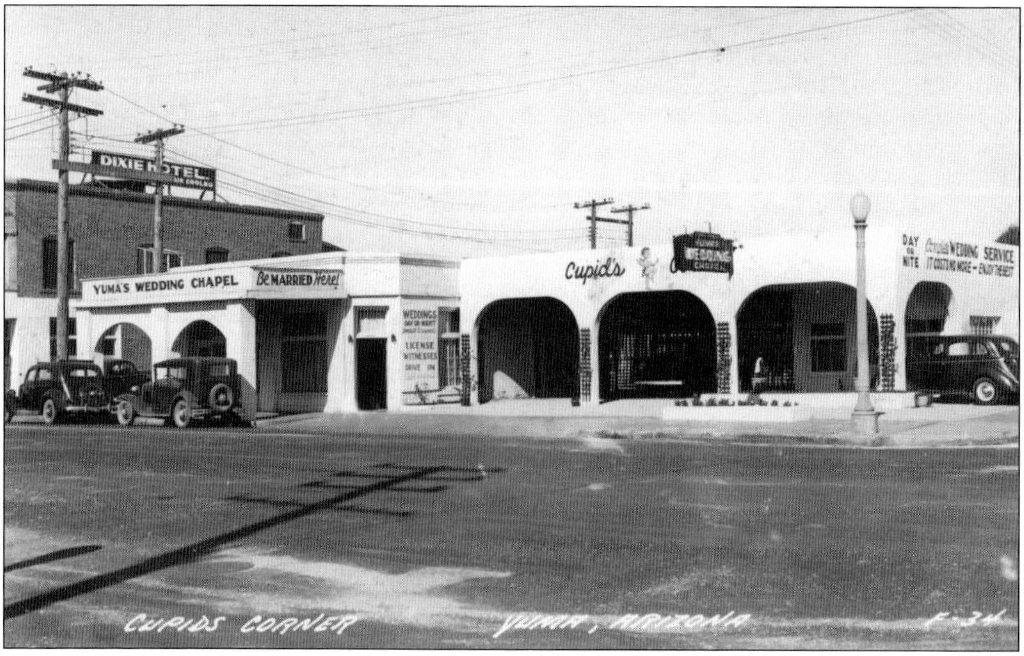

Cupids Corner, c. 1940 (Real-Photo Postcards). Prior to becoming a wedding chapel, the building was the Rio Garage. It was a convenient location, as it was only the second building as one entered Yuma from California. The location is near where the Highway 8 bridge goes over East First Street at Gila Street.

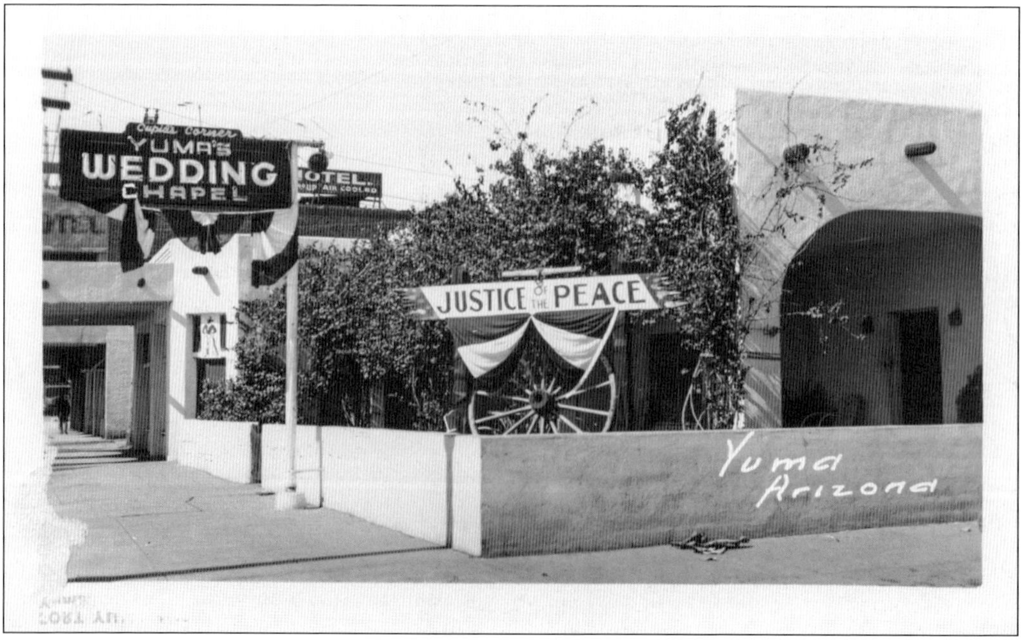

MISSION MARRIAGE CHAPEL, POSTMARKED SEPTEMBER 29, 1951 (ADVERTISING POSTCARD). The Mission Marriage Chapel was located at 133 East First Street near South Maiden Lane. The location is now an empty lot.

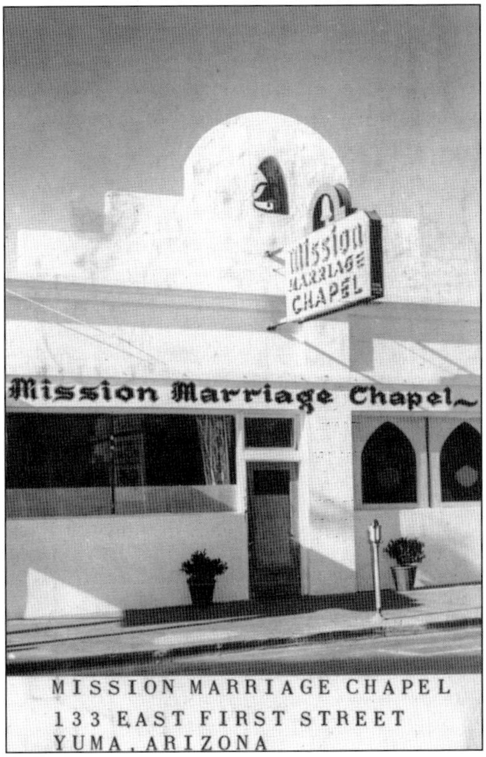

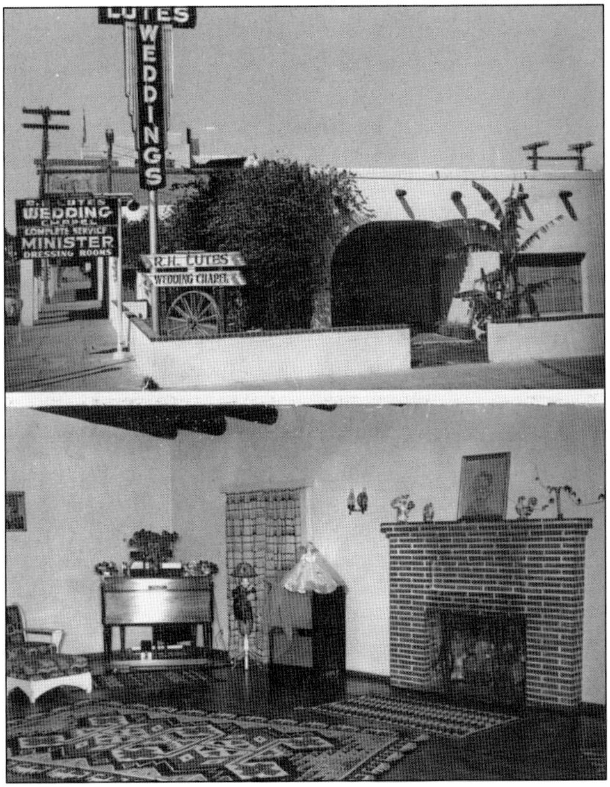

R.H. LUTES'S WEDDING CHAPEL, C. 1960S (ADVERTISING DOUBLE POSTCARD). Some of the Arizona laws listed on the postcard are "The laws of Arizona require the man to be 21 and the women to be 18. If under these ages they must have a notarized consent from the parent or guardian. The man cannot be married under 18, and the women under 16, even with parents' consent. Proof of age is required." (Published by William L. Timmons.)

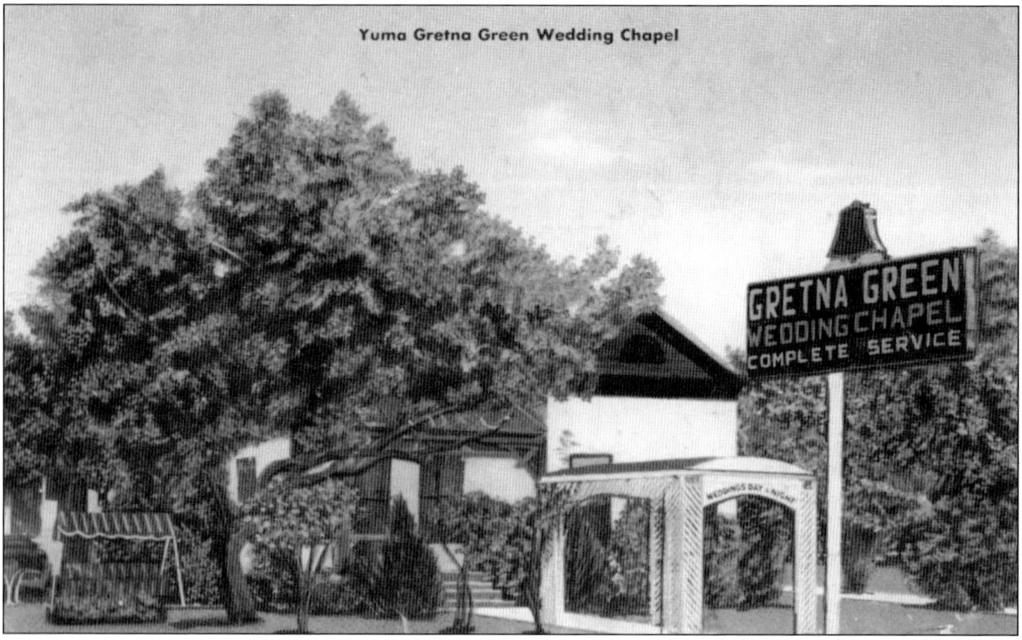

Gretna Green Wedding Chapel, Postmarked January 22, 1960 (Advertising Double Postcard). The reverse of the card reads, "Gretna Green Wedding Chapel, Yuma, Arizona. Is the oldest and most famous establishment of its kind in the entire Southwest, offering complete marriage service 24 hours of every day in the year. On Highway 80, 191 West First St." (Published by MWM Co.)

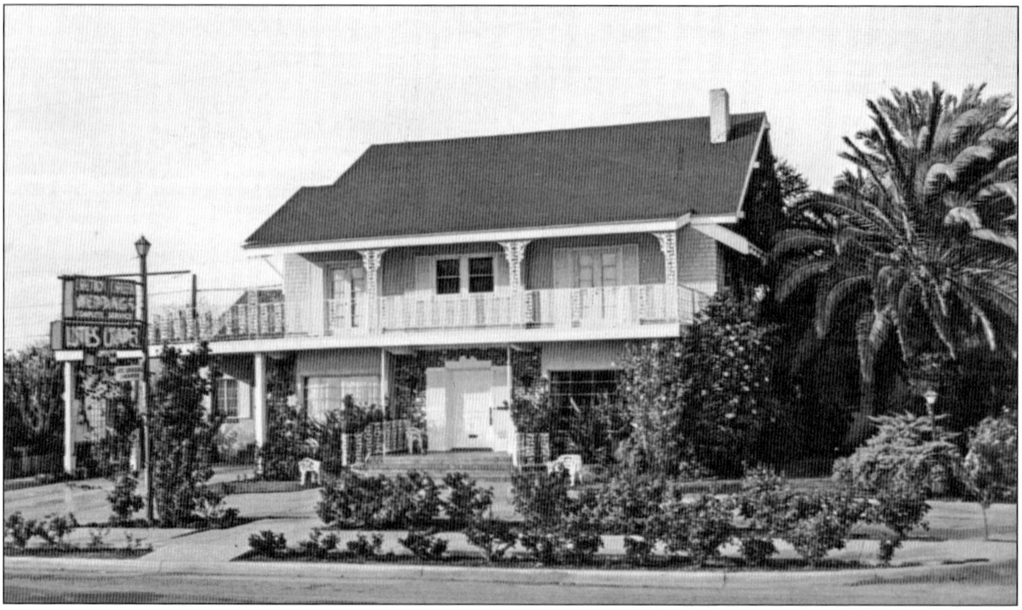

Lutes Gretna Green Wedding Chapel, c. 1960s (Advertising Postcard). The back of the card states, "Lutes Gretna Green Wedding Chapel, 500 First St.—Yuma, Arizona 85365, Marry in one hour. Complete service day or night including blood test, marriage license and ceremony. No waiting—No Publicity. Chapels in Yuma and Winterhaven." The chapel, on First Street, opened in 1955 and is still in business today. (Published by California Color Photos.)

Seven

NATIVE AMERICANS
FIRST PEOPLE TO YUMA

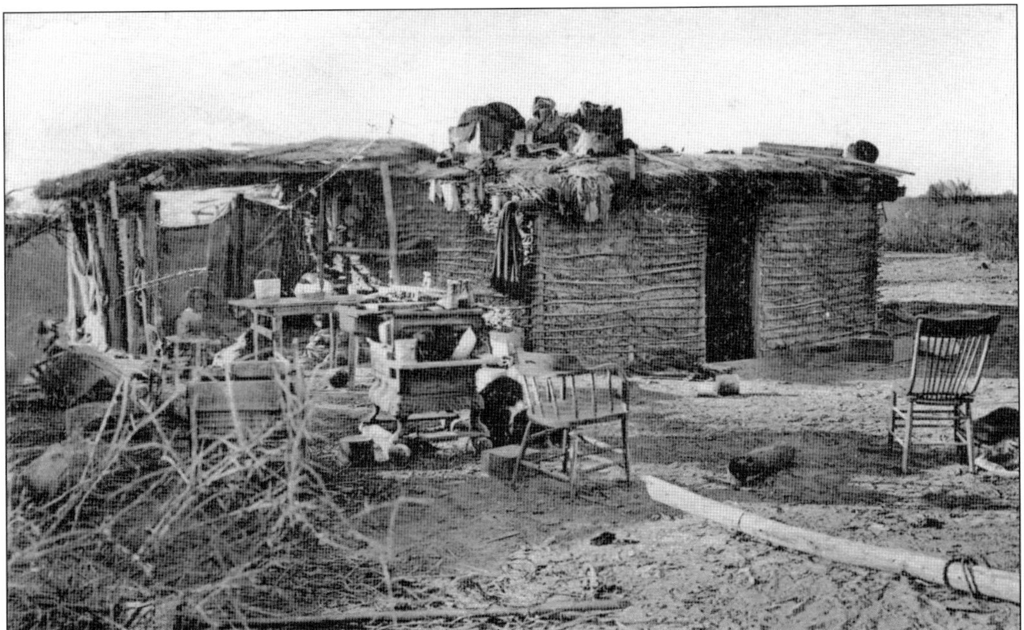

INDIAN RESIDENCE, POSTMARKED APRIL 24, 1908 (HAND-COLORED POSTCARD). Houses made of square wooden frames packed with clay and thatched with grass, known as earth houses, were common homes to the Cocopah and Quechan. The thick-walled architecture was perfect for the desert heat and cold night. (Published by the *Yuma Examiner.*)

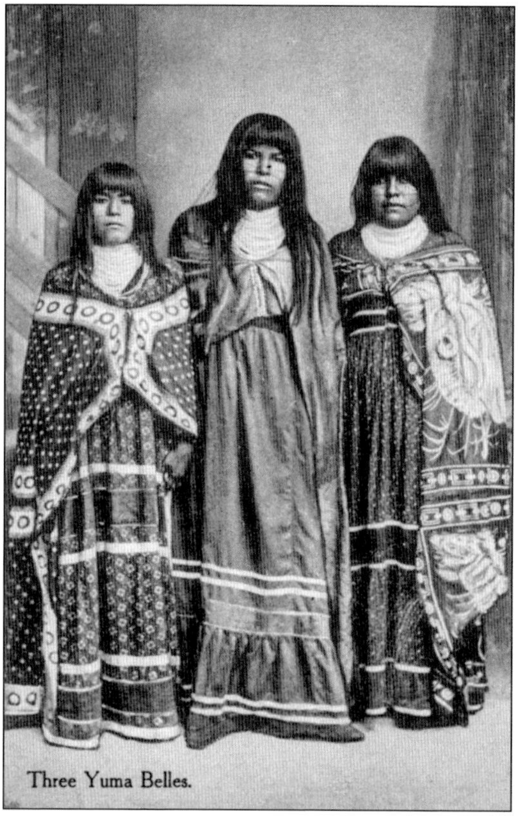

LEFT, THREE YUMA BELLES, C. 1910S (DIVIDED BACK POSTCARD); BELOW, YUMA INDIANS TODAY, C. 1910S (DIVIDED BACK POSTCARD). Prior to colonization, the Quechan women wore knee-length skirts made of willow bark and grass, and their upper torsos were exposed; men wore loincloths. As the Spanish, Europeans, and Americans became more prevalent in the Southwest, the Quechan were forced to dress in a more Western-cultured fashion. On special occasions, the women would wear colorful dresses, and if their faces were not already tattooed, they would add temporary tattoos or paint to their faces. (Below, published by Pacific Novelty Co.; courtesy of California State Library.)

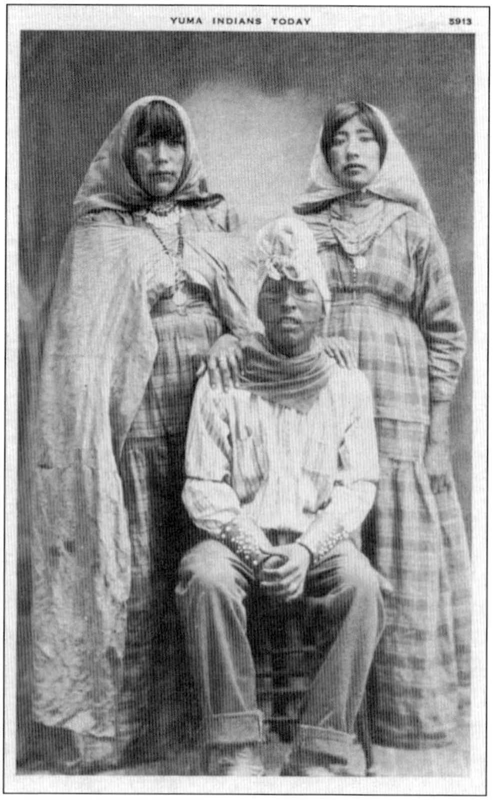

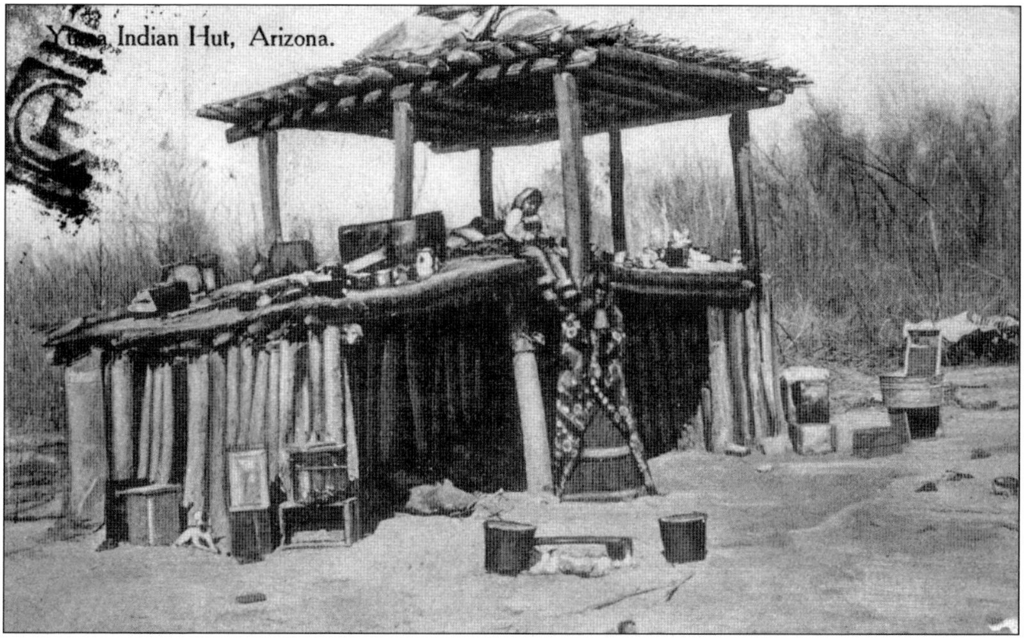

Indian Hut, Postmarked April 8, 1912 (Divided Back Postcard). Handwritten on the back of the card is the following: "Dear Folks, I am getting along good they say this is the hottest place in the U.S. There are lots of Indians here it is awfully sandy here we was late getting here to day."

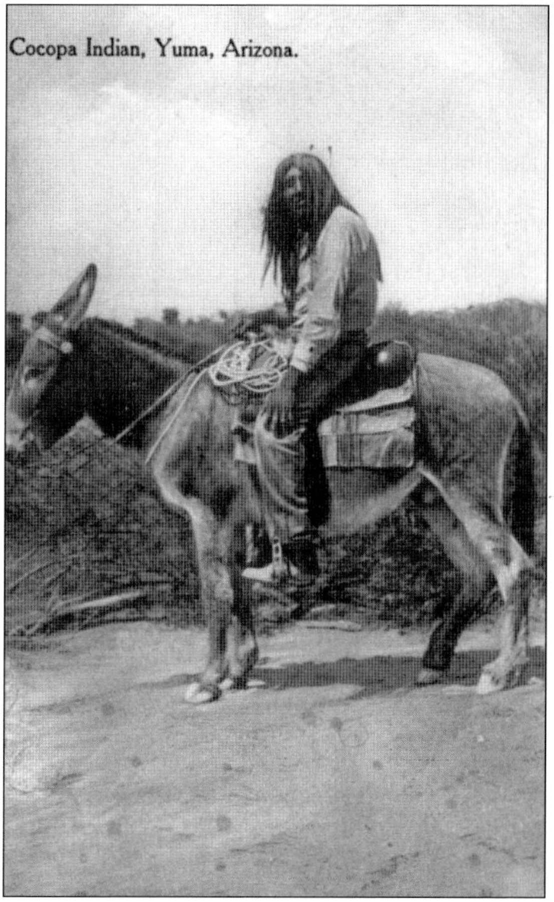

Cocopah Indian, Hand Dated May 1913 (Divided Back Postcard). The Cocopah people have lived along the lower portion of the Colorado River to the Gulf of California for centuries. The Cocopah (Kwapa), also known as the "River People," are one of seven descendant tribes from the Yuman language-speaking people who lived along the river. Having lived along and navigated the Colorado River for generations, the Cocopah and Quechan men became highly sought after for their skilled river navigation as riverboat pilots in the latter portion of the 1800s.

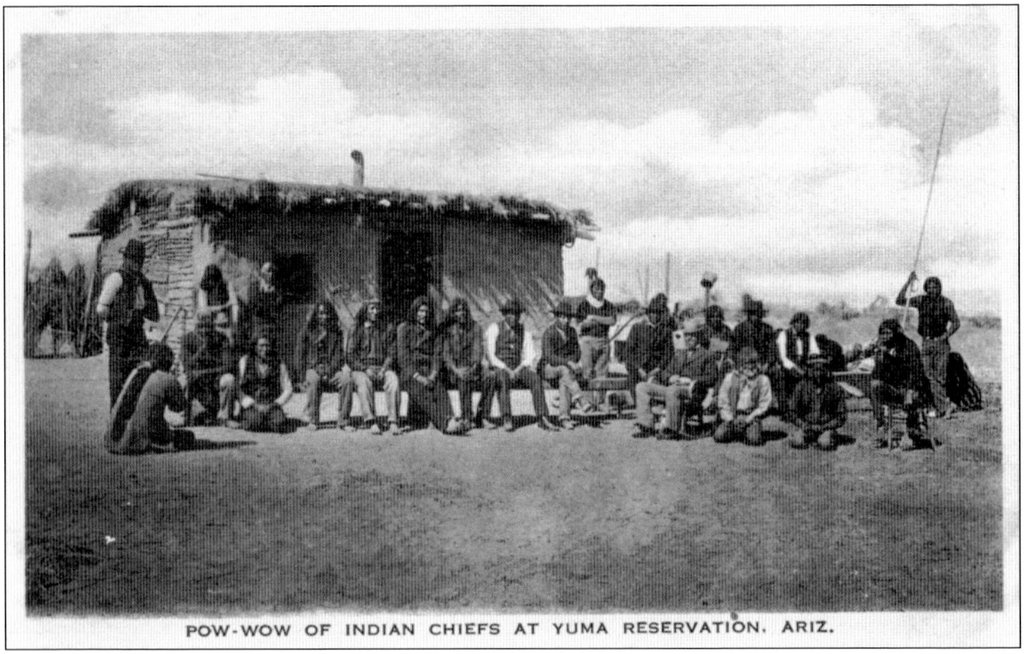

POWWOW, C. 1915 (ALBERTYPE POSTCARD). Once a private event held at the fort, the traditional powwow has grown since the 1960s to a more contemporary, public event. As it has for generations, the powwow is still held every year in mid-March. (Published by J. Homer Smith.)

FORT YUMA INDIAN SCHOOL, C. 1915 (HAND-COLORED POSTCARD). In the early days, the fort was used by soldiers guarding the border area. Between 1878 and 1880, the military abandoned the fort, which was taken over by the Catholic Sisters, who in turn established a school for Yuma Indians. The US government took over the school in 1895 to establish a boarding school. (Published by A.O. Boeres Co., Phoenix.)

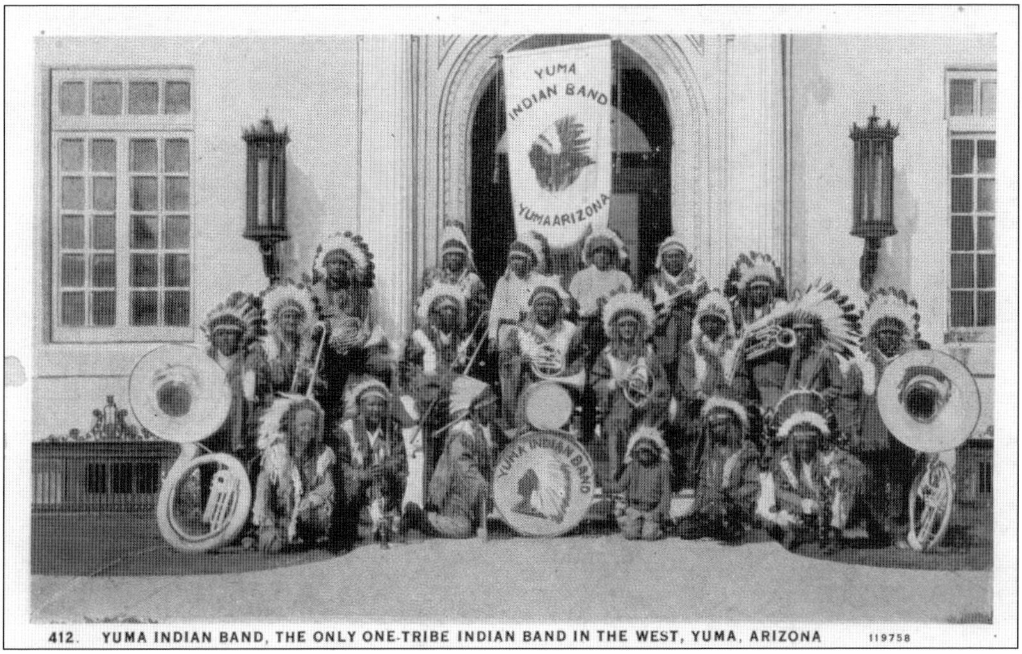

YUMA INDIAN BAND, C. 1928 (CURT TEICH POSTCARD). Fort Yuma's Indian Band was started back in the early 1900s. Dressed in traditional Indian clothing, the band would march through downtown Yuma, and it also participated in parades as far away as Prescott. The band was discontinued in the 1960s. (Published by Harry Herz.)

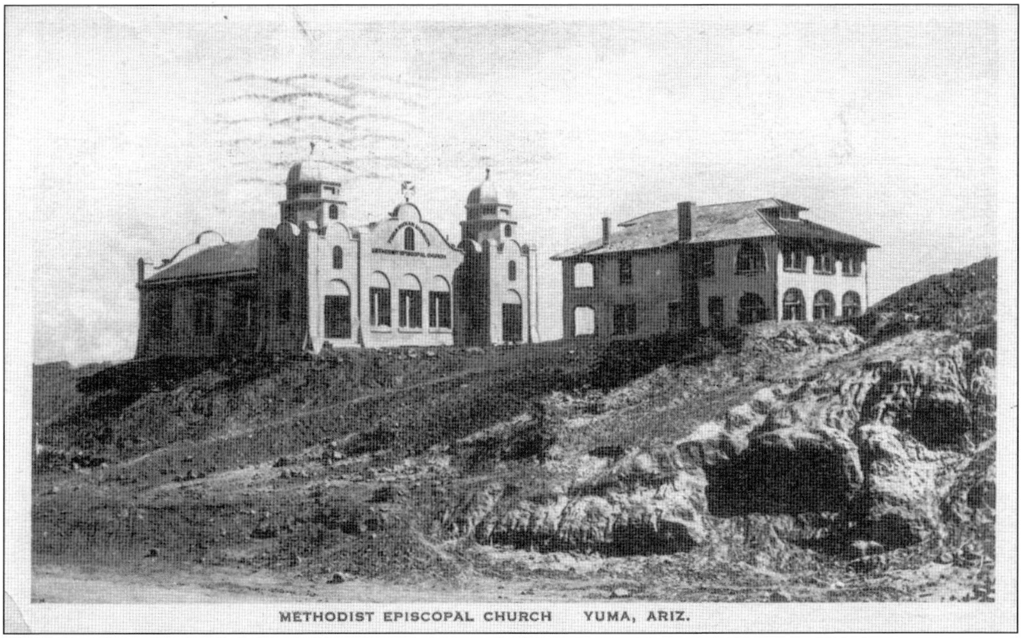

METHODIST EPISCOPAL CHURCH, POSTMARKED APRIL 17, 1935 (ALBERTYPE POSTCARD). The Fort Yuma United Methodist Indian Church is located on the Fort Yuma Indian Reservation. It was initially established as a mission and now serves the members of the Quechan Indian tribe. (Published by J. Homer Smith.)

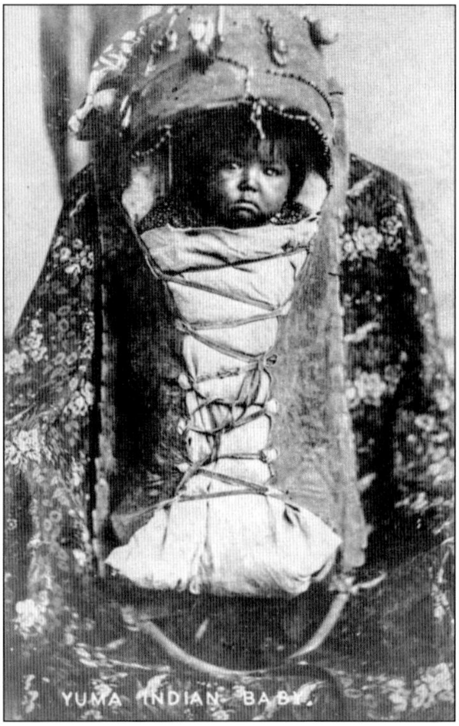

Yuma Indian Baby, c. 1940s (Real-Photo Postcard). A cradleboard is the traditional carrier for Native American babies. The baby is tightly wrapped in a small blanket and strapped or laced, as this baby is, to the cradleboard. The cradleboard can then be carried in the mother's arms or worn like a backpack for travel.

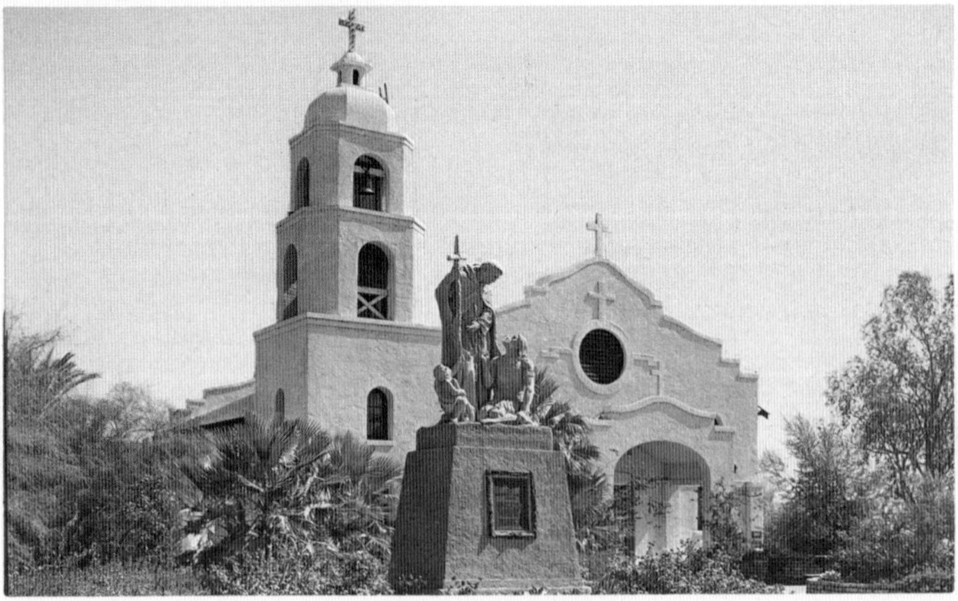

ST. THOMAS INDIAN MISSION

St. Thomas Indian Mission, Postmarked February 5, 1965 (Curt Teich Postcard Folder). This mission is a replica of the original Mission Puerto de Purisima Concepcion, which was constructed on the site in 1780. The following year, the Quechan Indians, fed up with mistreatment by the Spanish colonists, attacked and destroyed the mission and killed over 100 Spanish settlers. The new mission was dedicated in 1923. (Published by Yuma Color Cards.)

Eight

MISCELLANEOUS
FROM AGRICULTURE TO THE RIVER

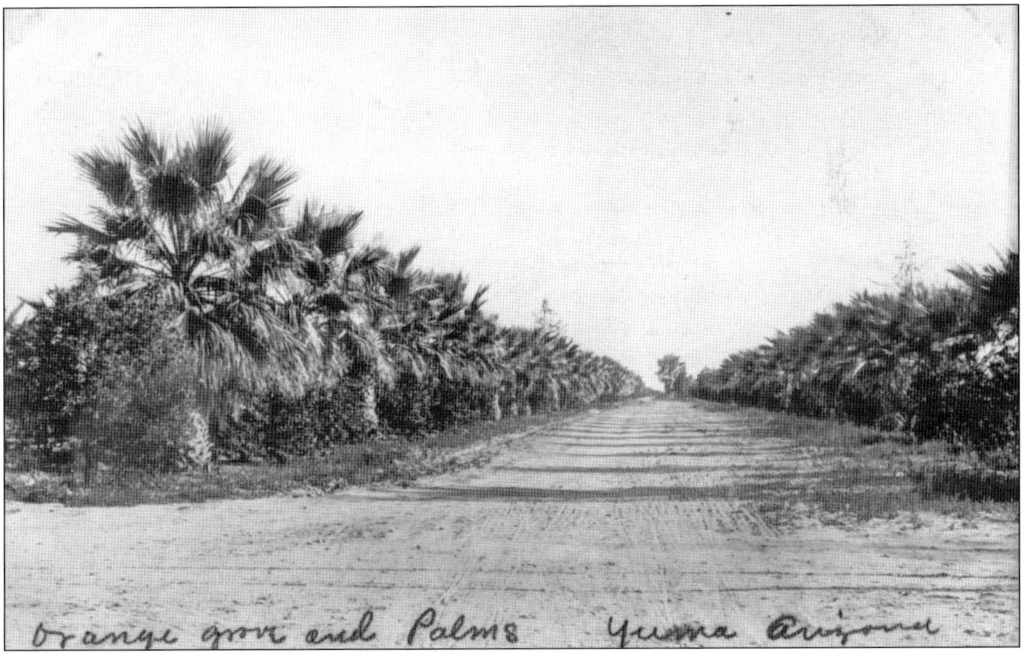

ORANGE GROVE, C. 1908 (REAL-PHOTO POSTCARD). Dating back to the 1880s, oranges and other citrus trees were planted to meet the high demand by miners. By the 1890s, over 1,500 acres were planted, and at its peak in the 1970s, production had reached over 80,000 acres. Now, with urban sprawl and competition from other agricultural products, citrus groves have declined to under 20,000 acres.

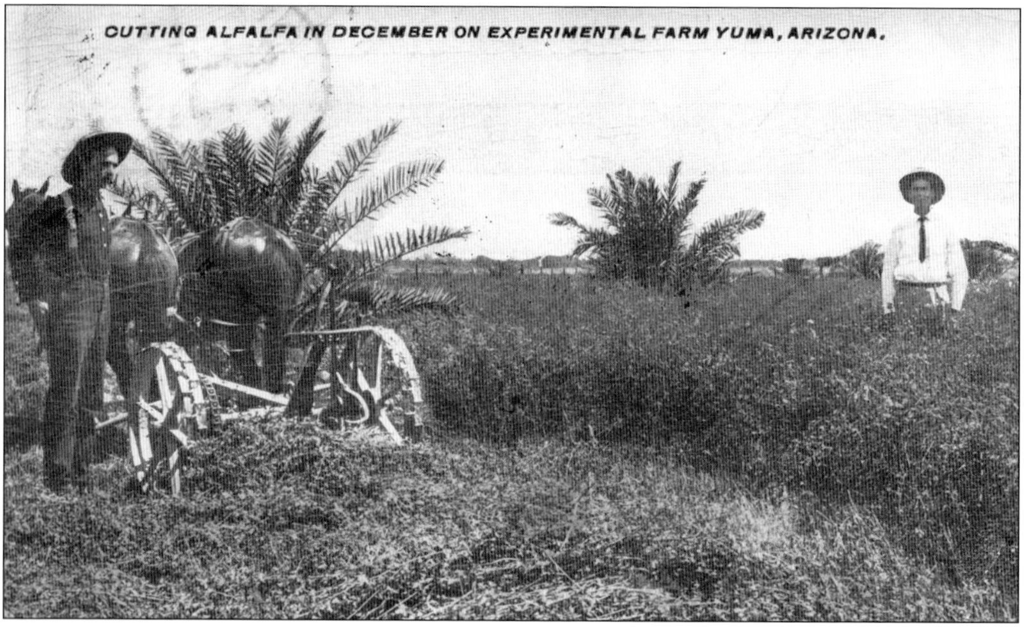

ALFALFA, POSTMARKED SEPTEMBER 23, 1911 (HAND-COLORED POSTCARD). Due to the climate, which allows for a 12-month growing season, Yuma's alfalfa can be harvested five to seven times a year, whereas most regions in the West harvest only two to four times a year. In 2010, Yuma County had 27,000 acres of alfalfa, grossing 243,000 tons. (Published by National Colortype Co.)

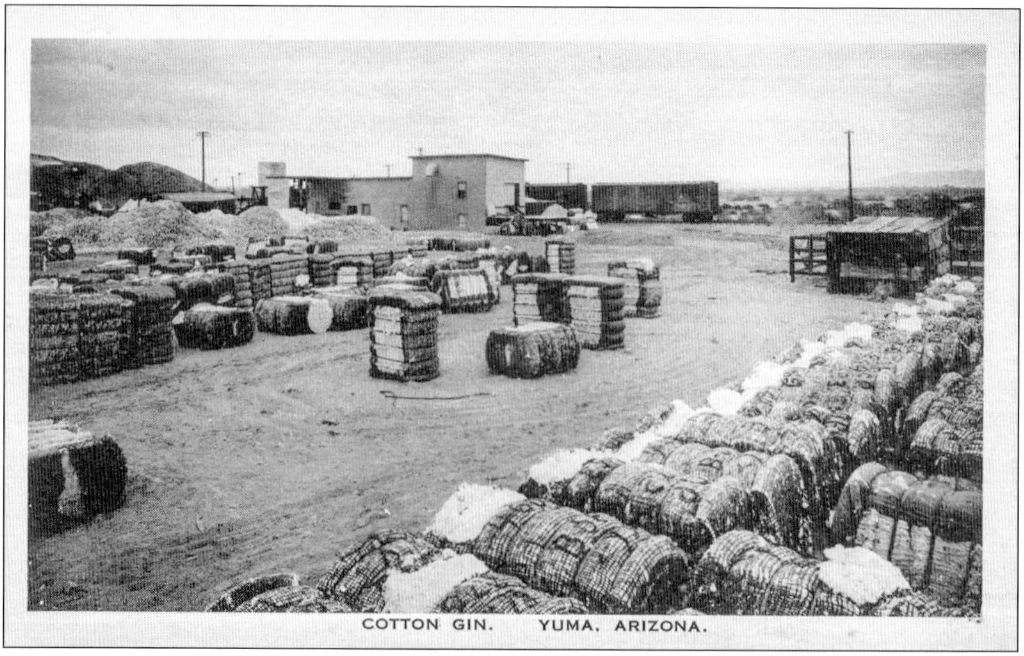

COTTON GIN, C. 1915 (REAL-PHOTO POSTCARD). Cotton has been grown in the Southwest by Native Americans for thousands of years and became a popular crop in the 1880s. Around World War I, cotton imports from Egypt were banned, so production in Yuma County heated up. There are currently about 20,000 acres of cotton in Yuma. (Published by J. Homer Smith.)

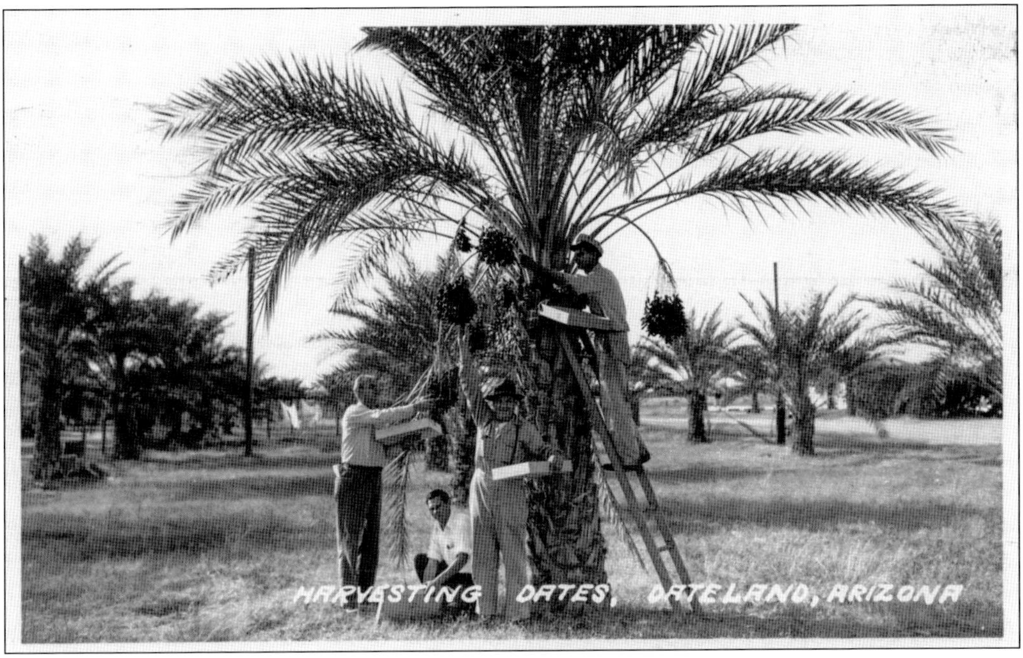

DATELAND, HARVESTING DATES, POSTMARKED APRIL 9, 1949 (REAL-PHOTO POSTCARD). As dates began to die off due to a disease outbreak in Morocco in the late 1920s, 11 offshoots were brought to the United States. In 1944, four of the original 11 offshoots were brought to Yuma, thus beginning the date industry in Yuma and the Southwest. The four date trees responsible for spurring the date industry are still alive in Yuma today. (Published by Lollesgard Specialty Co.)

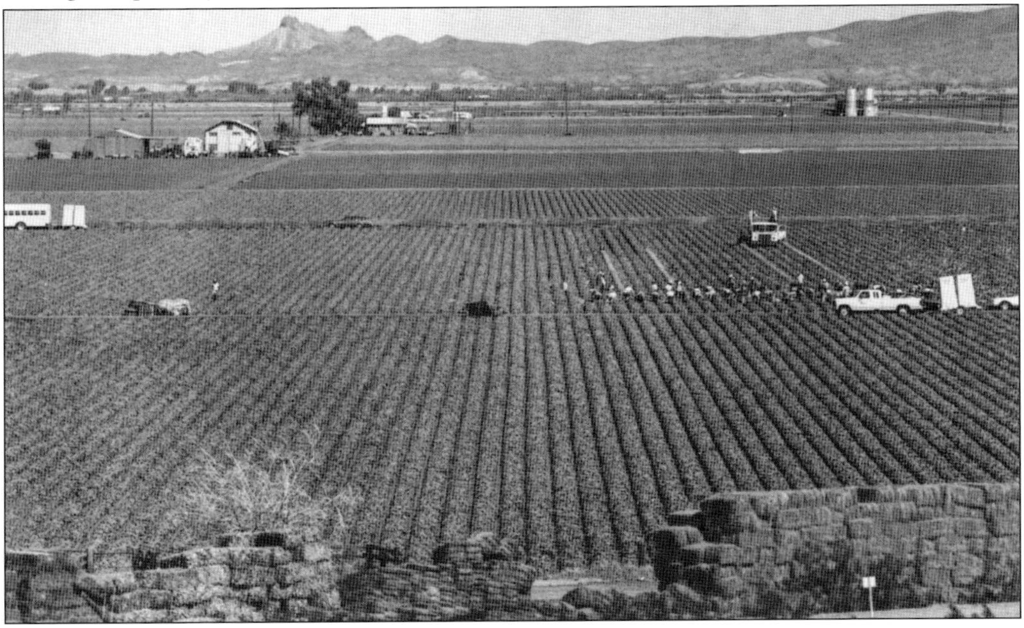

WINTER LETTUCE, C. 1970S (REAL-PHOTO POSTCARD). With the nation's longest growing season, Yuma County is the country's third-largest vegetable producer and is responsible for 90 percent of the leafy vegetables grown in the United States. (Published by Kendall Kards.)

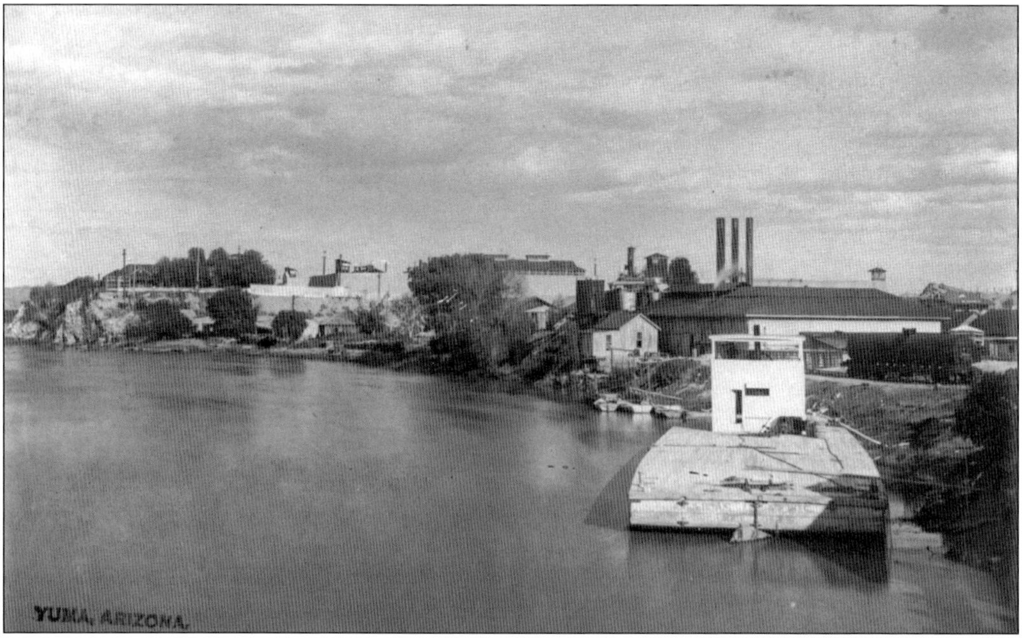

BARGE, C. 1910S (REAL-PHOTO POSTCARD). The Colorado River was once navigable from the Sea of Cortez to the Mojave area, a distance of 250 miles. With the introduction of the railroad in the late 1800s, steamships became less important for delivering goods to the desert region.

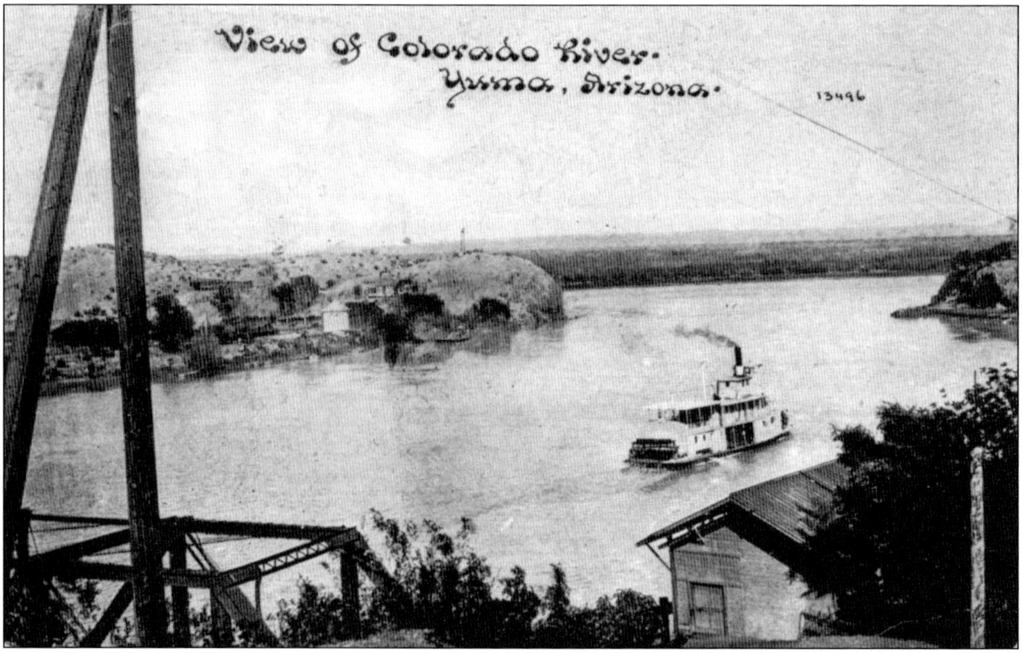

VIEW OF COLORADO RIVER, POSTMARKED JULY 27, 1911 (REAL-PHOTO POSTCARD). The first paddle steamer to reach Yuma was the *Uncle Sam* in 1852. The underpowered boat could only hold 35 tons of supplies and took 15 days to navigate the 120 miles from the Gulf of California to Yuma. The era of paddle wheelers ended with the railroad reaching Yuma in the late 1800s and the building of the Laguna Dam in 1908.

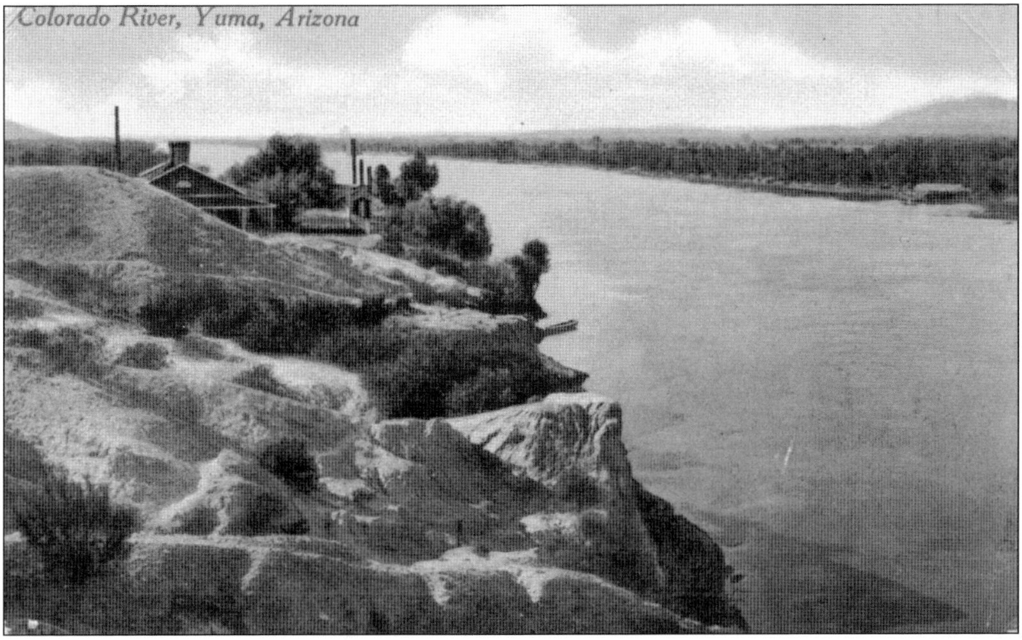

Colorado River, Postmarked December 23, 1912 (Divided Back Postcard). Starting high in the central Rocky Mountains, the Colorado River travels 1,450 miles through seven US and two Mexican states before reaching the Gulf of California. In the days before the river was dammed, flooding was common during winter months. The river would reach 15 miles wide in the low marshes of the Yuma Valley. (Published by Newman Post Card Co.)

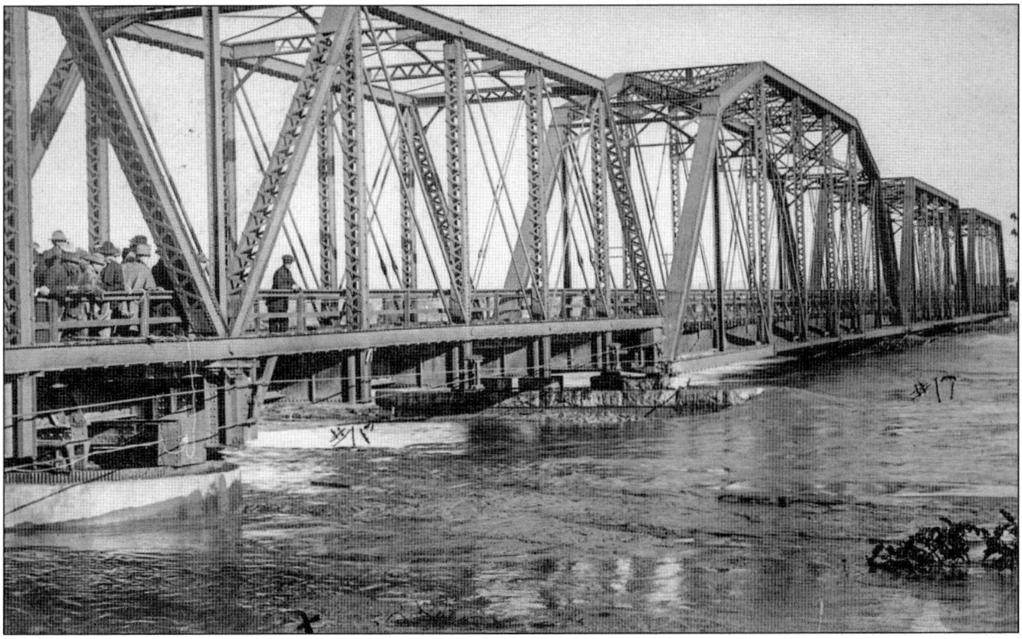

Southern Pacific Bridge, Postmarked March 10, 1916 (Real-Photo Postcard). The flood of January 1916 was one of the most devastating in Yuma history. The Colorado River reached over 35 feet, and with several breaks in the levees along the river, downtown Yuma was inundated with more than four feet of floodwater, leaving no store or business untouched.

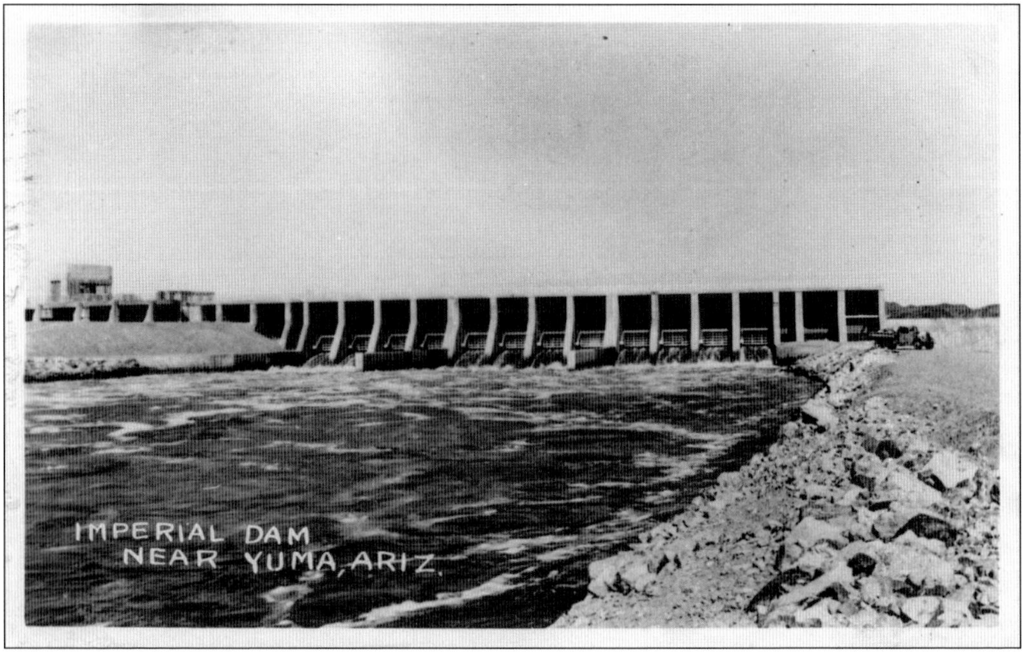

IMPERIAL DAM, C. 1940 (REAL-PHOTO POSTCARD). Completed in 1938, Imperial Dam, located about 20 miles north of Yuma on the Colorado River, is used to divert water to the All-American Canal and Gila Canal. The water is then shared between California, Arizona, and Mexico.

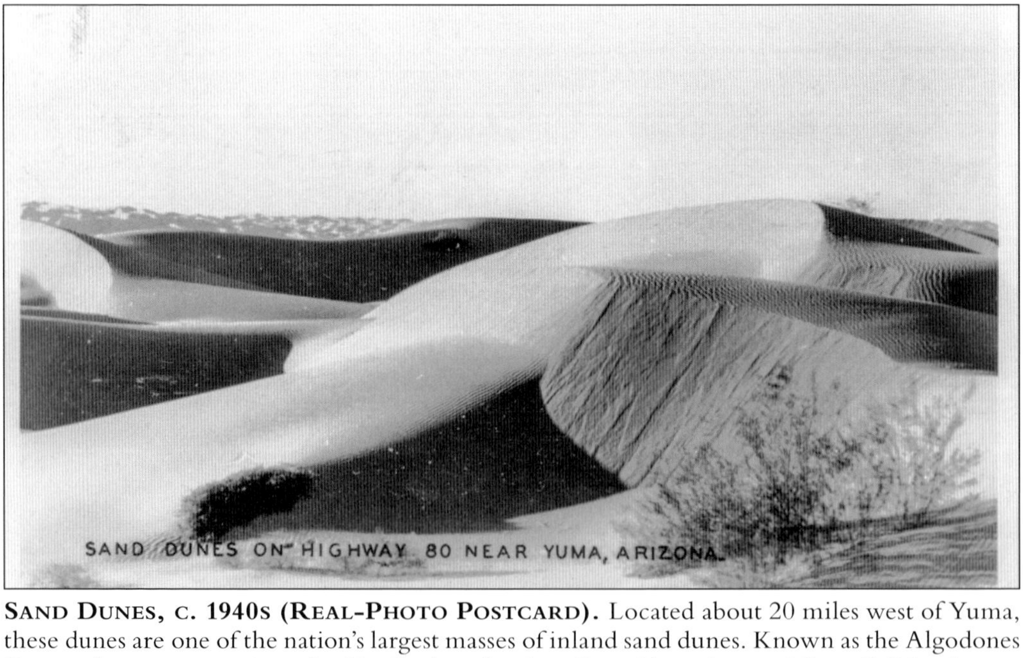

SAND DUNES, C. 1940S (REAL-PHOTO POSTCARD). Located about 20 miles west of Yuma, these dunes are one of the nation's largest masses of inland sand dunes. Known as the Algodones Dunes, they are approximately 45 miles long by six miles wide and extend from California near the Arizona border into the Mexican state of Baja California. The dunes are believed to have been formed over many hundreds of years from flooding of the Colorado River, which formed Lake Cahuilla. The last time the river flowed into the lake was as late as 1450. Lake Cahuilla encompassed much of the Imperial, Coachella, and Mexicali Valleys.

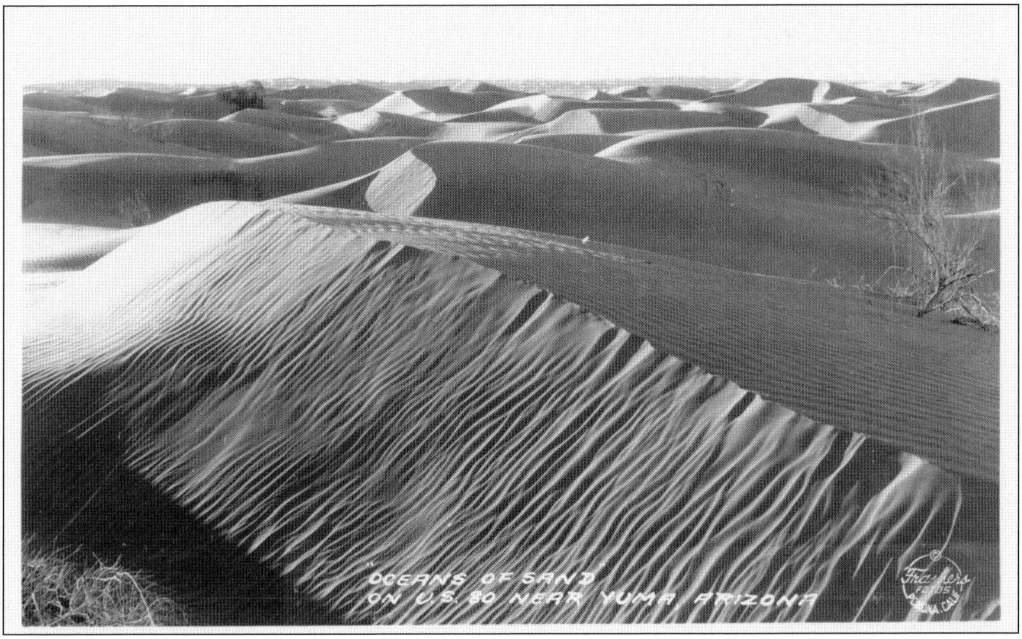

OCEANS OF SAND, C. 1940S (REAL-PHOTO POSTCARD). As the lake dried up, it left vast amounts of sand in its place. The prevailing westerly and northwesterly winds have carried the sand eastward to its present location. The dunes have continued to travel southeast at a rate of one foot a year. (Published by Frashers Fotos.)

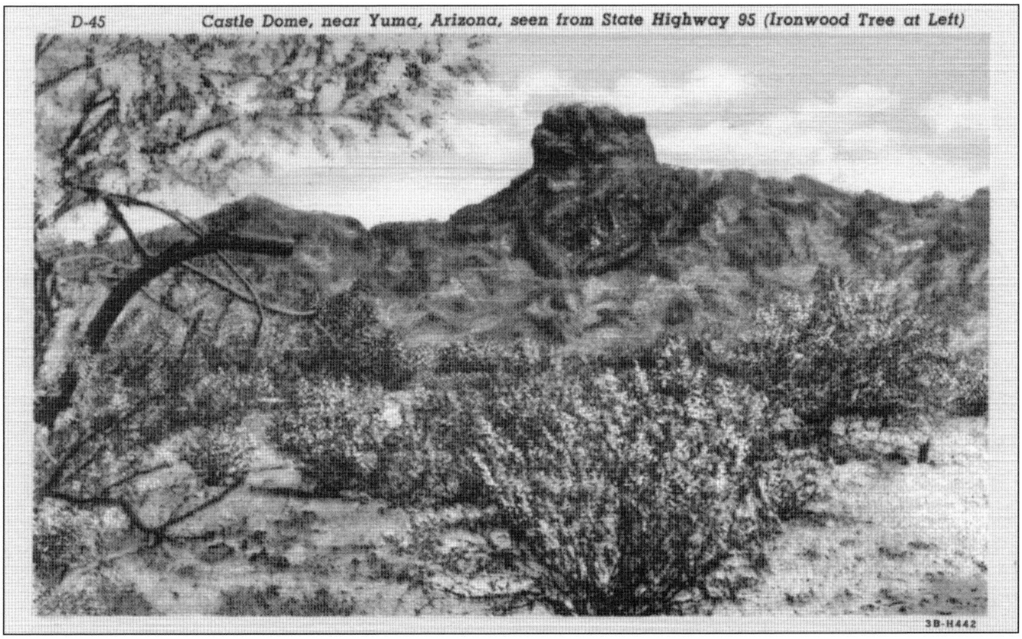

CASTLE DOME, C. 1943 (CURT TEICH POSTCARD). Located north of Yuma in the Kofa National Wildlife Refuge, Castle Dome Peak, with an elevation of 3,788 feet, can be seen from virtually anywhere in Yuma County. In the late 1800s, the city of Castle Dome was born with the high quality of silver and lead mines in the area. The city that was once larger in population than Yuma is now a living ghost town. (Published by Lollesgard Specialty Co.)

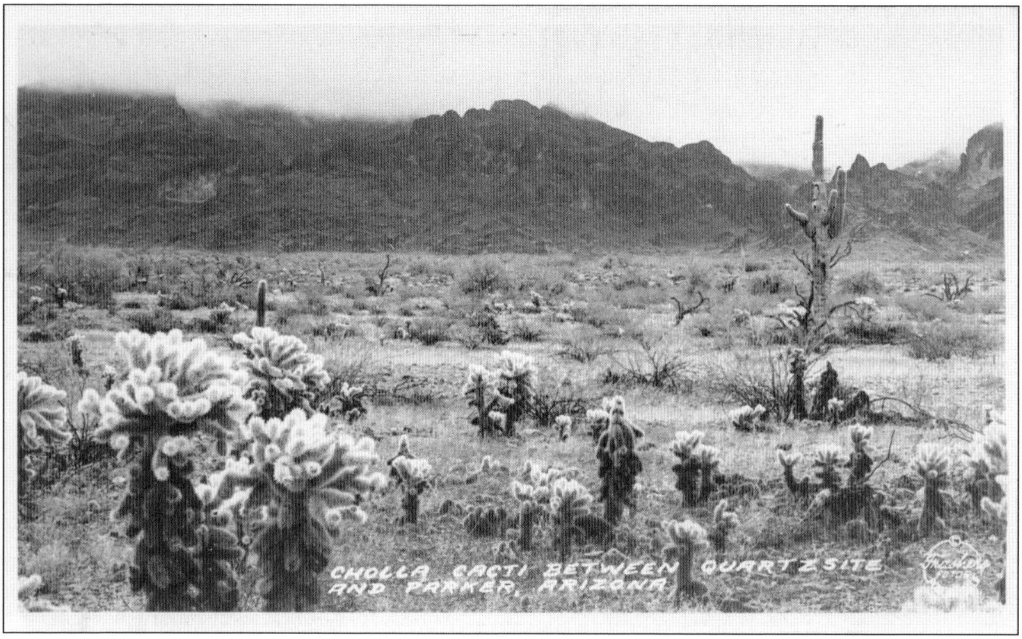

BETWEEN QUARTZSITE AND PARKER, POSTMARKED 1949 (REAL-PHOTO POSTCARD). There are over 20 species of the *Opuntia* genus of cacti in the North American deserts. Chollas come in many forms, from ground creepers to shrubs to trees, and vary in height from less than a foot to over 15 feet. (Published by Frashers Fotos.)

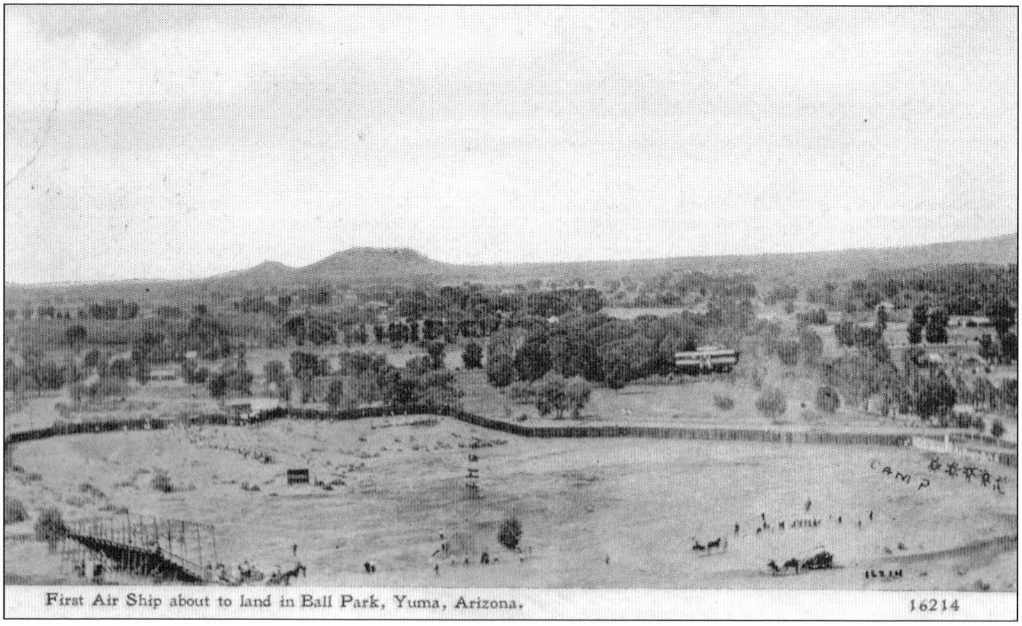

FIRST AIR FLIGHT IN ARIZONA, POSTMARKED NOVEMBER 2, 1912 (REAL-PHOTO POSTCARD). On October 25, 1911, Robert Fowler landed his Cole Flyer on the ball field that later became the site of the Landing Restaurant at 195 Fourth Avenue. The Cole Flyer was the first aircraft to fly into Arizona. Fowler took off for Maricopa on October 29 to continue the flight to the East Coast.

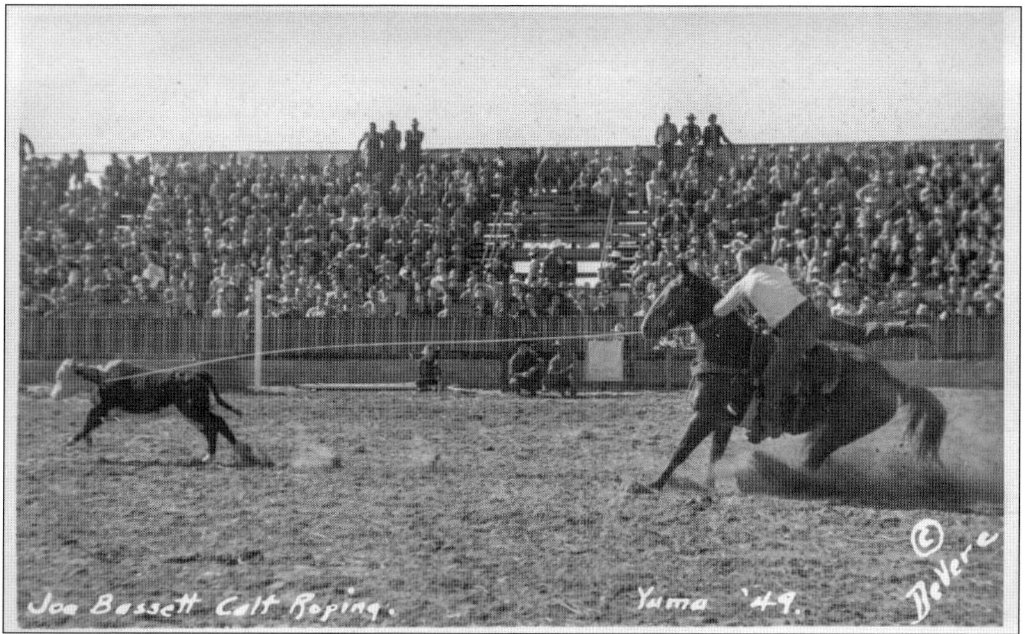

COLT ROPING, C. 1949 (REAL-PHOTO POSTCARD). Held on the second weekend in February, the Yuma Jaycees Silver Spur Rodeo has been a Yuma tradition since 1946. Some of the rodeo activities include bull riding, bronco riding, roping, and barrel racing. (Published by DeVere.)

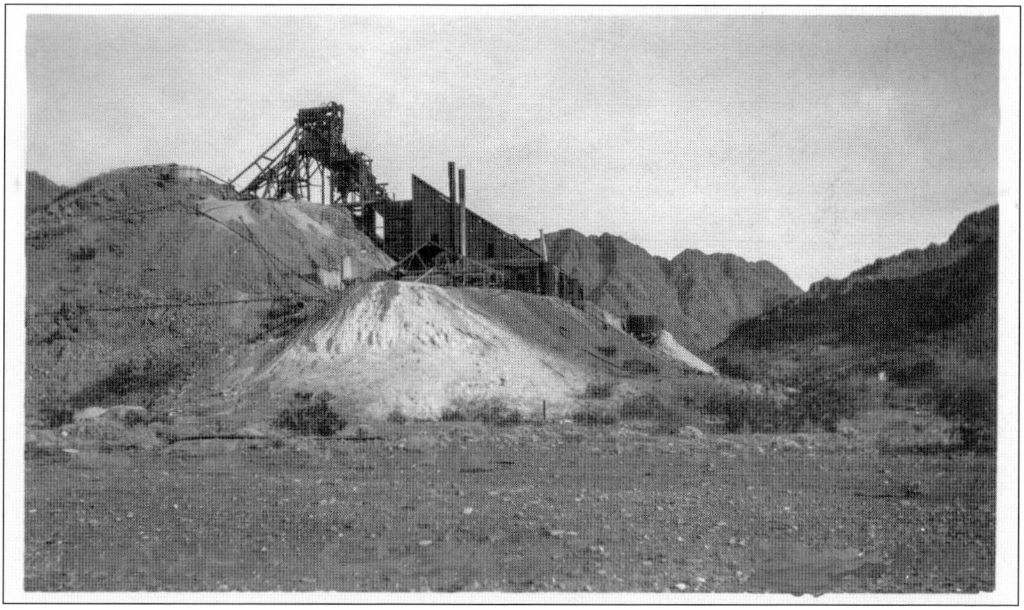

FORTUNA MINE, C. 1920S (REAL-PHOTO POSTCARD). The La Fortuna Gold Mine was discovered in 1894 and was worked consistently until 1904. It was then worked intermittently until 1942, when the last workings were shut down. The boomtown of Fortuna had a general store, blacksmith shops, cookhouses, saloons, homes, hotels, a stage and freight line, and a post office from 1896 to 1904. The mine produced 124,239 ounces of gold from 1896 through 1926. The site is located within the Barry M. Goldwater Gunnery Range and is managed by the US Marine Corps.

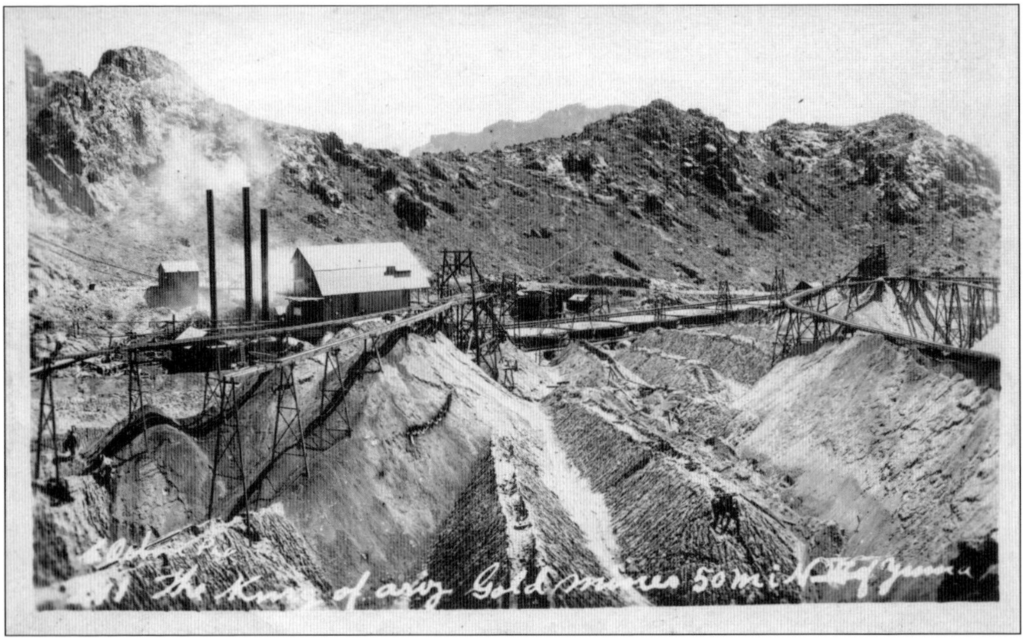

King of Arizona Gold Mine, c. 1910 (Real-Photo Postcard). Located in the Kofa Mountains about 50 miles north of Yuma, this site was discovered in 1896 and first began mine production in 1897. A small boomtown sprang up nearby, with a post office opening in June 1900. It closed in August 1928. The Kofa Mountains are named after the mine, which used to stamp its property "KofA," which also led to the mine being called the Kofa Mine. (Courtesy of John Taylor.)

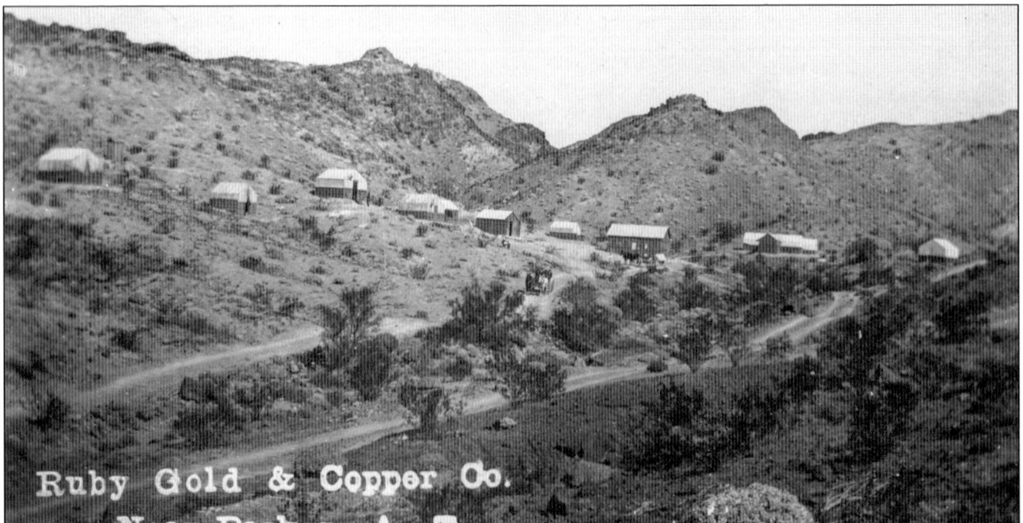

Ruby Gold and Copper Mine, Postmarked April 3, 1910 (Real-Photo Postcard). Also known as the Billy Mack Mine and the Billy Mack Ruby Mine, it was located in the Seneca (Cienega) Mining District about seven miles north of Parker. The mine was worked intermittently between 1909 and 1919, then again from 1943 to 1960, when it shut down for good. According to an April 1, 1958, report by the Arizona Department of Mineral Resources, the mine had been worked since 1870 and had 15 shafts, nine tunnels, and five crosscuts. (Courtesy of John Taylor.)

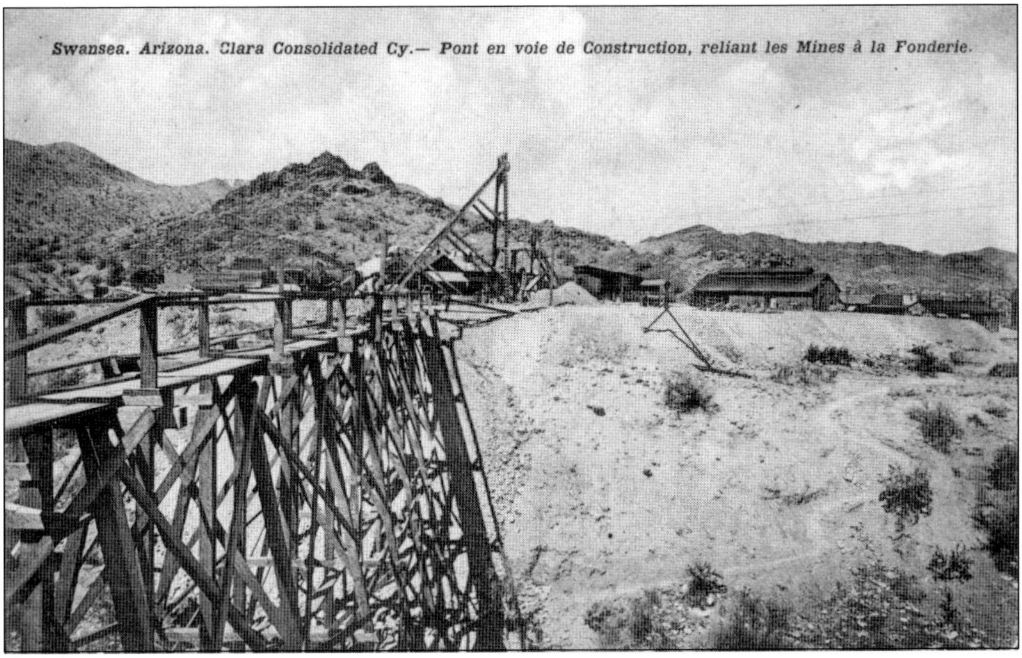

ABOVE, SWANSEA MINE, C. 1910 (REAL-PHOTO POSTCARD); BELOW, CAMP DE SWANSEA, C. 1910 (REAL-PHOTO POSTCARD). Miners began working the Swansea as early as the 1860s with little to show for their efforts. In the early 1900s, the Clara Consolidated Gold and Copper Mining Company began building in earnest, and by 1909, the town of Swansea established a post office. The town and mine were short lived; the company went bankrupt in 1912, and by 1924, it had lost its post office. Swansea was named after Swansea, Wales, where refined ore was originally shipped before it became too expensive to process. (Both, courtesy of John Taylor.)

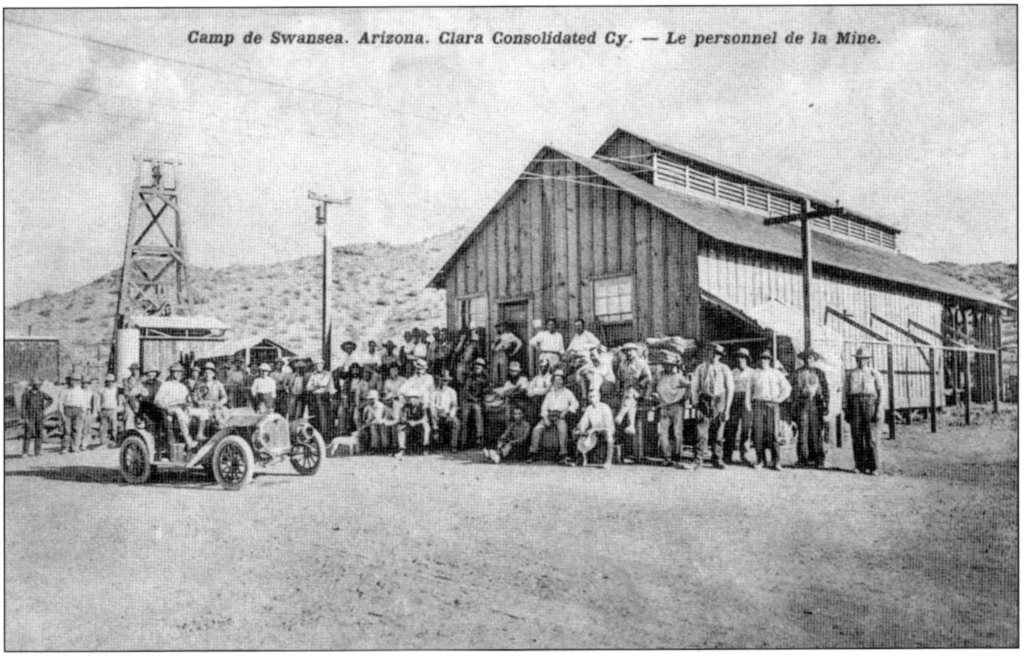

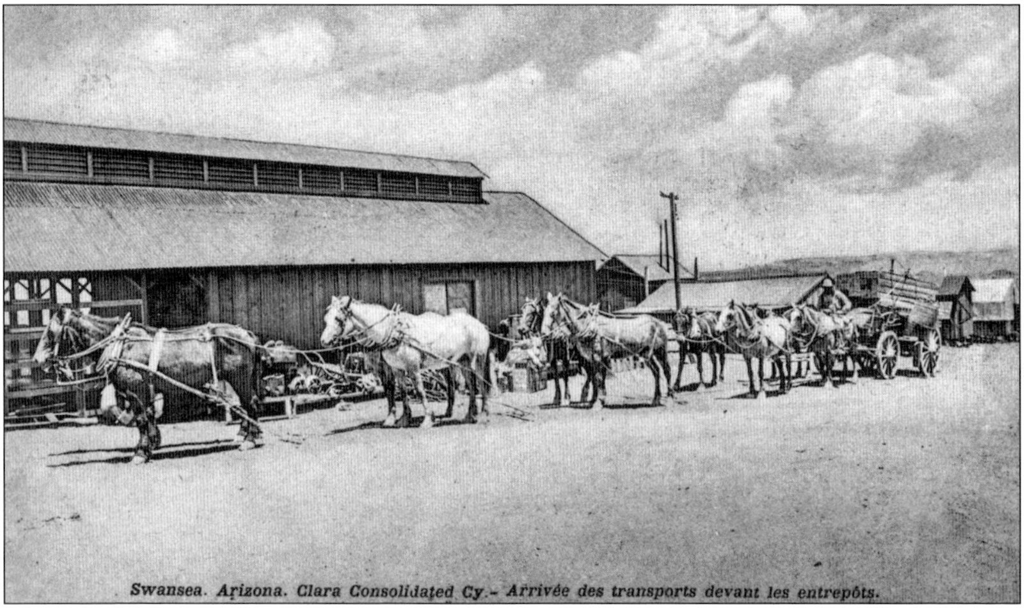

SWANSEA, HORSE TEAM C. 1910 (REAL-PHOTO POSTCARD). Swansea at its peak had as many as 750 people living there. By 1920, there was still a population of 337 people, but by 1937, Swansea was literally a ghost town. Today, Swansea is protected by the Bureau of Land Management, which has restored roofs of some of the buildings and established an interpretive trail for visitors.

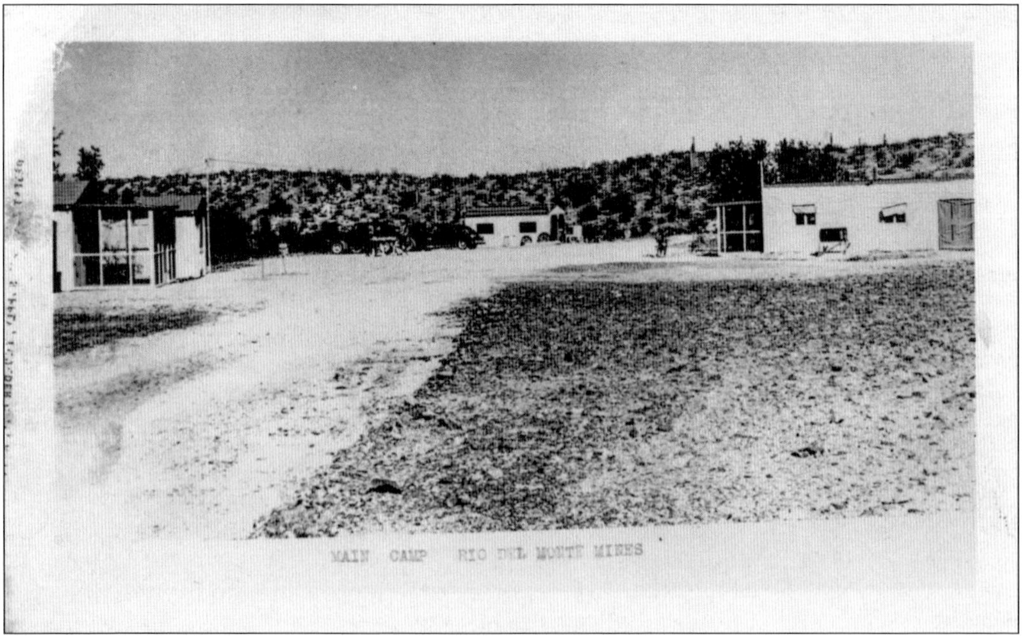

SALOME, RIO DEL MONTE MINES, C. 1940 (REAL-PHOTO POSTCARD). Located about four miles south of Salome, this mine was discovered in the 1890s and produced small amounts of gold and silver. A group of investors purchased the property around 1900 and sank several shafts totaling about 4,000 vertical feet. The site has been resold and abandoned a number of times through the years but is still in business today as a sand, gravel, and rock quarry.

Nine

LA PAZ COUNTY
THE OLD YUMA COUNTY

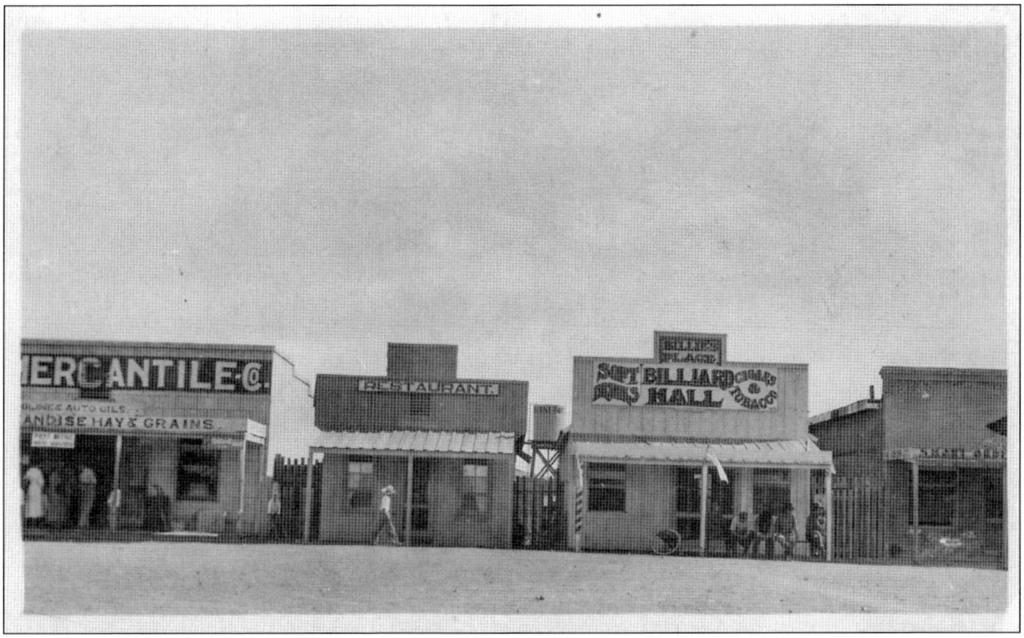

BOUSE, VIEW EAST SIDE OF RAILROAD TRACKS, HAND DATED 1909 (REAL-PHOTO POSTCARD). Miners and prospectors first arrived in the area in the 1860s, settling a small mining community. By 1906, the town was known as Brayton, after John Brayton, owner of the Brayton Mercantile Company. In January 1907, the town's name changed to Bouse, after Thomas Bouse, a wealthy local mine owner. By the early 1940s, Bouse was nothing more than a ghost town. In March 1943, Gen. George Patton developed a desert training facility there. Camp Bouse closed in April 1944, when all of the troops were transferred to Fort Knox, Kentucky. Now Bouse's economy is based on tourism, agriculture, and retirees. (Courtesy of Arizona Historical Society.)

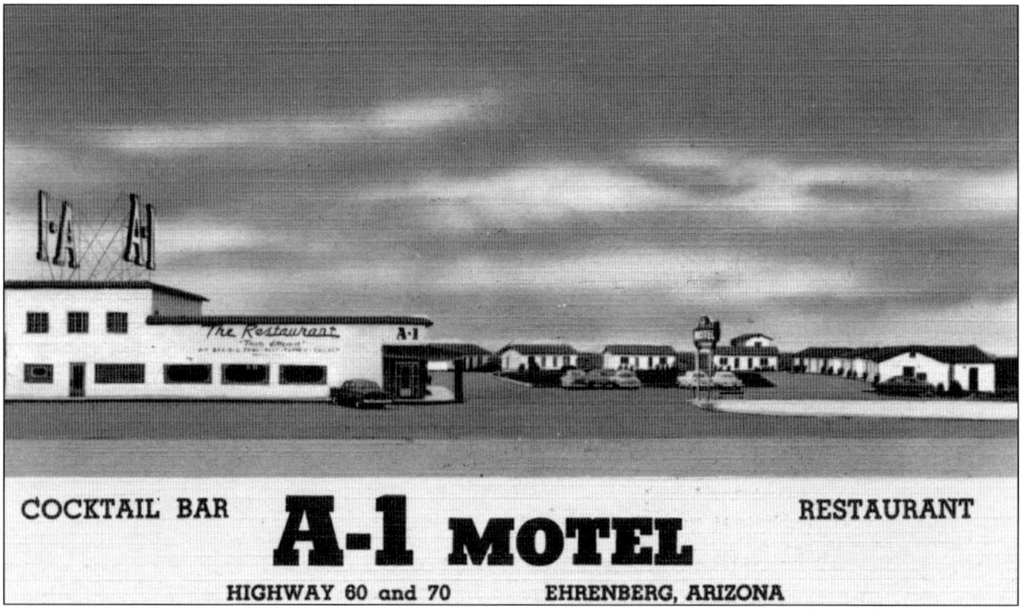

EHRENBERG, A-1 MOTEL, C. 1950S (LINEN ADVERTISING POSTCARD). Ehrenberg was founded in the early 1860s as Mineral City but changed its name in 1869 for its founder, Herman Ehrenberg. Built on the banks of the Colorado River, Ehrenberg was established to support steamboat traffic on the river. After the start of the 20th century, boat travel dwindled due to the railroad, and Ehrenberg began to decline. Most of the remaining old structures were demolished in the 1950s to make way for a trailer park. (Published by Colourpicture.)

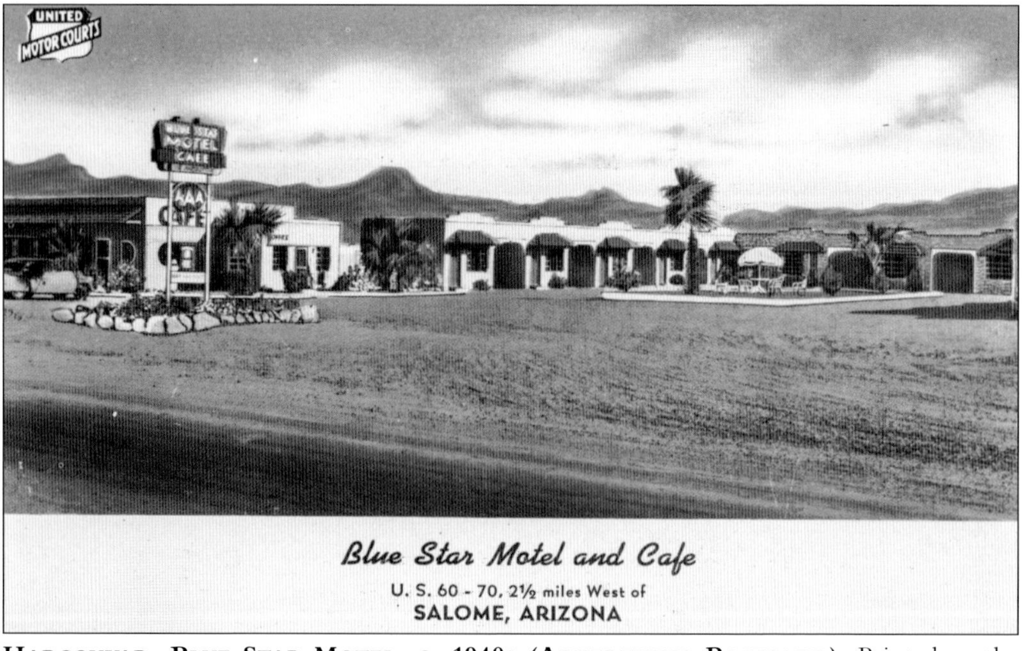

HARCOUVAR, BLUE STAR MOTEL, C. 1940S (ADVERTISING POSTCARD). Printed on the reverse is the following: "Blue Star Motel and Cafe, 2 1/2 miles West of Salome, Arizona. A new, air-cooled, fire-proof motel carpeted wall-to-wall. Panelray heat. Each unit with private shower. Garages. Excellent Cafe, open early and late." (Published by Colourpicture.)

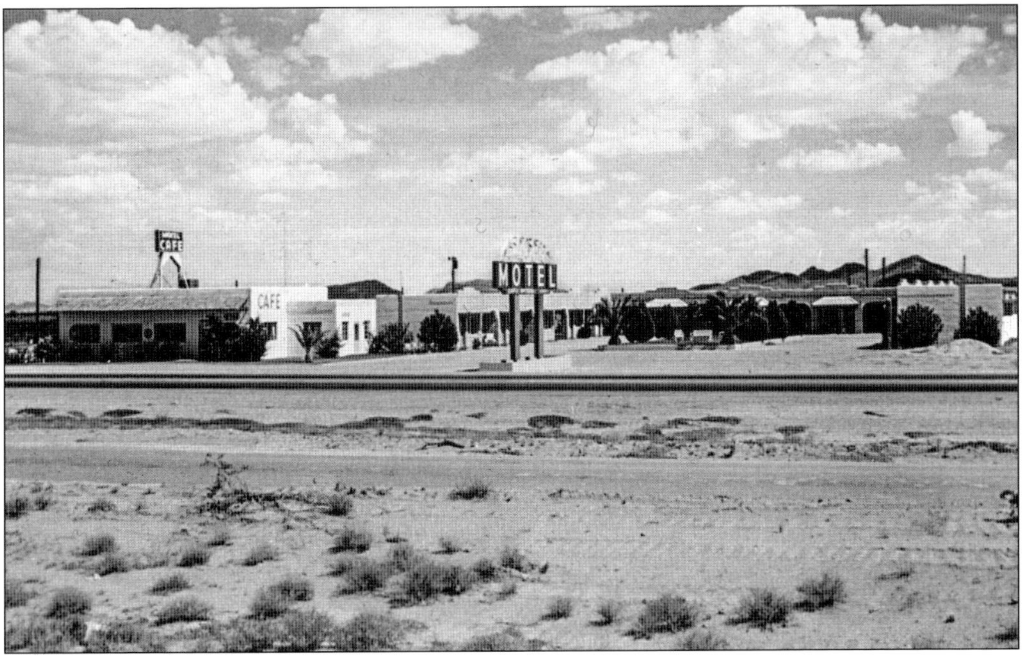

HARCOUVAR, AMBER HILLS MOTEL AND CAFÉ, C. 1950S (ADVERTISING POSTCARD). The Amber Hills Motel originally opened as the Blue Star Motel in the 1940s. Although faded with time, the Amber Hills Motel sign still stands today. The motel closed long ago but is seeing new life as office and retail space. (Published by Phoenix Specialty Advertising Co.)

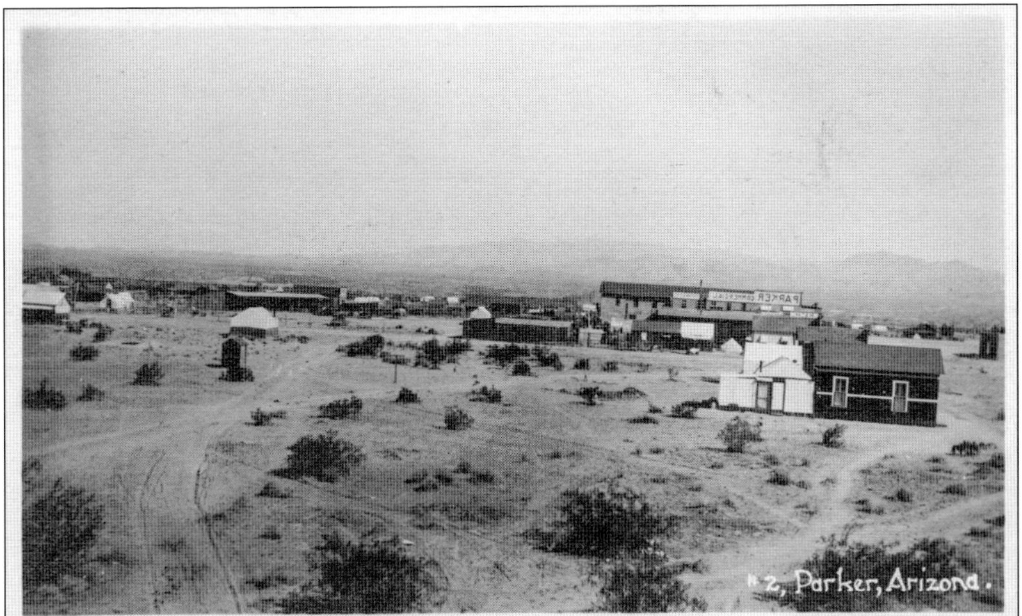

PARKER, TOWN VIEW, C. 1904–1918 (REAL-PHOTO POSTCARD). The origins of Parker are located four miles south of its present location on the Colorado River Indian Reservation. A post office was established in 1871 and named after Gen. Eli Parker, who was the commissioner of Indian Affairs when the Colorado River Indian Reservation was established in 1865.

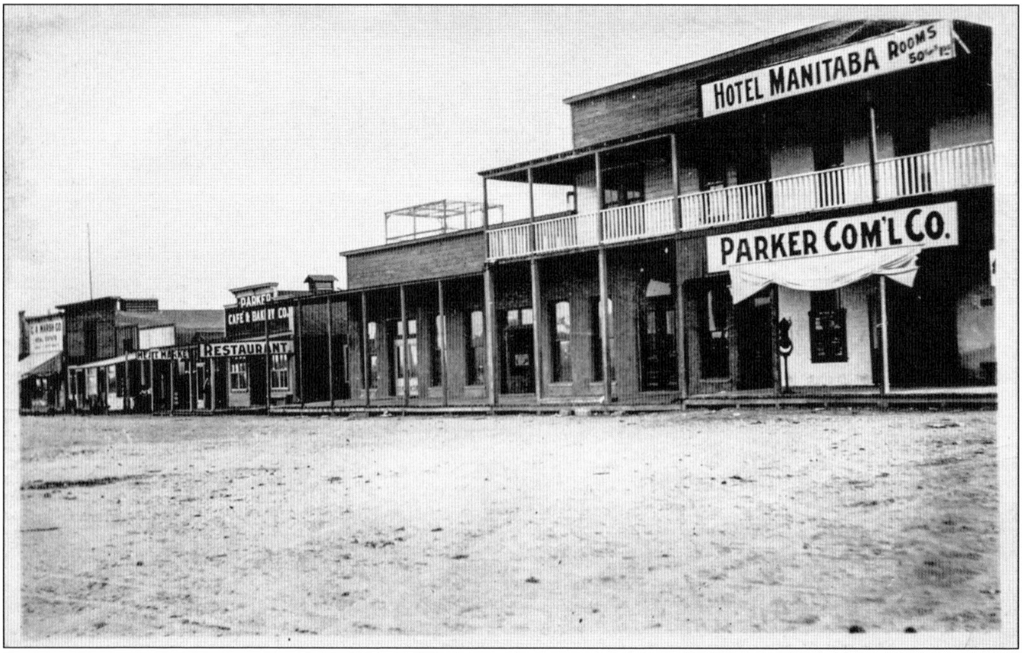

ABOVE, DOWNTOWN PARKER, C. 1908 (REAL-PHOTO POSTCARD); BELOW, PARKER, HOTEL MANITABA (REAL-PHOTO POSTCARD). Hotel Manitaba was named after Chief Manitaba, the tribal leader of the Colorado River Indian Reservation near Parker. According to the *Arizona Republican* newspaper of June 16, 1918, "Its accommodations for the traveling public are better than most towns of its size, there being two very good hotels—the Manitaba and the Parker Cut Out."

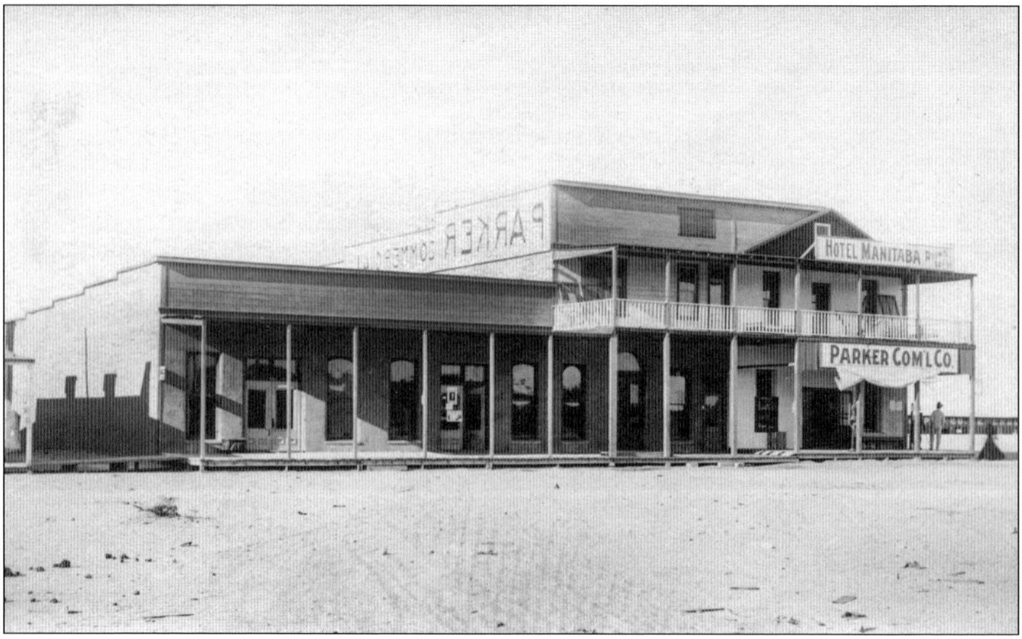

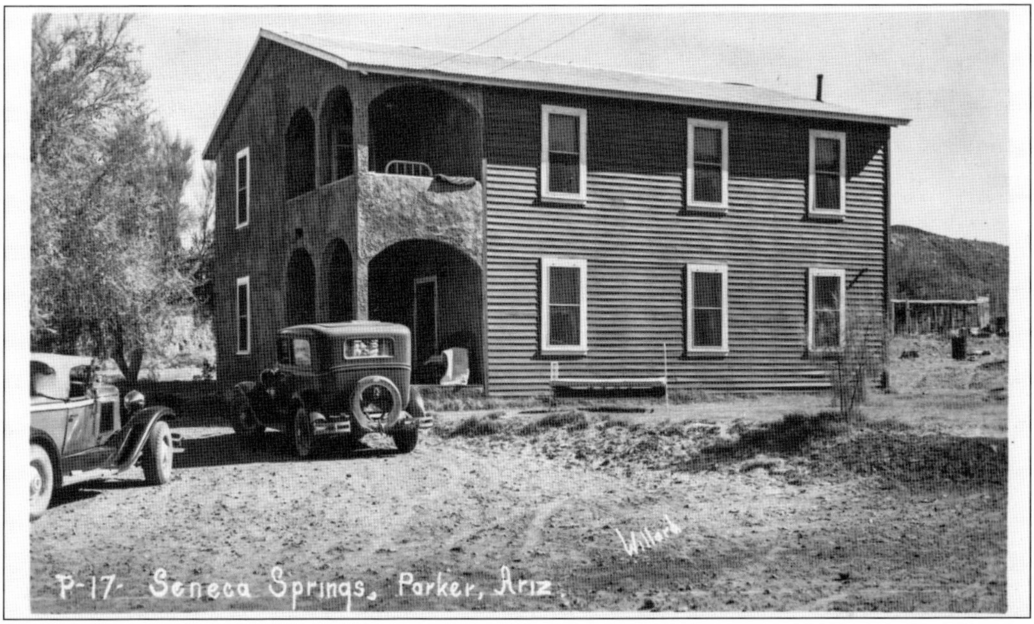

PARKER, SENECA SPRINGS, C. 1930S (REAL-PHOTO POSTCARD). One of the first settlers of Seneca Springs, or Cienega Springs, was Billy Mack, a local prospector who built his home there in 1884. Many years later, the area became known for its springs and guest ranch. An advertisement from the *Arizona Republic* of January 28, 1946, read: "Cienega Springs Guest Ranch, 80 acres on Parker Lake. Ten Cabins and 12-room hotel, all modern. Swimming pool, dance hall and store. Date Trees, palm grove and citrus trees. Water from springs. Will sell for $40,000." (Photograph by Stephen H. Willard.)

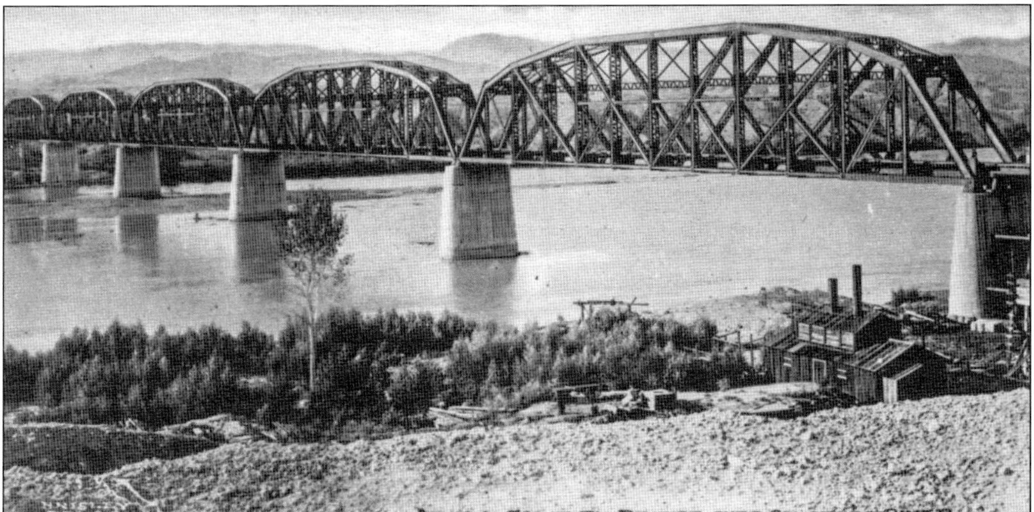

PARKER, COLORADO RIVER BRIDGE, C. 1910 (ALBERTYPE POSTCARD). Constructed by the Santa Fe Railroad, the bridge crossing the Colorado River from Parker to California opened in 1908. A two-lane bridge for automobile traffic opened in 1937, serving as the main thoroughfare between Parker and Earp, California, for almost 75 years. Construction began on a new bridge in 2011 and was completed in 2014, a year later than originally planned due to a fire. (Published by the Albertype Co.)

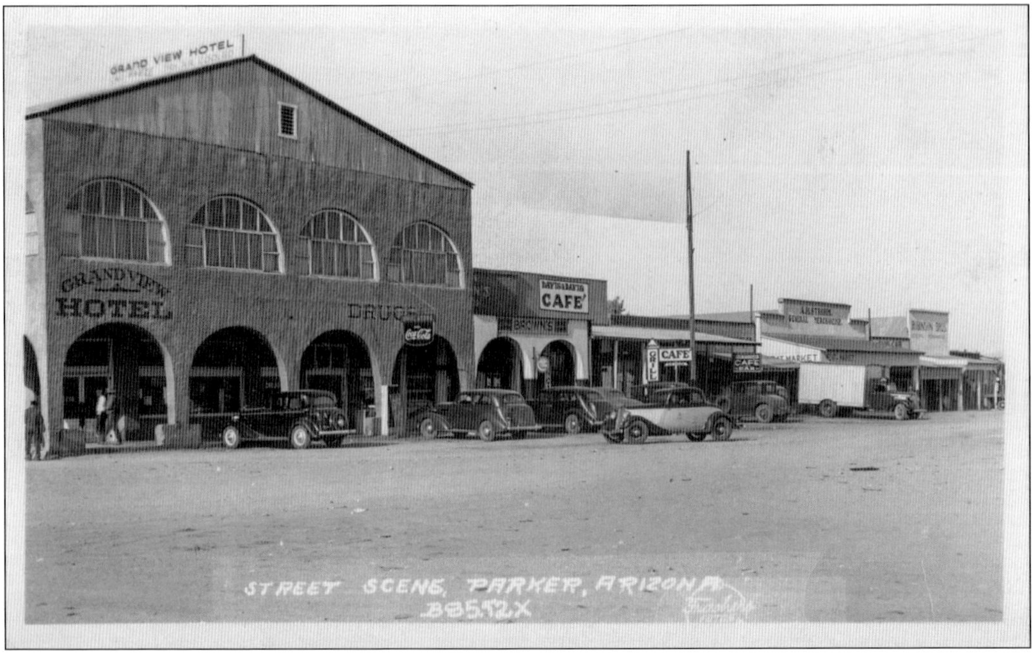

ABOVE, PARKER, STREET SCENE, C. 1938 (REAL-PHOTO POSTCARD); BELOW, PARKER, GRANDVIEW HOTEL, HAND DATED MARCH 19, 1971 (REAL-PHOTO POSTCARD). The Grandview Hotel was built in 1916 by Joe and Nellie Bush and was a city landmark until 1974, when it burned down. The hotel was sold to Frederick Hall and T.J. Carrigan in 1918. An advertisement in the June 16, 1918, edition of the *Arizona Republican* newspaper read, "THE NEW Grandview Hotel will Open About JULY FIRST. Parker's $30,000 contribution to the welfare of those visiting the district. Spacious Lobby, Porches, Writing and Rest Rooms. . . . The logical over-night stop from Arizona-to-the-Coast Automobile Tourist." (Above, published by Frashers; below, published by Columbia Wholesale Supply, photograph by Bill Strover.)

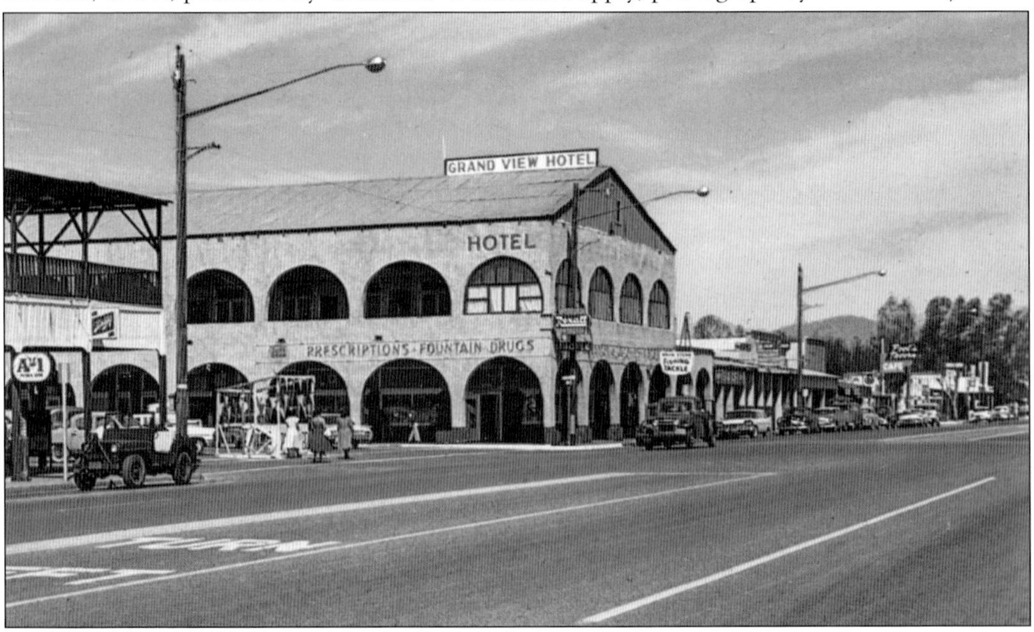

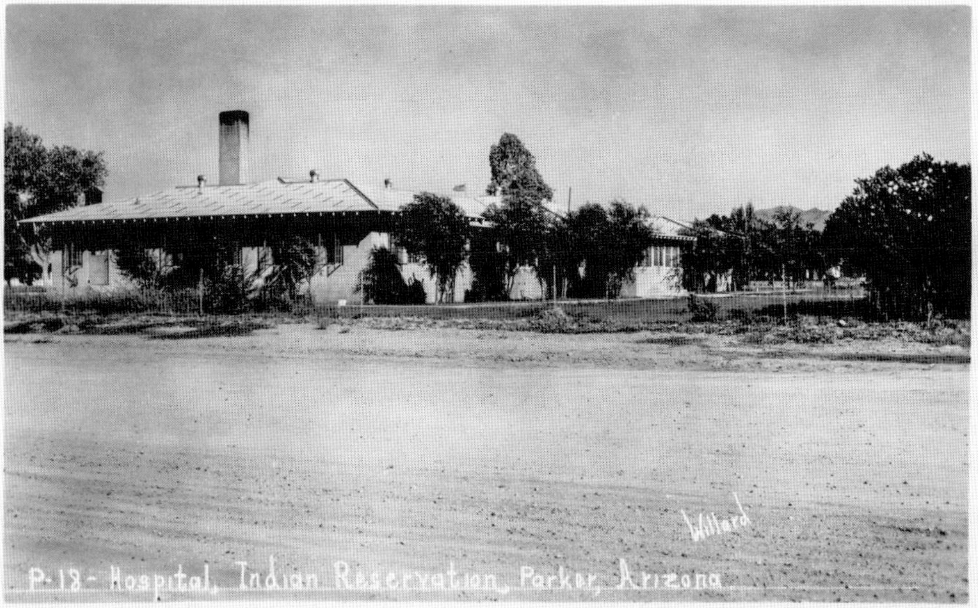

PARKER, INDIAN RESERVATION HOSPITAL, C. 1940 (REAL-PHOTO POSTCARD). The Colorado River Indian Reservation encompasses approximately 432 square miles along both sides of the Colorado River, with most of its territory being in La Paz County. It was established by Congress and approved by Pres. Abraham Lincoln on March 3, 1865, making it one of the oldest reservations in the nation. (Published by Willard.)

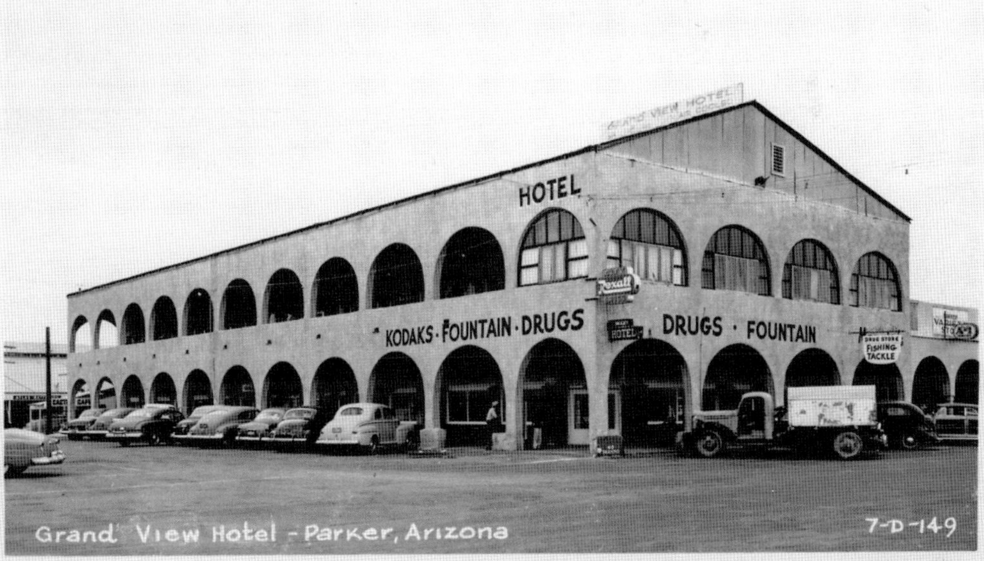

PARKER, GRANDVIEW HOTEL, C. 1940S (REAL-PHOTO POSTCARD). Built in 1916 for $33,000, the Grandview went up for sale in 1920 for the bargain price of $21,000. The hotel consisted of 23 rooms with porches, offices, a basement, and a large lobby and was bringing in $317 a month in sales and rent. The building also included a bank, a drugstore, a post office, a meat market, and a soft drink stand.

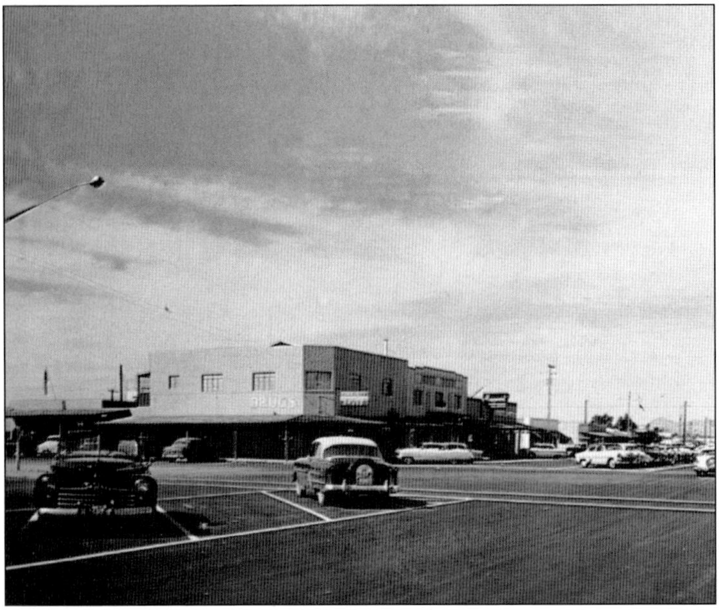

PARKER, STREET SCENE, C. 1950S (REAL-PHOTO POSTCARD). In 1905, the Parker Post Office moved north to the site of the present-day railroad, and by 1909, Capt. William Strover surveyed and laid out the foundation for the new town, encompassing about 973 acres. Parker officially incorporated in 1948 and became the county seat in 1983, when La Paz County was created. (Published by W.M. Cline Co.; photograph by Gene Aiken.)

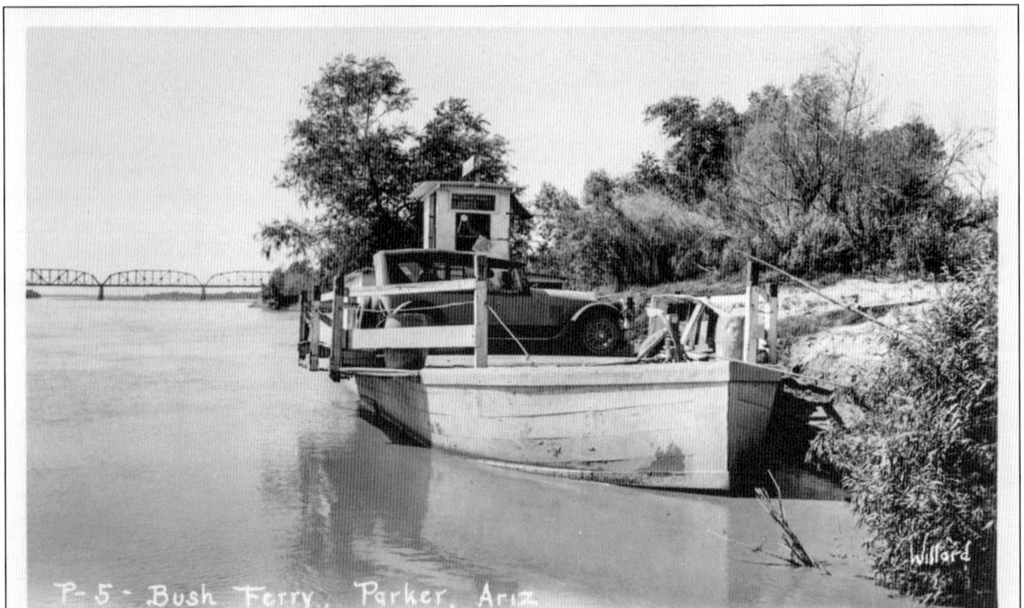

PARKER, CAR FERRY, C. 1930S (REAL-PHOTO POSTCARD). Joe Bush and his wife, Nellie, began a ferry service from Parker, across the Colorado River, to Earp, California, in 1910. The ferry operated for almost 27 years until 1937, when the bridge crossing the river was opened. On December 11, 1925, A.L. Borcherding drove onto the landing on the California side of the river to take the ferry across to Parker. As the automobile crossed the planks to the ferry, the vehicle lurched forward, smashing into the ferry guardrail and plunging into the river. Borcherding and his wife were able to free themselves from the submerged vehicle and were swept downriver. J.E. Bush, the ferryboat pilot, immediately cast off after them and was able to throw a preserver to the husband, but his wife disappeared underwater and drowned. (Published by Willard.)

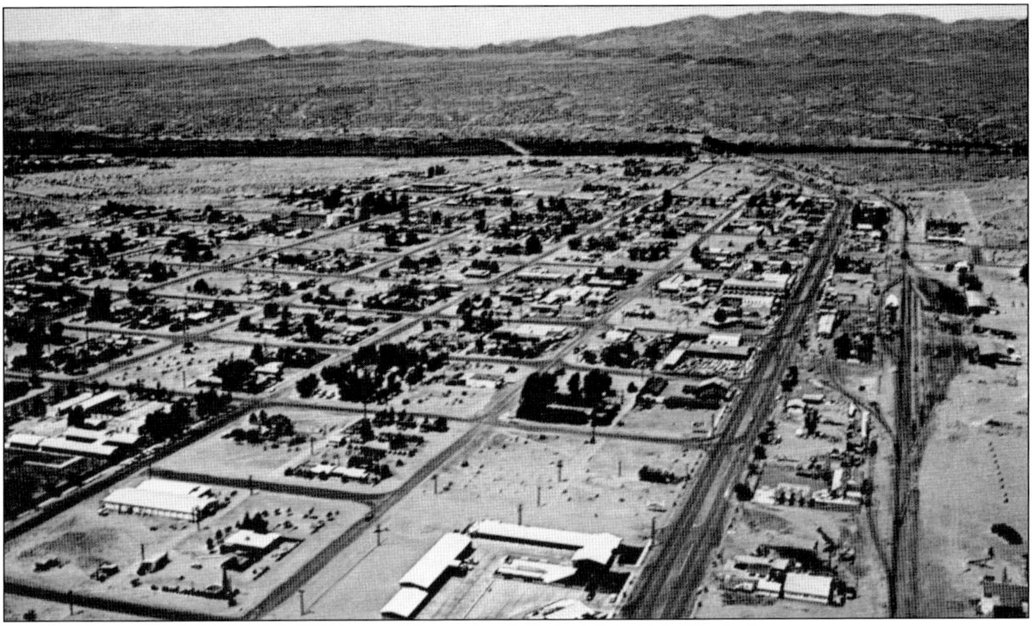

Parker, Town View, c. 1960s (Real-Photo Postcard). The back of the card reads, "The townsite is on the Colorado River Indian Reservation, on the southern tip of the famous '11-mile-strip' of the Colorado River below Parker Dam. Parker is the power boat racing capital of the southwest, and water sports are a part of everyday life. It is growing agriculture center, and also boasts a brand new riverside state Park." (Published by Bob Petley.)

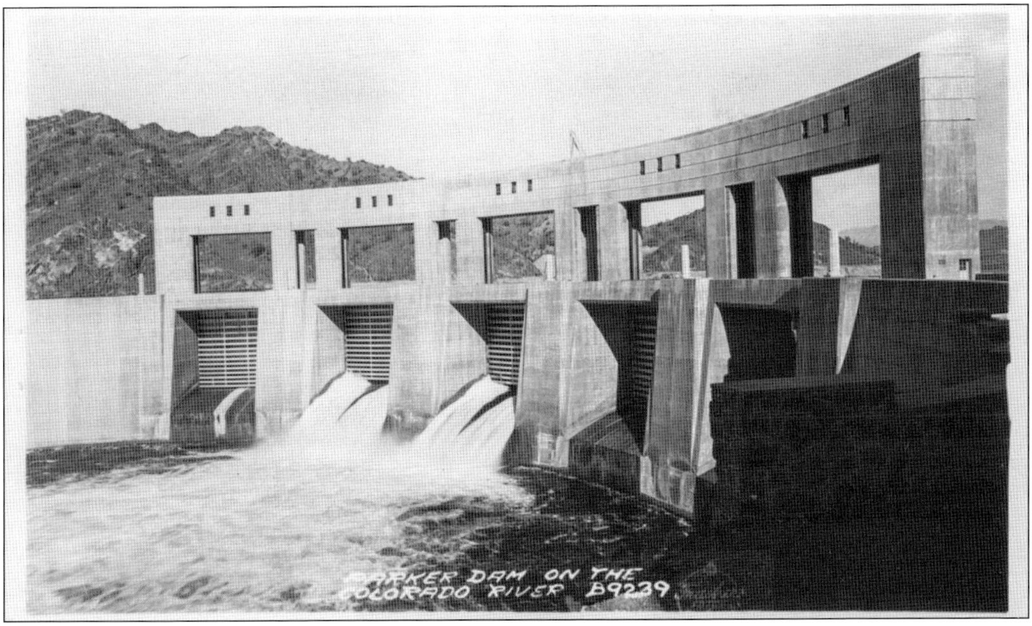

Parker Dam, c. 1940s (Real-Photo Postcard). Known as "the deepest dam in the world," Parker Dam is 320 feet high; 235 feet of that are below the riverbed. Engineers had to excavate down to bedrock, making 73 percent of the dam not visible. Construction began in 1934, but due to lawsuits and strikes, the dam was not completed until October 16, 1938. (Published by Frashers Fotos.)

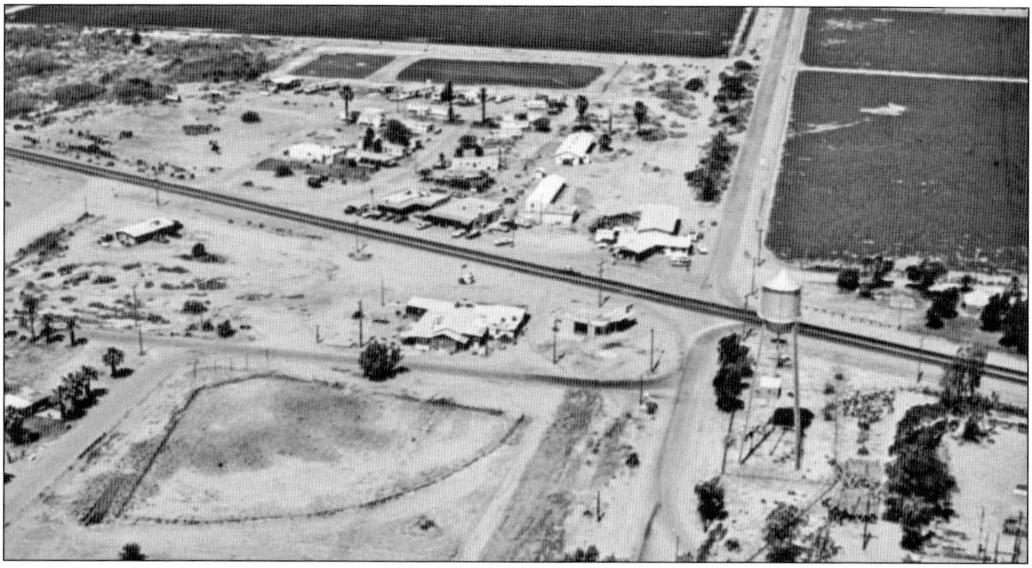

POSTON, AERIAL VIEW, C. 1960S (REAL-PHOTO POSTCARD). Named after Charles D. Poston, known as the "Father of Arizona," Poston was the site of one of the largest internment camps of Japanese Americans in the United States. Built on the Colorado River Indian Reservation against the wishes of the tribal council, the Poston War Relocation Center was separated into three camps that housed more than 17,000 people over a three-year period. (Published by Jim Jeffries.)

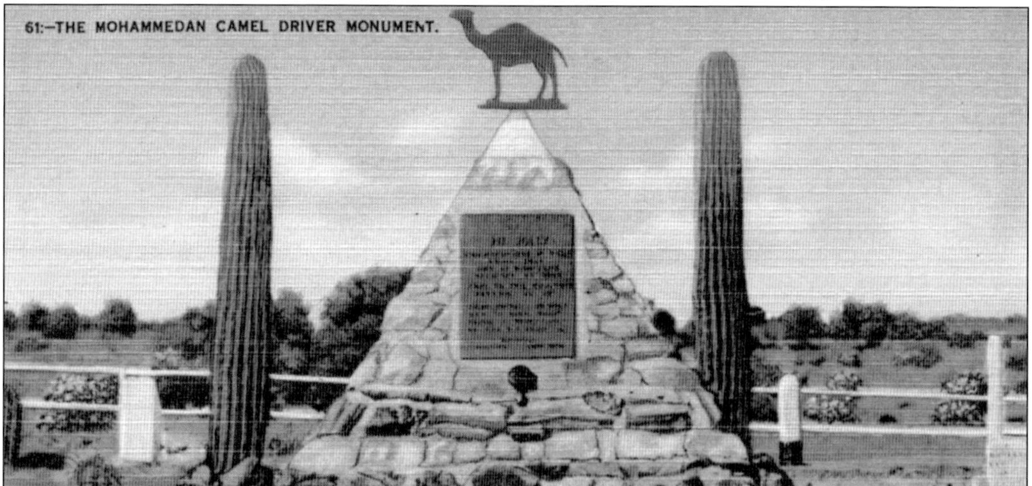

QUARTZSITE, HI JOLLY MONUMENT, HAND DATED AUGUST 16, 1949 (LINEN POSTCARD). Born Philip Tedro in Syria in 1828, he converted to Islam as a young adult and changed his name to Hadji Ali, or Hi Jolly. He served as a camel driver for the French Army in Algiers before signing on as the lead camel driver for the US Army in 1856. Thirty-three camels were brought to the United States as an experiment to transport cargo across the "Great American Desert." By 1864, the experiment was considered a failure, and the camels were sold off. After being discharged by the Army in 1870, Ali ran a freight service along the Colorado River mining district with a few camels he had purchased. When his business failed, Ali released the camels into the desert near Gila Bend. Using his birth name, Tedro, he became a US citizen in 1880 and was hired by the Army in 1885 to work with pack mules during the Geronimo campaign. He died in 1902 while living in Quartzsite and is buried in the Quartzsite Cemetery. (Published by Herz Post Cards.)

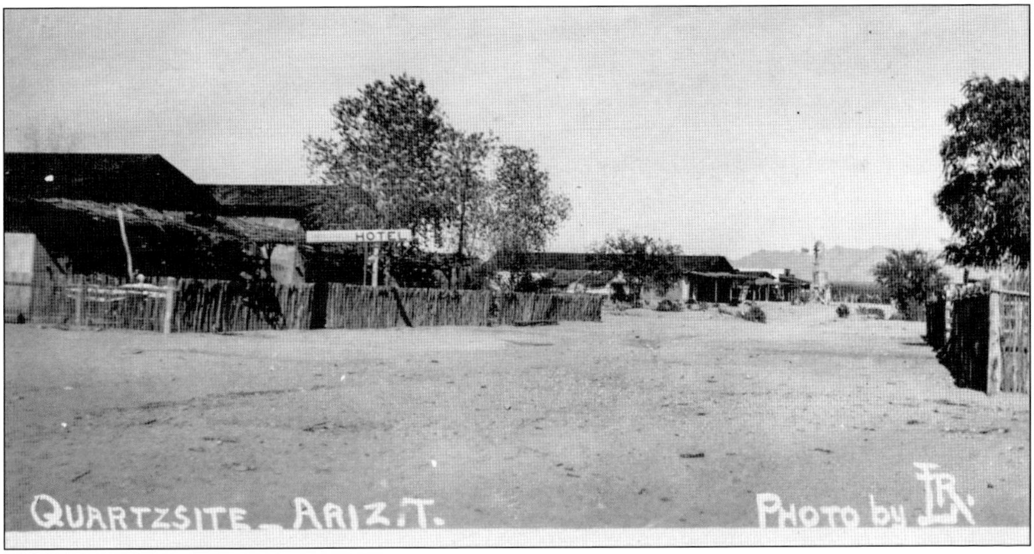

ABOVE, QUARTZSITE, STREET SCENE, C. 1908 (REAL-PHOTO POSTCARD); BELOW, QUARTZSITE, STREET SCENE, C. 1930S (REAL-PHOTO POSTCARD). In 1856, Charles Tyson constructed his own fort to protect miners and the local water supply. In 1866, Tyson built a stage station that was used by both Wells Fargo and the Butterfield stage lines. With the coming of the railroad, the usefulness of the town faded, and Tyson's Well became nearly a ghost town. A minor boom came to the area in 1897 with the discovery of gold, and the town was renamed Quartzsite due to the large fields of quartz. The boom was short-lived, and by 1900, there were only 20 people still living in Quartzsite. Today, Quartzsite's year-round population is just over 3,600 people; however, due to the mild winters, the population jumps into the tens of thousands during the winter months. Every January and February, one of the largest swap meets and gem shows is held in Quartzsite, drawing hundreds of thousands of people from all counties. (Below, published by Frashers Fotos.)

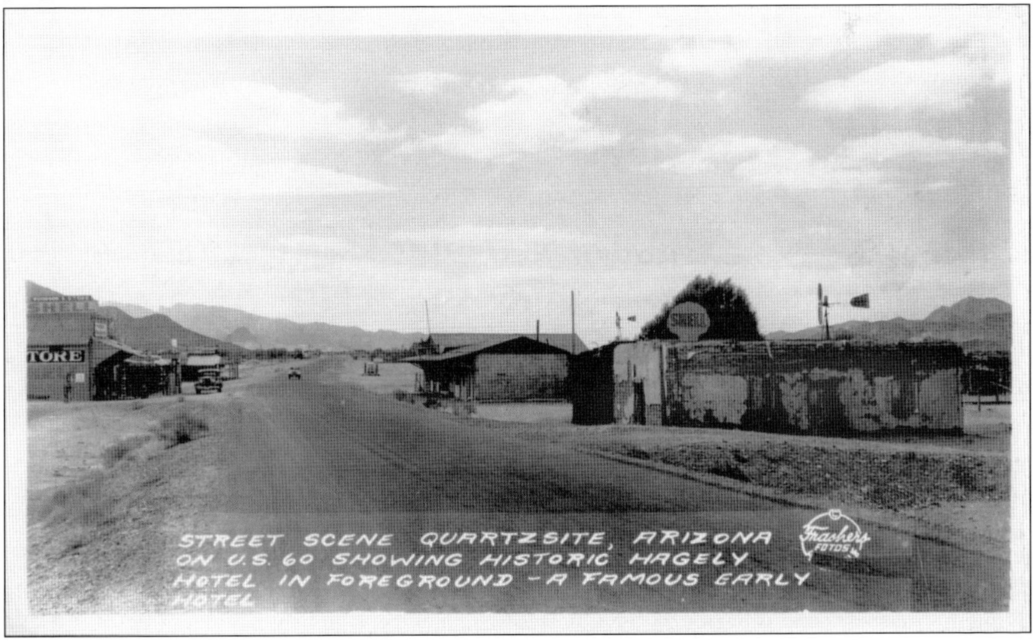

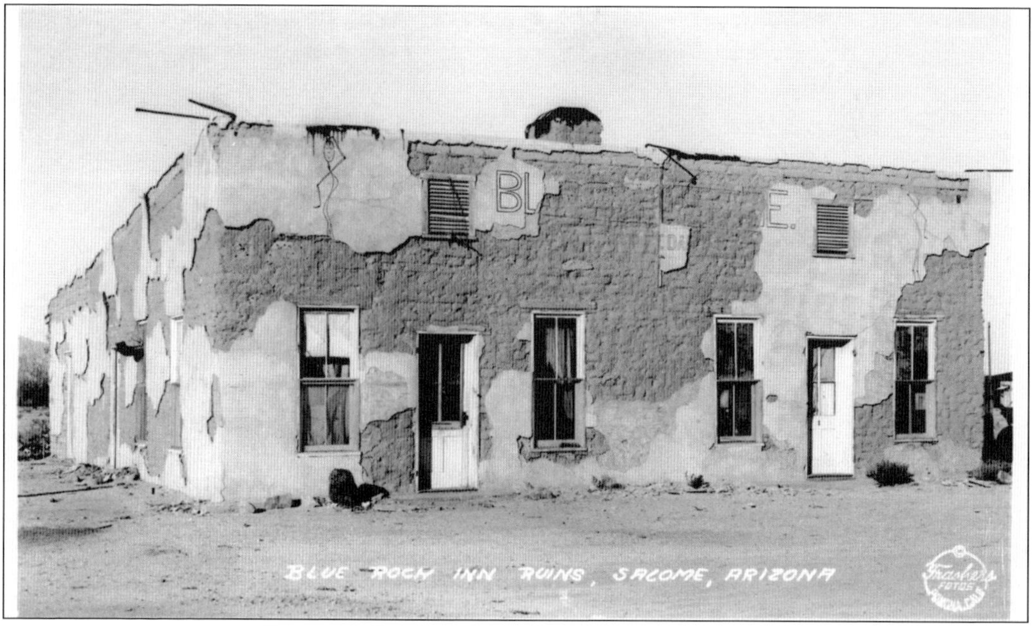

SALOME, BLUE ROCK INN, C. 1930S (REAL-PHOTO POSTCARD). One of Dick Wickenburg "Dick Wick" Hall's creations was the Blue Rock Inn. In the 1920s, the inn advertised that it had "eight inside rooms and 20,000 outside rooms." The inn was also on the Greasewood Golf Course, which was not a typical golf course but a course laid out in the desert among the cactus and rocks. Before being totally abandoned, the old inn was used as apartments. (Published by Frashers.)

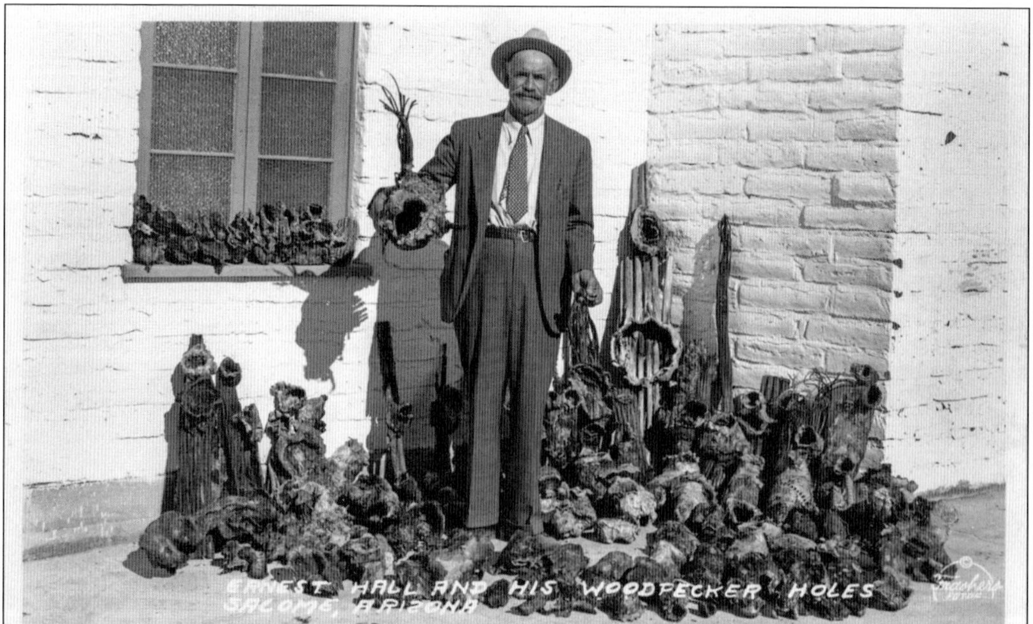

SALOME, WOODPECKER HOLES, C. 1940S (REAL-PHOTO POSTCARD). Ernest Hall (1880–1959) was a farmer, miner, stenographer, newspaperman, real estate salesman, justice of the peace for Salome, and Arizona secretary of state from 1921 to 1922. He was also a Republican state senator from 1917 to 1918. (Published by Frashers.)

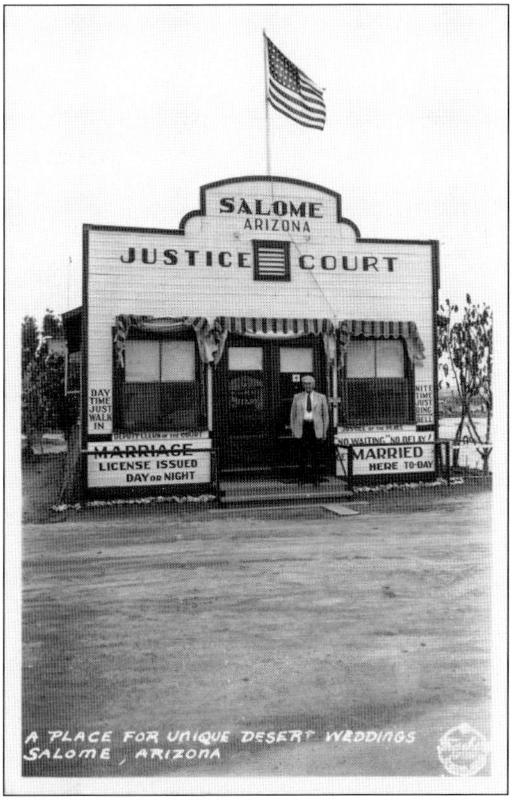

SALOME, JUSTICE COURT, C. 1940S (REAL-PHOTO POSTCARDS). Highway 60 was once the main highway between Los Angeles and Phoenix until the 1970s, when Interstate 10 was constructed. In the 1930s, California required a three-day waiting period for marriages, while Arizona had no such requirement. Salome became a popular wedding spot with Californians who also honeymooned in the local hotels. (Both, published by Frashers Fotos.)

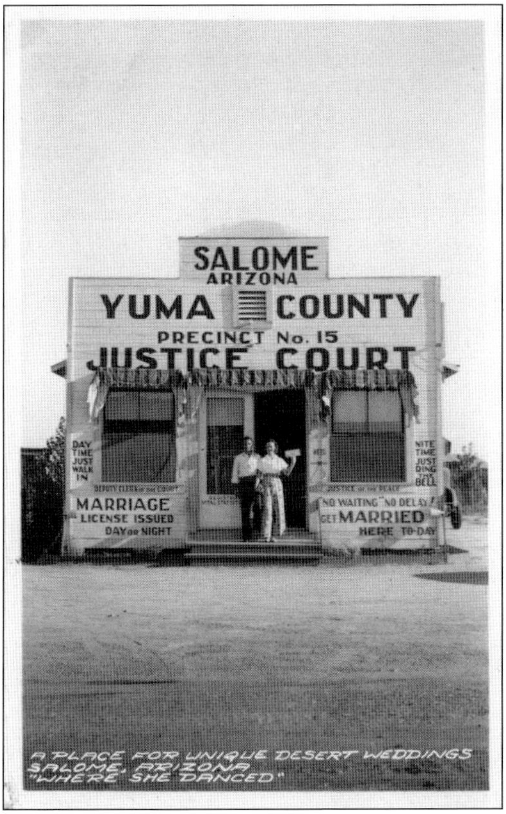

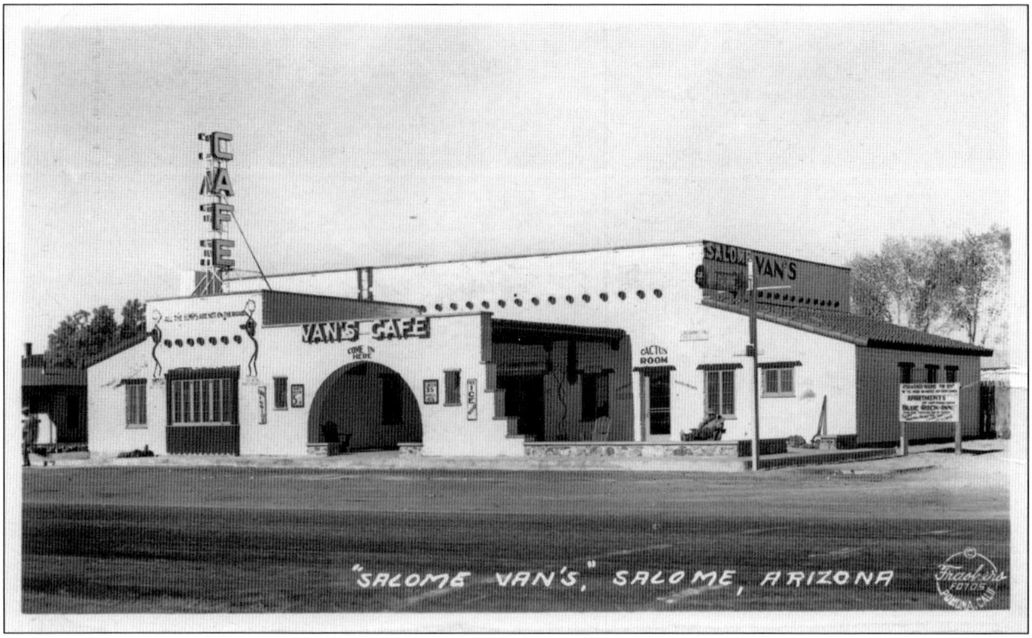

SALOME, VAN'S CAFE, C. 1940 (REAL-PHOTO POSTCARDS). Addie Lee "Van" Van Ordsdel and her ailing husband, Joseph, came to Salome in 1927, opening a gas station and Van's Café. Joseph died of pneumonia in December 1933, with Addie running the business until the late 1930s, when she retired and sold the cafe to the Sheffler brothers. They changed the name to Sheffler's Café. The café is now known as the Salome Restaurant and Don's Cactus Bar. (Both, published by Frashers Fotos.)

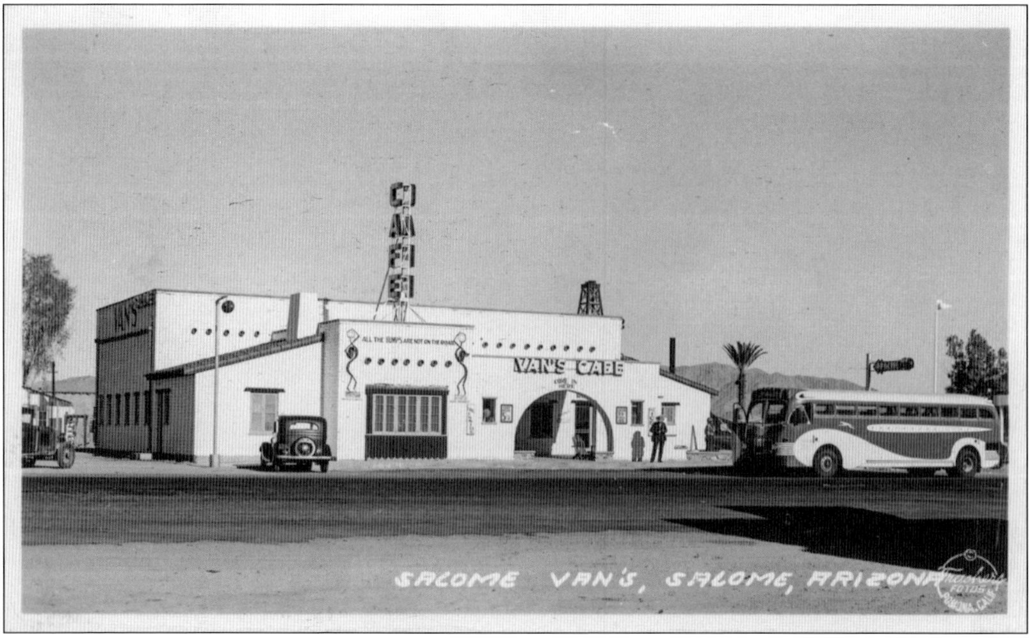

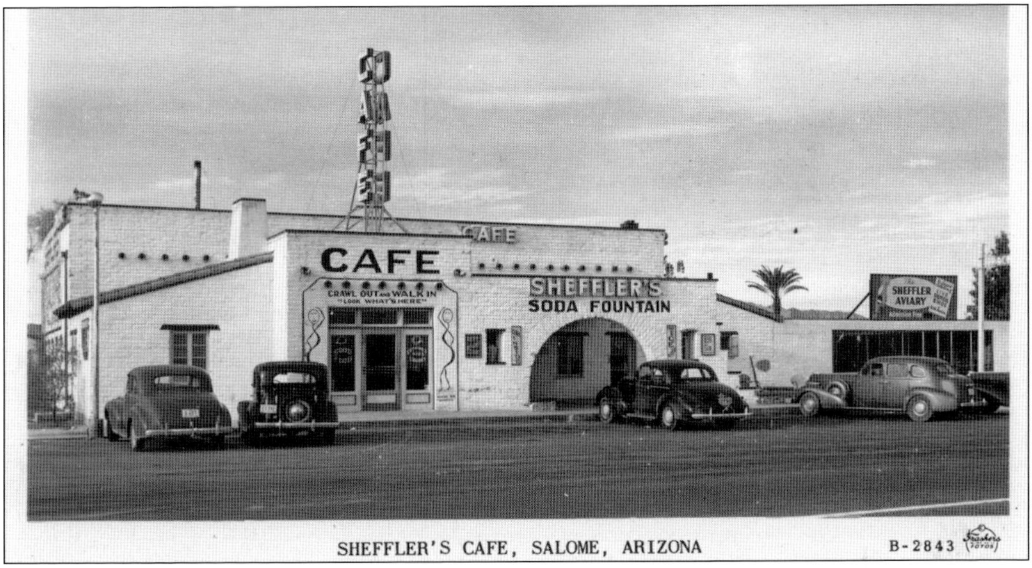

SALOME, SHEFFLER'S CAFÉ, C. 1941 (REAL-PHOTO POSTCARD). Brothers Russell "Bus" and William "Bill" Sheffler moved to Salome in 1939 when California outlawed gambling from ships anchored off the coast. The brothers supplied slot machines to the mob, which were then used on the boats. With the intent to create their own resort that Californians would flock to, the Shefflers constructed Sheffler's Motel and purchased Van's Café. Although appearing legitimate, the businesses were a front for the brothers' real interest, which was gambling and prostitution. (Published by Frashers.)

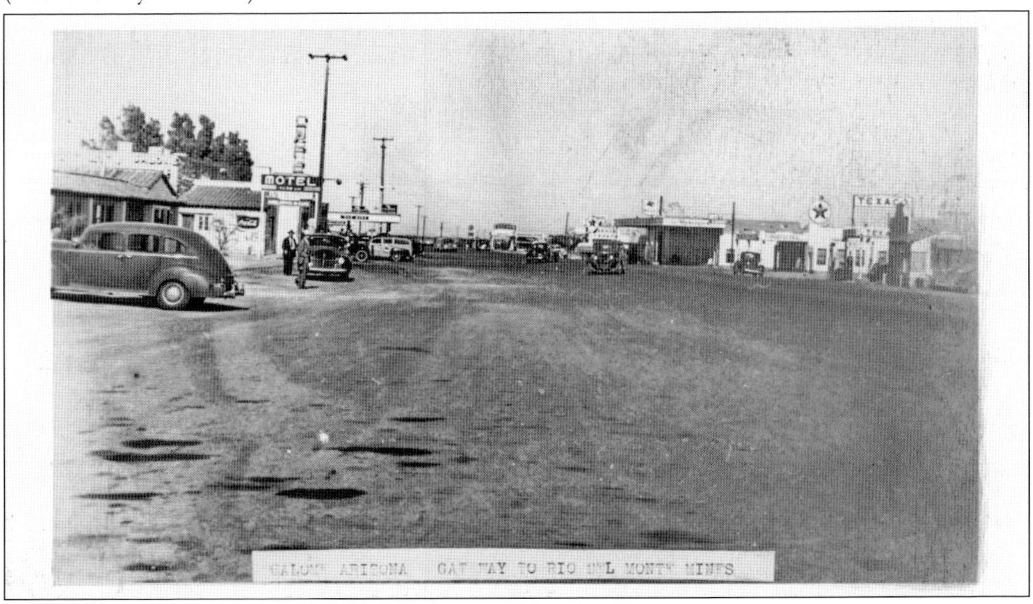

SALOME, MAIN STREET, C. 1940 (REAL-PHOTO POSTCARD). Salome was established in 1904 by Dick Wick Hall and his brother, Ernest, along with friend Charles H. Pratt and was named after Pratt's wife, Grace Salome Pratt. Ernest Hall (1880–1959) was a farmer, miner, stenographer, newspaperman, real estate salesman, and justice of the peace for Salome, and he served as Arizona secretary of state from 1921 to 1922. He was also a Republican state senator from 1917 to 1918.

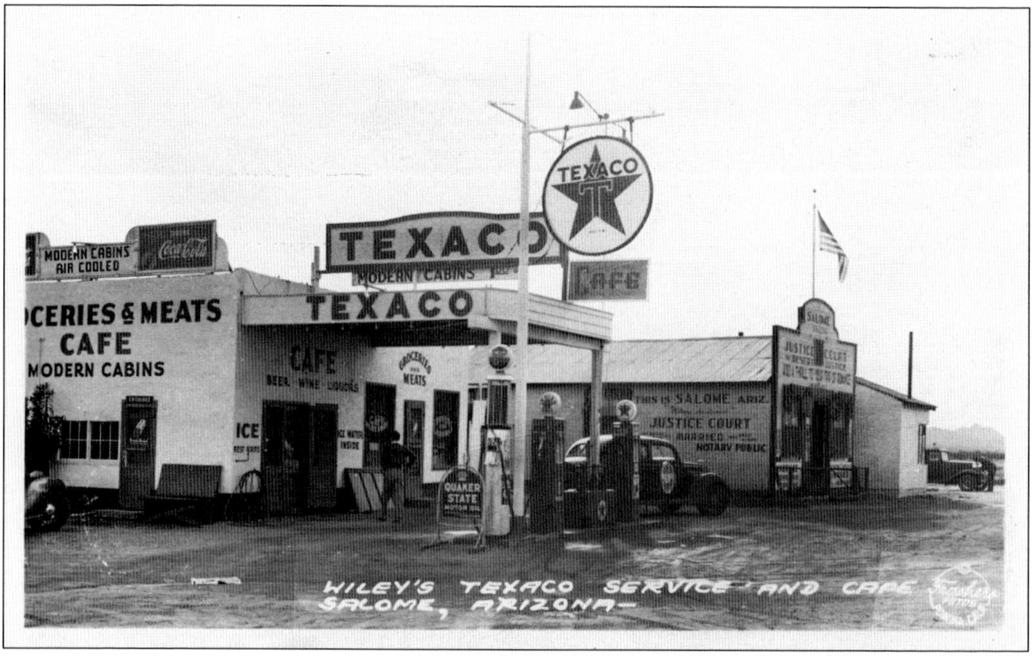

Above, Wiley's Texaco, c. 1940 (Real-Photo Postcard); Below, Salome, Schuler's Texaco Station, c. 1940s (Real-Photo Postcard). The national average cost of a gallon of gas in 1940 was 11¢, and in 1950, it rose to 18¢ a gallon. Accounting for inflation, 11¢ in 1940 is $1.95 today, and 18¢ in 1950 is $1.89 today. According to AAA, the highest average for a gallon of gas was in 2012, when regular gas hit $3.60 a gallon. Compare that to a national average of average of $2.50 in 2017. (Above, published by Frashers Fotos; below, published by Desert Photo Shoope.)

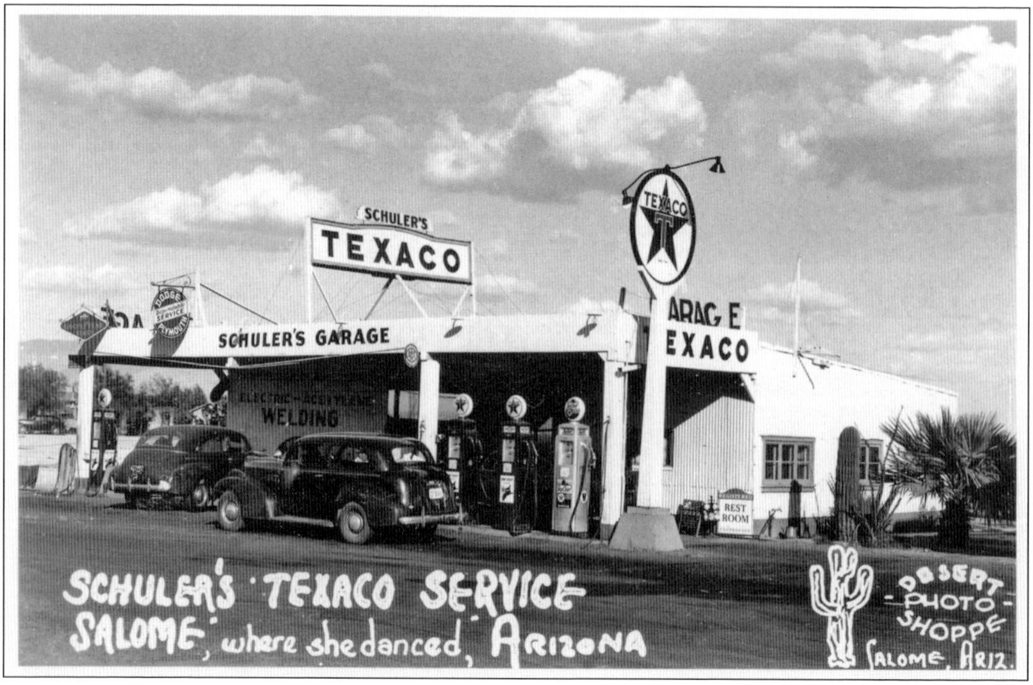

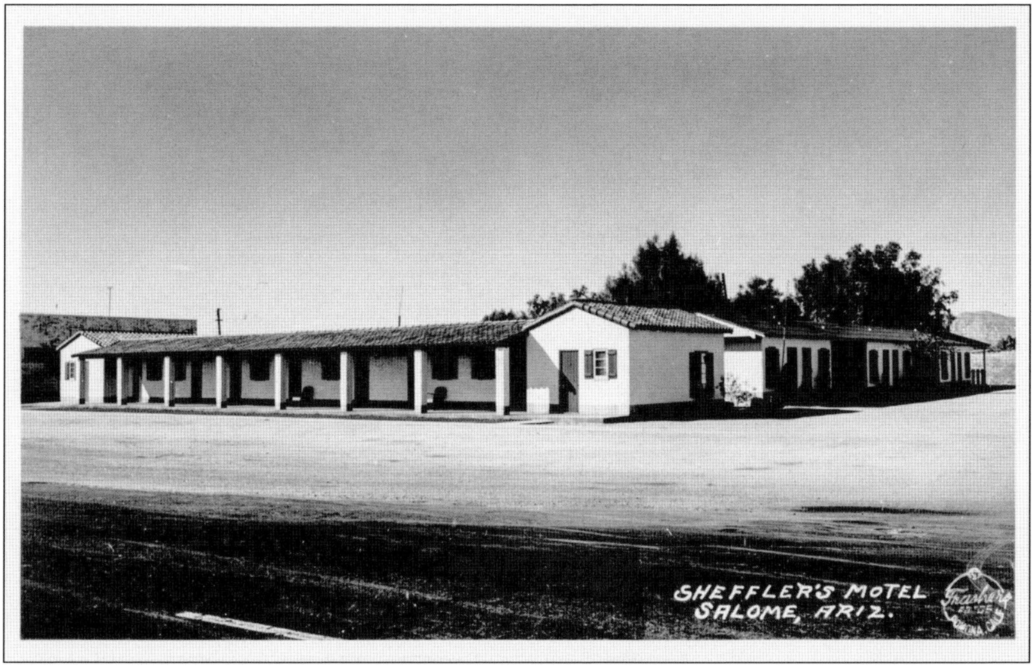

SALOME, SHEFFLER'S MOTEL, C. 1940S (REAL-PHOTO POSTCARDS). After brothers Russell and William Sheffler moved to Salome in 1939, they constructed Sheffler's Motel across the highway from their other interest, Sheffler's Café. (Both, published by Frashers Fotos.)

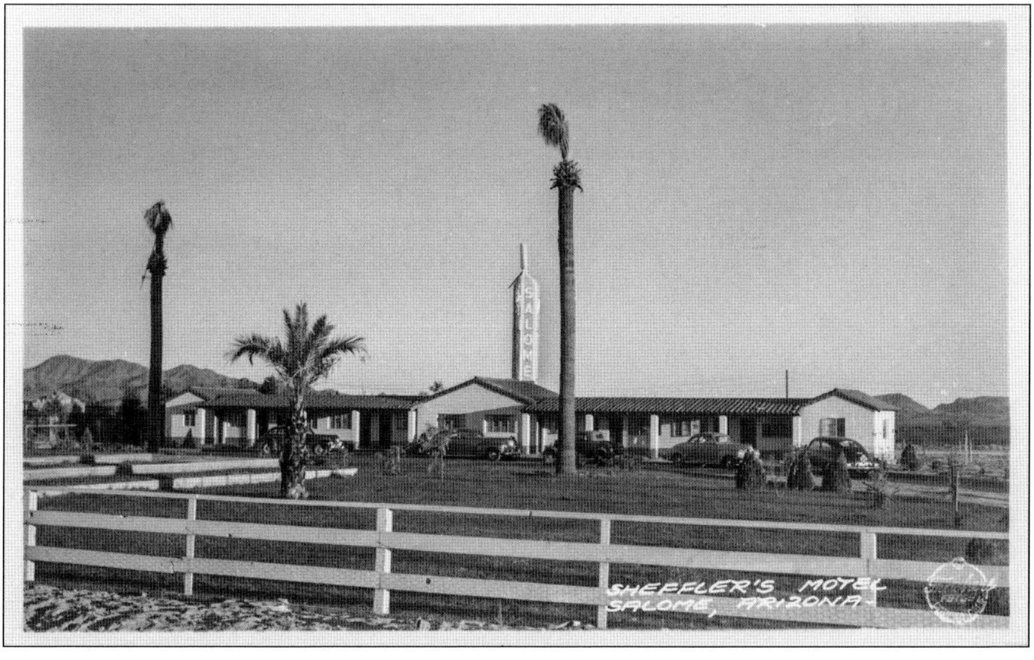

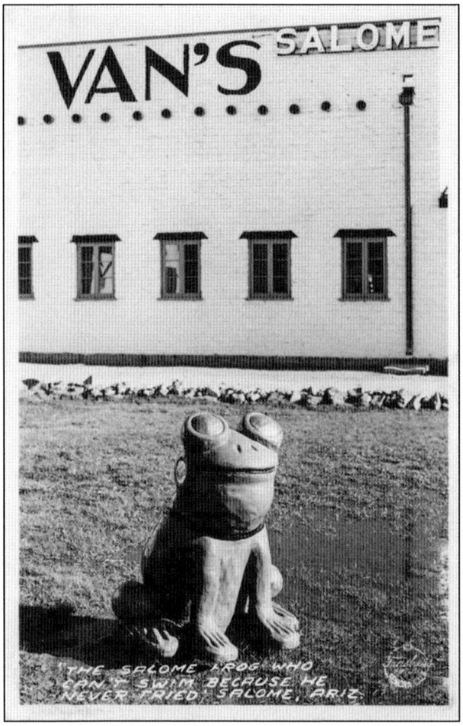

SALOME, THE SALOME FROG, POSTMARKED AUGUST 31, 1945 (REAL-PHOTO POSTCARD). One of the cofounders of Salome, Dick Wickenburg Hall (born DeForest Hall), was a humorist who lived in Salome and wrote the town's newsletter, the *Salome Sun*. One of the many characters he developed was the Salome frog. The frog was seven years old, weighed 18 pounds, and never learned to swim because of the lack of water holes in the desert. (Published by Frashers Fotos.)

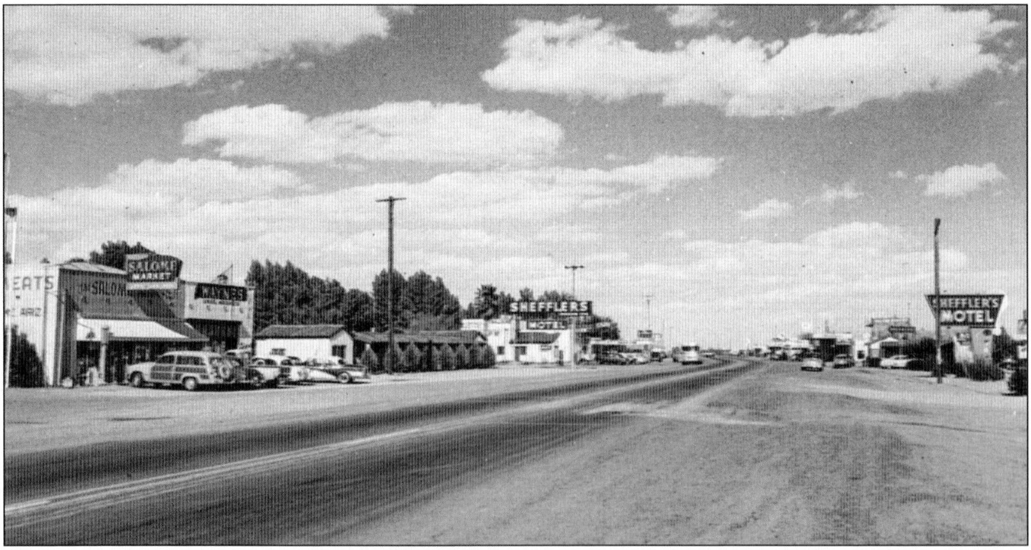

SALOME, MAIN STREET, C. 1950S (KODACHROME POSTCARD). The population numbers for Salome are not easily available, but according the US Census of 1920, a total of 73 people resided in Salome. By 1930, it increased to 189 people. It appears that Salome may have been included only in the county population totals, rather than as an individual town, for the remainder of the 20th century. The estimated population in 1990 was 689. The next available census with Salome being identified was in 2000, when the town's population reached 1,690 people. Ten years later, the population had declined by 160 people, to 1,530. By 2016, the population continued to slide, leaving Salome with 1,467 people. (Published by Petley Studios; photograph by Bob Van Luchene.)

Ten

Just across the Border Near Yuma County

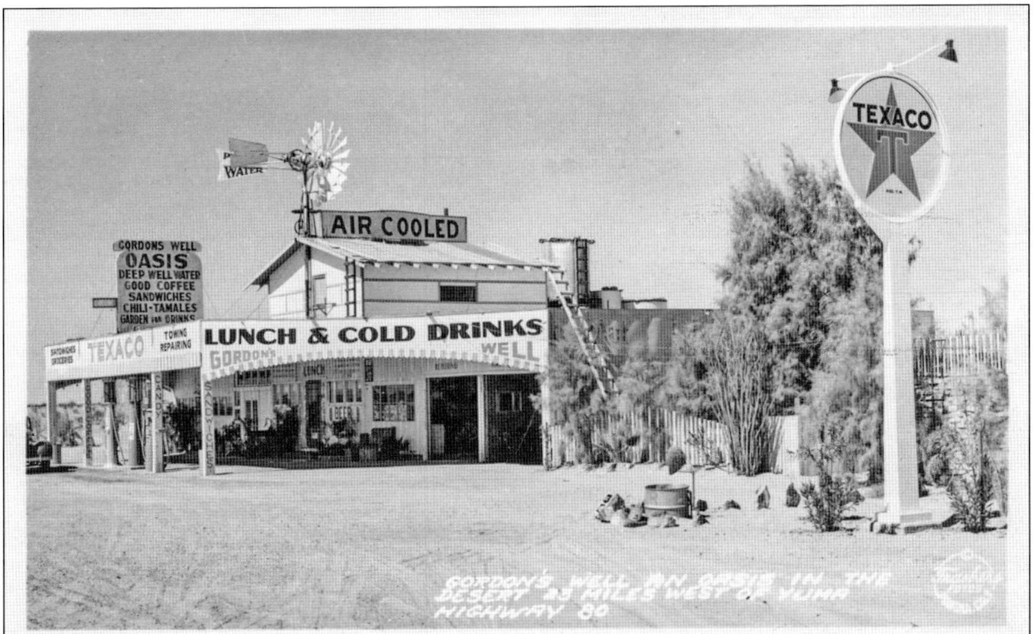

Gordon's Well, Patio Bar, Postmarked February 9, 1947 (Real-Photo Postcard). One of the premier spots in the Southwest for year-round off-road vehicles is the sand dunes surrounding Gordon's Well. The Gordon's Well service station, "An Oasis in the Desert," was established about 20 miles west of Yuma to service vehicles along the old plank highway. Although the structure is long gone, concrete remnants are still visible at the Gordon's Well RV Park and Storage that now occupies the site. The gas station was said to have once had camping sites along with bungalows accompanied by a tiki-themed restaurant and bar. (Published by Frashers Fotos.)

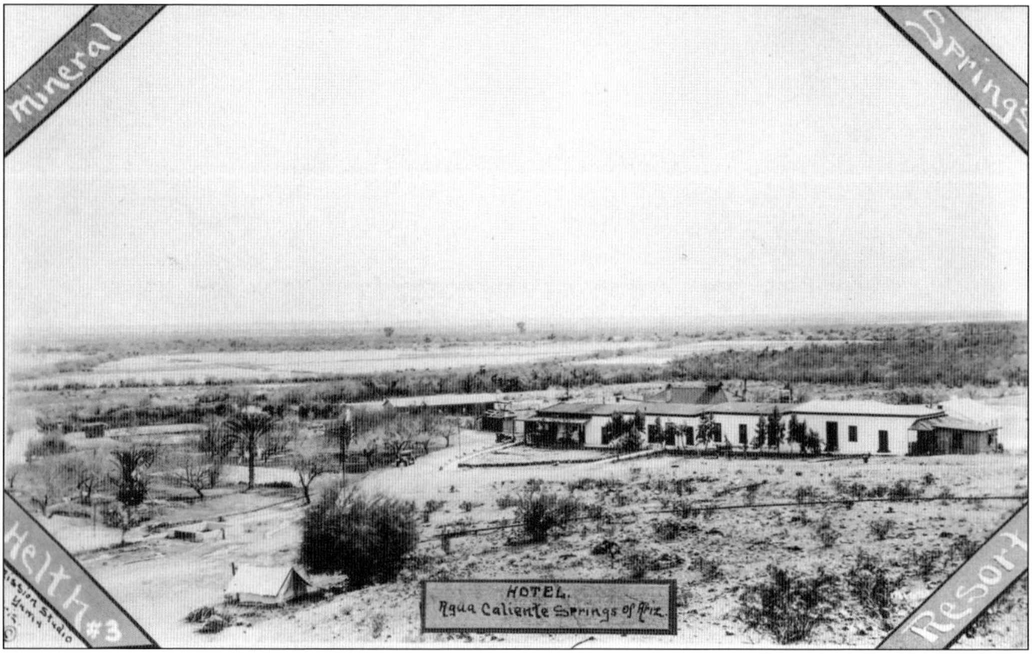

ABOVE, AGUA CALIENTE SPRINGS, C. 1908 (REAL-PHOTO POSTCARD); BELOW, HOTEL MODESTI, C. 1930S (REAL-PHOTO POSTCARD). The Agua Caliente Springs (Spanish for "hot water") is located in Maricopa County, literally within walking distance of the Yuma County border. It had been used by Native Americans for hundreds of years until settlers arrived in the mid-1800s and began farming. In 1897, a 22-room hotel was constructed, and years later, a swimming pool and other buildings were added. The springs dried up years ago from overpumping of water for irrigation. With the rerouting of the highway, the resort faded away and became a ghost town. Some structures, such as the hotel, have been maintained over the years, but most of the site remains as ruins. (Above, published by Mission Studio; below, published by Curteich.)

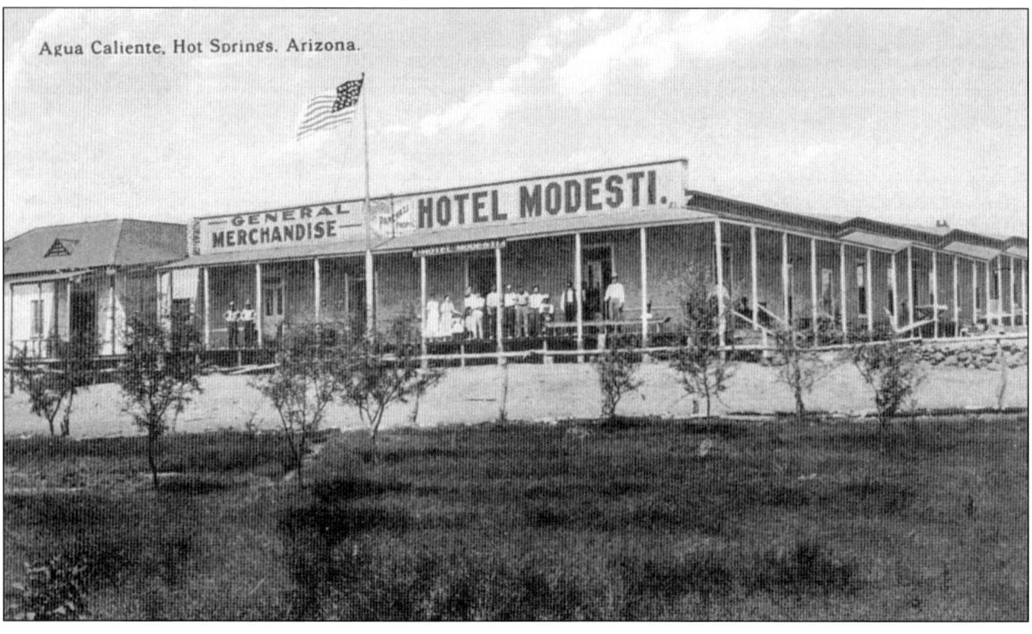

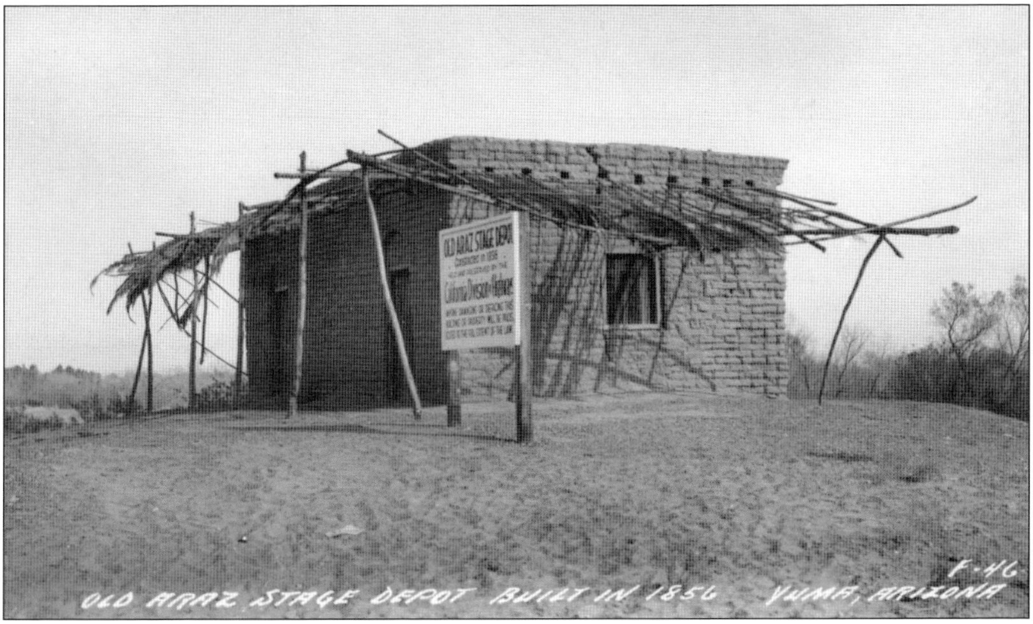

ARAZ, OLD ARAZ STAGE DEPOT, C. 1940S (REAL-PHOTO POSTCARD). Located a few miles west of Yuma on the south side of Highway 80, the Araz Stage Station is still visible to the passing motorist. Originally known as the Pilot Knob Station, it served the Butterfield Overland Stage line until 1877, when the train arrived in Yuma. (Published by L.L. Cook Co.)

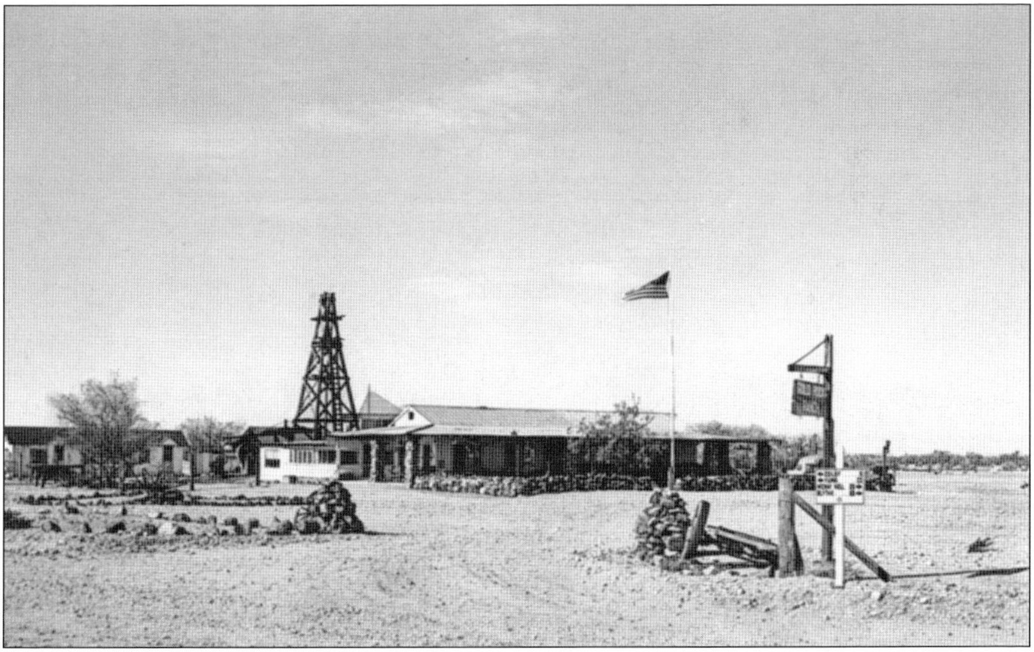

WINTERHAVEN, GOLD ROCK RANCH, C. 1960 (ADVERTISING POSTCARD). Five miles north of Ogilby, California, and about 20 miles from Yuma is the Gold Rock Ranch. The area is rich in gold mining history and is one of the area's best locations for four-wheel drive vehicles. The ranch itself appears today as it did back when this card was produced in the 1960s. (Published by Arco Studios.)

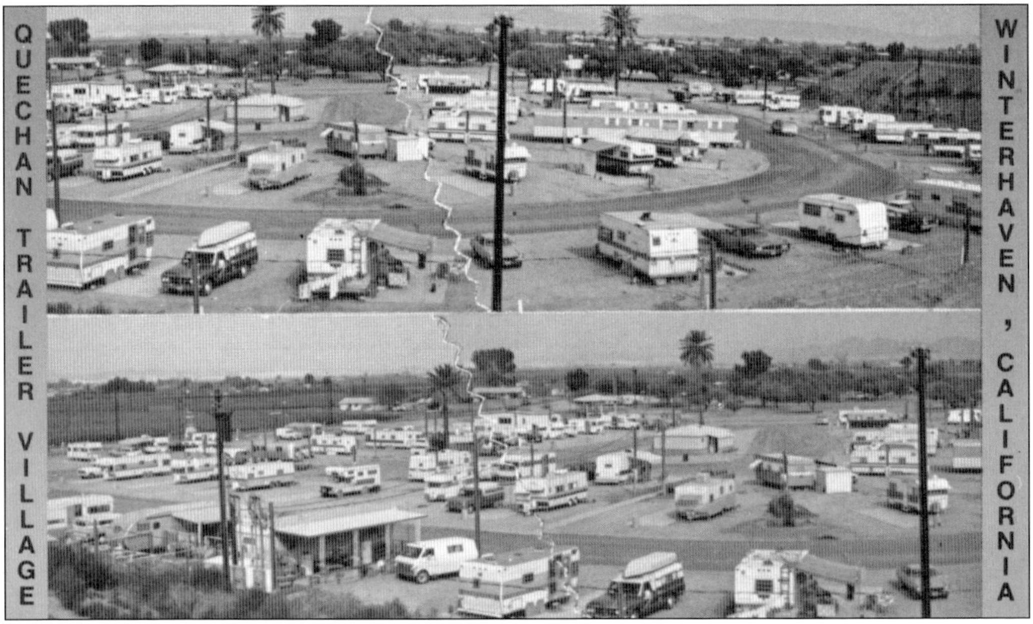

WINTERHAVEN, QUECHAN TRAILER VILLAGE, C. 1970 (ADVERTISING POSTCARD). Once located on Agnes and Indian Hill Roads, the lot where the trailer village once stood is now a vacant lot. (Published by Kendall Photography.)

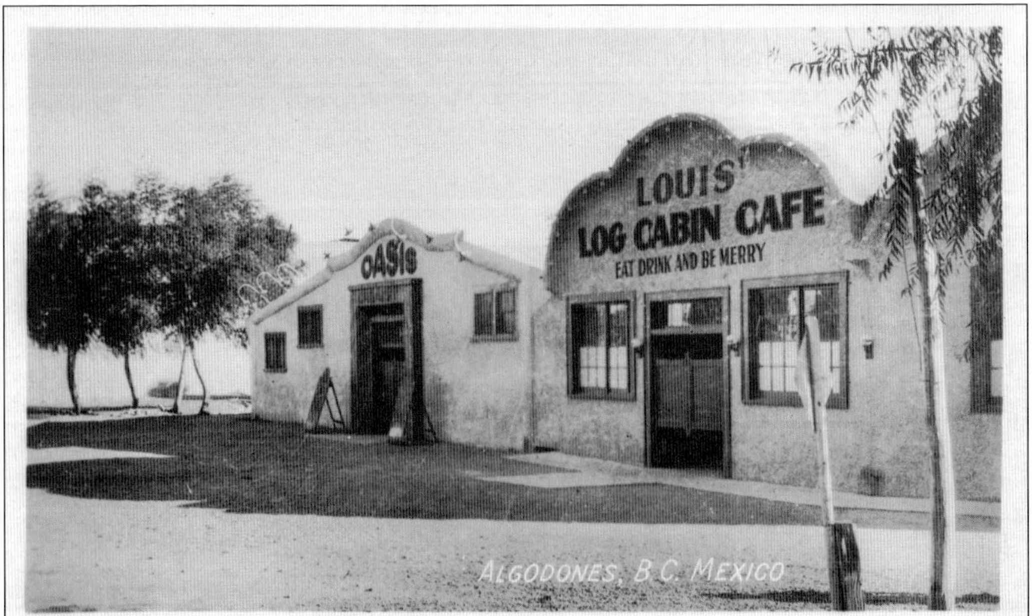

ALGODONES, MEXICO, LOUIS' LOG CABIN CAFÉ, C. 1930S (REAL-PHOTO POSTCARD). Louis' Log Cabin ran advertisements in 1925, during the height of Prohibition in the United States, in the Yuma *Morning Star* newspaper announcing "Special Stages" leaving Yuma at the Sharpensteen Service Station every hour on the hour from 9:00 a.m. to 1:00 a.m. Return trips left Louis' Log Cabin on the half hour.

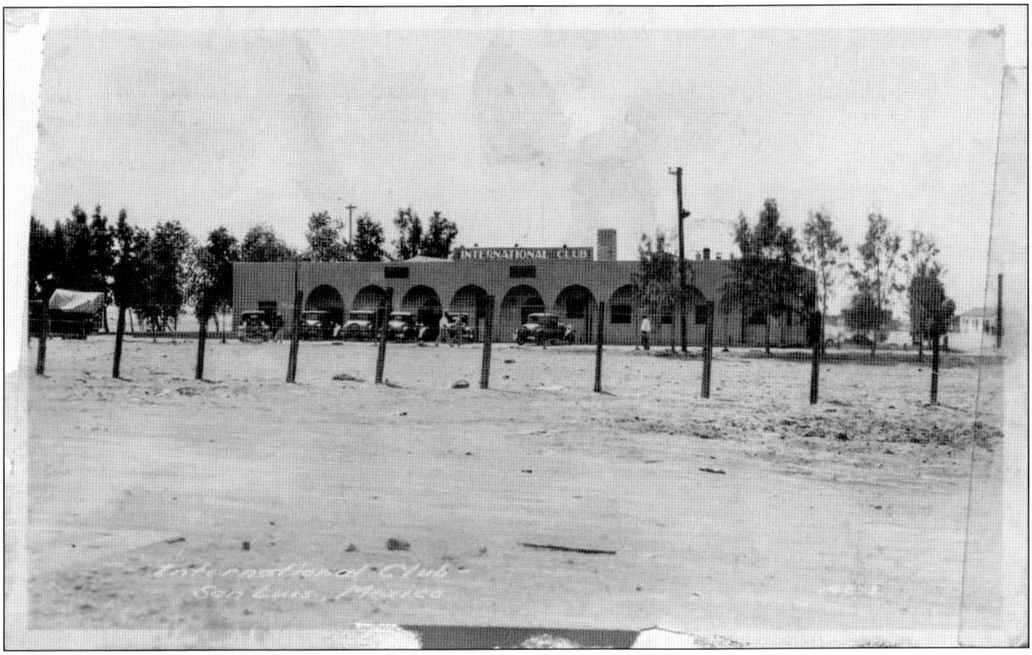

SAN LUIS, MEXICO, INTERNATIONAL CLUB, C. 1920S (REAL-PHOTO POSTCARD). Located just across the border, the International Club attracted Americans from the 1920s through the 1940s. The club boasted a café, dining room, dancing with American bands, and a bar. Gambling was allowed until 1932, when the Mexican government shut down all gambling operations. In July 1960, the International Club was sold and renamed La Fiesta. Note the barbed wire fence that once separated the American and Mexican border. (Courtesy of Louie Gradias.)

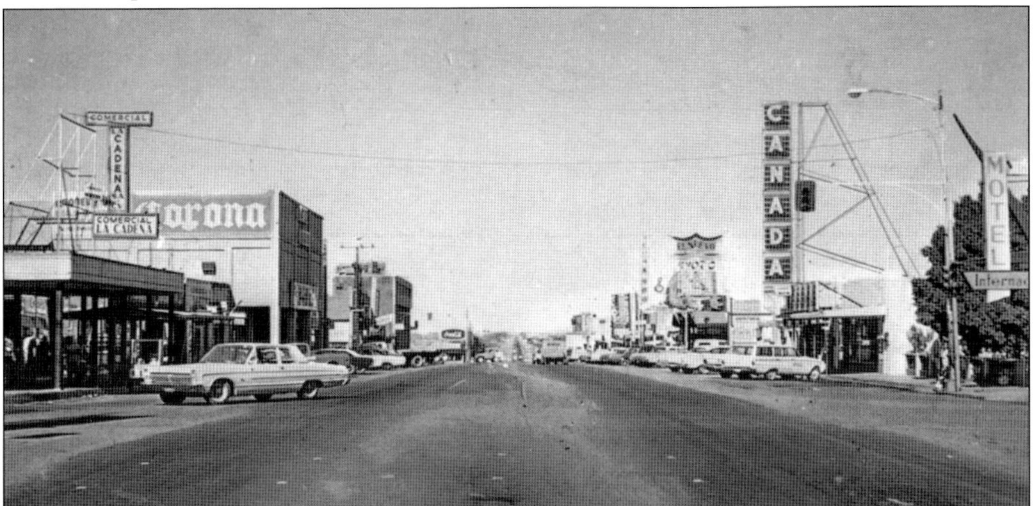

SAN LUIS RIO COLORADO, MEXICO, SHOPPING DISTRICT, C. 1960S (REAL-PHOTO POSTCARD). Located across the border from San Luis, Arizona, San Luis Rio Colorado was established in the early 1900s as an agricultural town to support the local military. The town now sees as many as 40,000 workers cross the border every day during peak winter lettuce season. The city is the fourth largest in the state of Sonora with a population of over 160,000 people. (Published by Mexico Fotografico.)

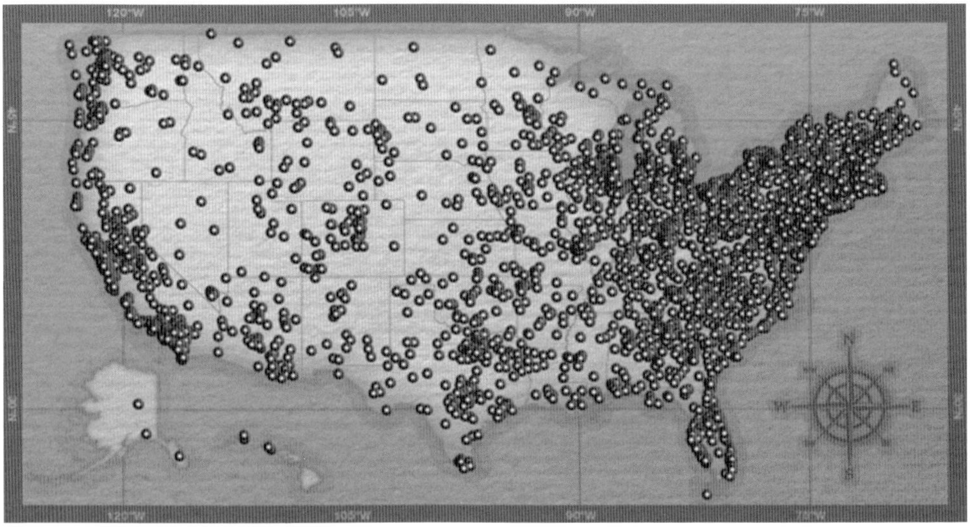

Consistent with our mission to preserve history on a local level, this book was printed in South Carolina on American-made paper and manufactured entirely in the United States. Products carrying the accredited Forest Stewardship Council (FSC) label are printed on 100 percent FSC-certified paper.

MADE IN THE USA